NUTCASES

MEDICAL LAW

AUSTRALIA
Law Book Company
Sydney

CANADA and USA
Carswell
Toronto

HONG KONG
Sweet & Maxwell Asia

NEW ZEALAND
Brookers
Wellington

SINGAPORE and MALAYSIA
Sweet & Maxwell Asia
Singapore and Kuala Lumpur

NUTCASES

MEDICAL LAW

FIRST EDITION

by

GWYN TOVEY, LL.B (Hons),
PGCE(FE), MCP
Senior Lecturer in Law
University of Glamorgan

London • Sweet & Maxwell • 2008

Published in 2008 by Sweet & Maxwell Limited of
100 Avenue Road, London NW3 3PF
Typeset by YHT Ltd, London
Printed in the Netherlands by Krips of Meppel

No natural forests were destroyed to make this product.
Only farmed timber was used and re-planted.

A CIP catalogue record for this book is available
from the British Library.

ISBN 978 1 847 03003 0

©
Sweet & Maxwell
2008

CONTENTS

TABLE OF CASES

TABLE OF STATUTES

1. THE MODERN NHS

The Impact of National and International Obligations on the NHS

Key Principle: **Provisions relating to a person's health, and the regulation and continuing evolution of the NHS, are subjected not only to the laws of England and Wales and to laws of the European Union, but also to the influence of International law.**

Provisions under International Law

United Nations Declaration of Human Rights 1948, Art.25 provides that:
Everyone has the right to a standard of living adequate for the health and well-being of himself and his family, including food, clothing, housing and medical care and necessary social services...

Article 12 of the United Nations International Covenant on Economic, Social and Cultural Rights 1966 defines health as; "the right of everyone to the enjoyment of the highest attainable standard of physical and mental health".

Furthermore, the European Social Charter 1961, Arts 11 and 13 contains two noteworthy provisions relating to health care, viz:

Article 11—The right to protection of health
With a view to ensuring the effective exercise of the right to protection of health, the Contracting Parties undertake, either directly or in co-operation with public or private organisations, to take appropriate measures designed inter alia:

1   to remove as far as possible the causes of ill-health;

2   to provide advisory and educational facilities for the promotion of health and the encouragement of individual responsibility in matters of health;

3   to prevent as far as possible epidemic, endemic and other diseases.

Article 13—The right to social and medical assistance

With a view to ensuring the effective exercise of the right to social and medical assistance, the Contracting Parties undertake:

1   to ensure that any person who is without adequate resources and who is unable to secure such resources either by his own efforts or from other sources, in particular by benefits under a social security scheme, be granted adequate assistance, and, in case of sickness, the care necessitated by his condition;

2   to ensure that persons receiving such assistance shall not, for that reason, suffer from a diminution of their political or social rights;

3   to provide that everyone may receive by appropriate public or private services such advice and personal help as may be required to prevent, to remove, or to alleviate personal or family want;...

Commentary

The provisions above are amongst those cited by those who wish to debate whether there is a right to health care. Aiming to base an argument from a platform that entirely ignores an individual's responsibilities for his own health care and, moreover, takes no account of the economics of health care is futile, however. Indeed, the economics of health care becomes a significant factor given that the overall spending for the NHS is projected to be more than £90 billion pounds in 2007/08. Cost is also very much a factor taken into consideration by NICE (The National Institute for Health and Clinical Excellence) in their recommendations of what new and expensive drugs should be available via the NHS. This is discussed below in the section on the allocation of scarce medical resources. That there is no "absolute right" to health care is clear from the wording of s.3 of the NHS Act 2006, below.

With reference to international treaties, the UK is a *dualist* state. This means that international law is regarded as distinct from domestic, or internal, law. Accordingly, before a treaty becomes part of English law, it has to be enacted in statutory form. In the absence of an enactment, the international provisions remain as mere aspirations. The unenforceable aspirations of international law in respect of human health protection contrasts with the express provision of Art.152 EC that has been

given the force of law in England and Wales via the European
Communities Act 1972:

European Community Law

Article 152 EC

1. A high level of human health protection shall be ensured
   in the definition and implementation of all Community
   policies and activities....

. . .

4. [The "co-decision" procedure for making secondary EC
   legislation may be used to adopt]:

   (a) Measures setting high standards of quality and
       safety of organs and substances of human origin,
       blood and blood derivatives; these measures shall
       not prevent any Member State from maintaining or
       introducing more stringent protective measures;
   (b) ...measures in the phytosanitary fields which have
       as their direct objective the protection of public
       health;
   (c) Incentive measures designed to protect and improve
       human health, excluding any harmonisation of the
       laws and regulations of the Member States.

Commentary

Article 152 EC is the sole Article constituting Title XIII—"Public
Health" in the current EC Treaty. However, the non-binding EU
Charter of Fundamental Rights and Freedoms also espouses
rights to health care and the right to benefit from medical
treatment.

Later in this chapter, it will be noted that Art.49 EC—freedom
to provide/receive services within the European Union—may
play a part in enabling a patient residing in England or Wales to
avail himself of medical treatment elsewhere in the EU with the
cost of treatment being borne by the NHS.

The Laws of England and Wales

Key Principle: **The National Health Service Act 2006, The National Health Service (Wales) Act 2006 and the National Health Service (Consequential Provisions) Act 2006 are the three principal statutes that contain the major provisions relating to the administration of the NHS. In particular, the NHS Act 2006 places statutory duties on the Secretary of State for Health, whereas under the NHS (Wales) Act, those duties are to be discharged by the Minister for Health and Social Services. Some provisions of the 2006 Acts will be amended when the Health and Social Care Act 2008 comes into force.**

NHS Act 2006, section 1

1. Secretary of State's duty to promote health service

(1) The Secretary of State must continue the promotion in England of a comprehensive health service designed to secure improvement—

   (a) in the physical and mental health of the people of England, and

   (b) in the prevention, diagnosis and treatment of illness.

(2) The Secretary of State must for that purpose provide or secure the provision of services in accordance with this Act.

(3) The services so provided must be free of charge except in so far as the making and recovery of charges is expressly provided for by or under any enactment, whenever passed.

Commentary

For Wales, substitute "Secretary of State" with "Welsh Ministers". Apart from other differences which will be noted below, in Wales the "services so provided [that] must be free of charge" includes, as from April 1, 2007, free prescription items for everyone. The Welsh Assembly Government had made a commitment in 2003 to abolish prescription charges, and in January 2007, Dr Brian Gibbons, the then Assembly Health Minister, said:

"The main reason for providing free prescriptions is to ensure people are not put off getting medication they need due to cost. This is the simplest and most effective way of resolving health inequalities and inconsistencies in prescribing"

The free prescriptions enables those living in Wales to enjoy a health care system that is nearer to one of the founding principles of the NHS when the National Health Service Act 1946 came into force in July 1948, i.e. free at the point of need.

Some commentators believe this significant difference is sufficient to claim that either we have a two-tier NHS within England and Wales or we don't have a "National" health service at all. Indeed, it has been claimed that devolution has created four different health care systems within the UK and that "We basically have four different systems, albeit with the same set of values," according to Dr Gill Morgan, the chief executive of the NHS Confederation (as reported in the Daily Telegraph, Thursday January 3 2008).

NHS Act 2006 (continued)

Sections 3, 8 and 9, below, all apply to England, i.e. they are all part of the NHS Act 2006. There are relatively minor variations in the NHS (Wales) Act 2006.

Provision of particular services

3. Secretary of State's duty as to provision of certain services
   (1) The Secretary of State must provide throughout England, to such extent as he considers necessary to meet all reasonable requirements—

   (a) hospital accommodation,
   (b) other accommodation for the purpose of any service provided under this Act,
   (c) medical, dental, ophthalmic, nursing and ambulance services,
   (d) such other services or facilities for the care of pregnant women, women who are breastfeeding and young children as he considers are appropriate as part of the health service,
   (e) such other services or facilities for the prevention of illness, the care of persons suffering from illness and the after-care of persons who have suffered from illness as he considers are appropriate as part of the health service,
   (f) such other services or facilities as are required for the diagnosis and treatment of illness.

See also: Sch.1, para.8, which provides that:

The Secretary of State must arrange, to such extent as he considers necessary to meet all reasonable requirements, for—

(a) the giving of advice on contraception;

(b) the medical examination of persons seeking advice on contraception;

(c) the treatment of such persons; and

(d) the supply of contraceptive substances and appliances.

Commentary

The duty placed on the Secretary of State by Sch.1, para.8, previously was contained in s.5(1)(b) of the NHS Act 1977. There, the Secretary of State had a duty to arrange, to such extent as he considered necessary to meet all reasonable requirements in England *and Wales* ... and the duties (the same as in the NHS Act 2006) were comma delineated in a single paragraph rather than four sub-paragraphs, (a)–(d). However, the National Health Service (Consequential Provisions) Act 2006 repealed the entire 1977 Act.

8.   Secretary of State's directions to health service bodies

(1) The Secretary of State may give directions to any of the bodies mentioned in subsection (2) about its exercise of any functions.

(2) The bodies are—

(a) Strategic Health Authorities;
(b) Primary Care Trusts;
(c) NHS trusts; and
(d) Special Health Authorities.

Commentary

The roles of Strategic Health Authorities, Primary Care Trusts and NHS Trusts are noted, below, followed by an analysis of some of the most significant Special Health Authorities. England, but not Wales, has Strategic Health Authorities; and the Welsh equivalents of England's Primary Care trusts are Local Health Boards.

Strategic and Special Health Authorities: Sections 13 and 28 of the NHS Act 2006

Key Principle: **In England, 10 Strategic Health Authorities plan and administer the NHS for their areas which, together, cover the whole of England. By contrast, *Special* Health authorities are free from regional restrictions: they provide services for the NHS throughout England and Wales**

Strategic Health Authorities: Section 13 of the NHS Act 2006

PART 2 [NHS Act 2006]

HEALTH SERVICE BODIES

CHAPTER 1

STRATEGIC HEALTH AUTHORITIES

13. Strategic Health Authorities
  (1) The Strategic Health Authorities established by the Secretary of State continue in existence.

  . . .

  (6) The Secretary of State must act under this section so as to ensure that the areas for which Strategic Health Authorities are at any time established together comprise the whole of England.

  . . .

  (10) Schedule 2 makes further provision about Strategic Health Authorities.

Commentary
For nearly the first 50 years of the NHS, the local/regional administration was under the jurisdiction of only two different bodies: first, from the inception of the NHS up to 1974 by Regional Hospital Boards, then 1974–1996 by Regional Health Authorities. The bodies were created to manage the local NHS on behalf of the secretary of state. However, the pace of change

in the administration of the NHS over the past decade has been remarkable. Regional Health Authorities were replaced by Health Authorities from 1996–2002. Then, in 2002, 28 Strategic Health Authorities replaced the previous 95 health authorities. However, there has been further reorganisation since then and the 28 strategic health authorities (SHAs) of 2002 vintage were reduced, by way of amalgamations, to 10 new Strategic Health Authorities from, as from July 1, 2006. The new Strategic Health Authorities cater for populations ranging in size from London, catering for a population of nearly 7.5 million people to the North East, catering for a population of just over 2.5 million.

The following commentary has been extracted from the "Strategic Health Authorities", Department of Health NHS Factsheet, which may be viewed at: http://www.info.doh.gov.uk/nhsfactsheets.nsf/vwHelp/Strategic%20health%20authorities?OpenDocument [Accessed February 28, 2008].

"The health authorities have a strategic role. This means they are responsible for:

- developing plans for improving health services in their local area;
- making sure local health services are of a high quality and are performing well;
- increasing the capacity of local health services—so they can provide more services; and
- making sure national priorities—for example, programmes for improving cancer services—are integrated into local health service plans.

"Strategic Health Authorities manage the NHS locally and are a key link between the Department of Health and the NHS. They hold all local NHS organisations (apart from NHS Foundation Trusts) to account for performance."

A map showing the areas administered by the "2002" SHAs and the areas covered by the amalgamated "2006 SHAs" may be located online at: http://nlhcms.library.nhs.uk/nlhdocs/SHA-map.pdf [Accessed February 28, 2008].

Within each SHA, the NHS is further divided into a number of trusts that have the prime responsibility for providing the NHS services within that region. The principal budget-controllers are the Primary Care Trusts (PCTs).

Primary Care Trusts and NHS Trusts

Key Principle: **Primary Care Trusts, which were created under s.2 of the Health Act 1999, with the provisions being inserted after s.16 of the NHS Act 1977, are now provided for by s.18 of the NHS Act 2006.**

CHAPTER 2 [NHS Act 2006]

PRIMARY CARE TRUSTS

18. Primary Care Trusts

(1) The Primary Care Trusts established by the Secretary of State continue in existence.

(2) But the Secretary of State may by order (a "PCT order")—

(a) vary the area in England for which a Primary Care Trust is established;
(b) abolish a Primary Care Trust;
(c) establish a new Primary Care Trust for the area in England specified in the order with a view to it exercising functions in relation to the health service.

(3) The Secretary of State must act under this section so as to ensure that the areas for which Primary Care Trusts are at any time established together comprise the whole of England.

(4) A Primary Care Trust must exercise its functions in accordance with any prohibitions or restrictions in a PCT order relating to it.

. . .

(8) Schedule 3 makes further provision about Primary Care Trusts.

19. Exercise of Primary Care Trust functions

(1) This section applies to functions exercisable by a Primary Care Trust under or by virtue of this Act (including this section) or any prescribed provision of any other Act.

(2) Regulations may provide for any functions to which this section applies to be exercised—

   (a) by another Primary Care Trust;

   (b) by a Special Health Authority; or

   (c) jointly with any one or more of the bodies mentioned in subs.(3).

(3) The bodies are—

   (a) Strategic Health Authorities;

   (b) NHS trusts;

   (c) Local Health Boards; and

   (d) other Primary Care Trusts.

. . .

20. Strategic Health Authority directions to Primary Care Trusts

(1) A Strategic Health Authority may give directions to a Primary Care Trust about its exercise of any function.

(2) Directions under this section are subject to any directions given under s.8.

Commentary

Formerly, family practitioner services were organised by health authorities and they replaced family health service authorities in this respect. Whereas the Health Act 1999 provided the Secretary of State with the discretion to create Primary Care Trusts, which, inter alia, would organise the "first-line" of care by way of GPs, etc. the discretion under the 1999 Act was replaced by a duty under the NHS Reform and Health Care professions Act 2002, s.2. Currently, the role of Primary Care Trusts (PCTs) includes the planning and securing of primary care in their geographical areas. This is achieved via the provision of GPs, pharmacists, dentists, and opticians. GPs may remain independent contractors or work under a contract with the PCT (see next chapter). PCTs also make provisions for secondary care via hospitals and ambulance services.

It is generally thought that PCTs control about 75 per cent of the NHS budget—and, as noted, above, the NHS budget for 2007/08 has been estimated at being in excess of £90 billion!

NHS Trusts are provided for by ss.25–27 and Sch.5 of the NHS Act 2006. In essence, NHS Trusts run the NHS hospitals and employ the majority of the NHS workforce.

This URL links to easy-to-read information about trusts: http://www.nhs.uk/aboutnhs/howtheNHSworks/

authoritiesandtrusts/Pages/Authoritiesandtrusts.aspx   [Accessed February 28, 2008].

Key principle: **All NHS organisations—Strategic Health Authorities, PCTs, NHS Trusts, etc.—have a duty to monitor and, so far as is practicable, continuously improve the quality of the services they provide.**

Health and Social Care (Community Health and Standards) Act 2003

Section 45 Quality in health care
(1) It is the duty of each NHS body to put and keep in place arrangements for the purpose of monitoring and improving the quality of health care provided by and for that body.

(2) In this part "heath care" means—

   (a) Services provided to individuals for or in connection with the prevention, diagnosis or treatment of illness; and
   (b) the promotion and protection of public health.

In subs.(2)(a), "illness" has the meaning given by s.275 of the [NHS] Act 2006.

Commentary
When in force, the Health and Social Care Act 2008 will amend the NHS Act 2006 by placing a duty on Primary Care Trusts (PCTs) requiring them to make arrangements to secure continuous improvement in the quality of health care provided by or for them. This duty (which was contained in cl.129 of the Health and Social Care Bill 2007) will replace s.45 of the Health and Social care (Community Health and Standards) Act 2003.

Special Health Authorities—section 28 of the NHS Act 2006

CHAPTER 4

SPECIAL HEALTH AUTHORITIES

28. Special Health Authorities

(1) The Secretary of State may by order establish special bodies for the purpose of exercising any functions which may be conferred on them by or under this Act.

. . .

(2) A body established under this section is called a Special Health Authority.

. . .

(8) Schedule 6 makes further provision about Special Health Authorities.

Commentary

Special Health Authorities are organisations that provide services for the English and Welsh NHS. They are independent organisations with their own board, but still fall under ministerial direction. Sch.6, para.1 of the NHS Act 2006 provides that "Each Special Health Authority is a body corporate". Half-a-dozen of, perhaps, the most noteworthy Special Health Authorities might include:

National Patient Safety Agency

In essence, this Special Health Authority co-ordinates the efforts of all those involved in healthcare, and disseminates information so that all involved can learn from patient safety incidents occurring in the NHS. So, for example, guidance issued in February 2007 focused on the promotion, support and use of auto identification (barcoding and similar technologies) to increase patient safety and improve efficiency. It was claimed that there was evidence of demonstrable improvements to patient safety when coding systems were used to match patients to their care. The improvements were evidenced by: reduced medication errors, reduced risk of wrong site surgery, accurate track and trace of surgical instruments, equipment and other devices and much better record keeping. (Coding for success: simple technology for safer patient care, published February 16, 2007).

The newly created National Research Ethics Services, established on April 1, 2007, has become part of the NPSA. For further information, go to: http://www.nres.npsa.nhs.uk/ [Accessed February 28, 2008] and see brief notes on NRES in Ch.12, Research.

NHS Blood and Transplant

This was established as a Special Health Authority in October 2005 to provide a reliable, efficient supply of blood, organs and associated services to the NHS. Links from the home page: http://www.nhsbt.nhs.uk/ [Accessed February 28, 2008] locate information on services such as the Cord Blood Bank set up in 1996 "to collect, process, store and supply cord blood for the sole purpose of providing a life saving product from something that is normally thrown away"; and provide the statistic that nearly 15 million people—24 per cent of the population—have registered their wishes to help others to live after their deaths by placing their names on the NHS Organ Donor Register.

NHS Direct
The Mission statement of NHS Direct is:

"To provide information and advice about health, illness and health services, to enable patients to make decisions about their healthcare and that of their families".

NHS Direct claims to be far more than a telephone help-line and, indeed, since the inception of the NHS Direct digital TV service, it claims to have more than 2 million people per month accessing its services. In fact, during the outbreak of the norovirus "winter vomiting virus" over the Christmas / new year period, 2007/ 2008, alone, 1.2 million people asked NHS Direct staff for advice.

NHS Direct became the first national organisation to apply for Foundation Trust status. (Previously, the only Foundation Trusts were hospitals and mental health services). The public consultation on NHS Direct's application to become an NHS Foundation Trust closed on Monday, March 31, 2008.

The URL for NHS Direct is: http://www.nhsdirect.nhs.uk/ [Accessed February 28, 2008].

NHS Institute for Innovation and improvement
The NHS Institute for Innovation and Improvement claims to support the NHS to "transform healthcare for patients and the public by rapidly developing and spreading new ways of working, new technology and world-class leadership."

"The Productive Operating Theatre" is one of the programmes developed by NHS Institute for Innovation and Improvement. The stated aim of this project was to: "give frontline NHS organisations and staff the knowledge and practical improvement tools they need to:

- **measure** and compare their performance locally and nationally;

- **improve** theatre performance dramatically, giving patients a better experience, increasing the reliability and safety of care, improving efficiency by reducing waste, and driving down waiting times."

The URL for this Special Health Authority is: http://www.institute.nhs.uk/ [Accessed February 28, 2008]

NHS Litigation Authority
The NHS Litigation Authority was established in 1995 and a summary of its expressed functions is:

(i) to ensure claims are dealt with consistently and with due regard to the proper interests of the NHS and its patients;

(ii) to manage the financial consequences of such claims and to advise the Department of Health of the likely future costs;

(iii) to advise the Department of Health on both specific and general issues arising out of claims against the NHS;

(iv) to manage and raise the standards of risk management throughout the NHS;

(v) to assist NHS bodies to comply with the Human Rights Act 1998 by providing a central source of information on relevant case-law development;

(vi) to provide mechanisms for the proper, prompt and cost-effective resolution of disputes between NHS primary care organisations and those providing, or seeking to provide, services for patients; and

(vii) to provide advice about, and assistance with, litigation concerning equal pay claims involving NHS bodies in England.

Further information relating to this Special Health Authority may be traced from this URL: http://www.nhsla.com/home.htm [Accessed February 28, 2008].

NICE (National Institute for Health and Clinical Excellence)
This Special Health Authority was established as the National Institute for Clinical Excellence (NICE) in 1999. In 2005, it merged with the Health Development Agency and became the National Institute for Health and Clinical Excellence but it retained its acronym, NICE. NICE is responsible for providing national guidance on the promotion of good health and the prevention and treatment of ill health. Its expressed functions are to produce "best practice" guidance in three areas of health:

- public health—via guidance on the promotion of good health and the prevention of ill health for those working in the NHS, local authorities and the wider public and voluntary sector;

- health technologies—via guidance on the use of new and existing medicines, treatments and procedures within the NHS; and

- clinical practice—via guidance on the appropriate treatment and care of people with specific diseases and conditions within the NHS.

Commentary
Undoubtedly, the most critical comments about NICE have followed controversial decisions to reject a drug for use in the NHS on the grounds that it was not cost effective—perhaps because only a small proportion of patients for whom the drug was intended would find them beneficial. One example relates to Sutent and Nexavar for the treatment of kidney cancer where the cost of treatment per patient may reach £2,500 per month. Another example relates to the use of High Intensity Focused Ultrasound (HIFU) labelled "a life-saving treatment" for

prostate cancer which, for a "one-off" treatment, costs about £13,000. By way of comparison, it costs about £3,000 for radiotherapy, which takes six weeks, and £5,000 for surgery. However, there is evidence that HIFU has eliminated 90 per cent of prostate tumours, and five years after treatment, 80 per cent of patients exhibit no indication of the cancer recurring.

Pharmaceutical companies aggrieved at the decisions of NICE have now started to seek judicial review, although, perhaps, with very limited success: *R. (on the application of Eisai Ltd) v NICE* [2007] EWHC 1941 (Admin) where the determination of NICE that a drug to treat the sufferers of Alzheimer's disease of moderate severity, only, was upheld.

Decided cases on the allocation of scarce resources are noted below under the heading "Healthcare and Resource Allocation", and the use by NICE of the QALY (Quality Adjusted Life Year) in determining the treatments that constitute value for money is discussed in Ch.3, Ethics.

The URL for NICE is: http://www.nice.org.uk/ [Accessed February 28, 2008].

Complaints about NHS bodies: National Health Service (Complaints) Regulations 2004, SI 2004/1768 (as amended)

Key Principle: **Notwithstanding the aims and expectations that arise from the performance of competent NHS treatment, not everyone's expectations are met and regulations have been enacted so that complaints that follow are treated sympathetically, promptly and formally.**

Complaints about NHS bodies:

The National Health Service (Complaints) Regulations 2004, SI 2004/1768

Interpretation
2.–(1) In these regulations—
"NHS body" means a Strategic Health Authority, an NHS Trust which operates from premises wholly or mainly in England, a Primary Care Trust and a Special Health Authority to which s.2 of the Health Service Commissioners Act 1993 applies;...

Part II Handling and Consideration of Complaints By NHS Bodies

Arrangements for the handling and consideration of complaints

3.–(1) Each NHS body must make arrangements in accordance with these Regulations for the handling and consideration of complaints.

(2) The arrangements must be accessible and such as to ensure that complaints are dealt with speedily and efficiently, and that complainants are treated courteously and sympathetically and as far as possible involved in decisions about how their complaints are handled and considered.

(3) The arrangements must be in writing and a copy must be given, free of charge, to any person who makes a request for one. . . .

Responsibility for complaints arrangements

4. Each NHS body must designate one of its members, or in the case of an NHS trust a member of its board of directors, to take responsibility for ensuring compliance with the arrangements made under these Regulations and that action is taken in the light of the outcome of any investigation.

Complaints manager

5.–(1) Each NHS body must designate a person, in these Regulations referred to as a complaints manager, to manage the procedures for handling and considering complaints and in particular—

(a) to perform the functions of the complaints manager under this Part; and

(b) to perform such other functions in relation to complaints as the NHS body may require.

Complaints to NHS bodies

6. Subject to reg.7, a complaint to an NHS body may be about any matter reasonably connected with the exercise of its functions including in particular, in the case of an

NHS trust or Primary Care Trust, any matter reasonably connected with—

(a) its provision of health care or any other services ...; and

(b) the function of commissioning health care or other services under an NHS contract or making arrangements for the provision of such care for other services with an independent provider or with an NHS foundation trust.

Matters excluded from consideration under the arrangements

7. The following complaints are excluded from the scope of the arrangements required under this Part—

(b) a complaint made by a primary care provider...

(f) a complaint which is being or has been investigated by the Health Service Commissioner;

(g) a complaint arising out of an NHS body's alleged failure to comply with a data subject request under the Data Protection Act 1998 or a request for information under the Freedom of Information Act 2000;

(h) a complaint about which the complainant has stated in writing that he intends to take legal proceedings;...

Persons who may make complaints

8.–(1) A complaint may be made by—

(a) a patient; or

(b) any person who is affected by or likely to be affected by the action, omission or decision of the NHS body which is the subject of the complaint.

(2) A complaint may be made by a person (in these Regulations referred to as a representative) acting on behalf of a person mentioned in para.1 in any case where that person—

(a) has died;

(b) is a child;

(c) is unable by reason of physical or mental incapacity to make the complaint himself; or

(d) has requested the representative to act on his behalf.

Making a complaint

9.–(1) Where a person wishes to make a complaint under these Regulations, he may make the complaint to the complaints manager or any other member of the staff of the NHS body which is the subject of the complaint.

(2) A complaint may be made orally or in writing (including electronically) and—

  (a) where it is made orally, the complaints manager must make a written record of the complaint which includes the name of the complainant, the subject matter of the complaint and the date on which it was made; and

  (b) where it is made in writing, the complaints manager must make a written record of the date on which it was received.

Commentary

Given that the bodies to which complaints may be addressed are those specified in reg.2(1), they exclude foundation trusts (in England) at the first (local resolution) level and primary care providers—complaints procedures for the latter are discussed in Ch.2.

Regulation 9 provides for the initiation of local resolution by the complainant submitting the complaint to "the NHS body which is the subject of the complaint", and reg.10 provides for a general time limit of six months in which to lodge the complaint, although in particular circumstances the complaint may be investigated after this time.

Regulation 13(3) (as amended) now provides for the complainant to receive a written response within 25 working days beginning on the date on which the complaint was made and to be made aware of his (the complainant's) right to refer his complaint to the second stage of resolution (should it be necessary) via the independent Healthcare Commission (see below).

The general rule in reg.7(h) that the complaints regulations exclude "a complaint about which the complainant has stated in writing that he intends to take legal proceedings" applies also to the Healthcare Commission: reg.15(3)(a).

If reference of the complaint to the Healthcare Commission fails to resolve the matter, a further reference to the Health Service Commissioner (the Ombudsman) is possible under reg.16(2)(g) and s.10 of the Health Service Commissioners Act

1993. This requires the complaint to be made in writing generally within one year of the incident giving rise to the complaint.

Whereas a convention seemed to be developing that investigation by the Ombudsman would preclude the complainant from pursuing legal action, there is, in fact, no legal basis for this: court action may be pursued on the basis of evidence established by the Ombudsman.

Forthcoming Mergers

Key Principle: **The Commission for Health Audit and Inspection (CHAI), usually known as The "Healthcare Commission", and the Commission for Social Care Inspection (CSCI) which, at present, are distinct bodies, are scheduled to merge under the proposed Health and Social Care Act 2008.**

Health and Social Care (Community Health and Standards) Act 2003

PART 2

STANDARDS

CHAPTER 1

REGULATORY BODIES

Section 41 The Commission for Healthcare Audit and Inspection
   (1)   There is to be a body corporate known as the Commission for Healthcare Audit and Inspection (in this part referred to the CHAI)

   ...

Section 42 The Commission for Social Care Inspection
   (1)   There is to be a body corporate known as the Commission for Social care Inspection (in this Part referred to as the CSCI)

   ...

Commentary

Amongst the functions the Commission for Healthcare Audit and Inspection—better known as the Healthcare Commission—carries out in England are: the regulation and inspection of NHS, private and voluntary healthcare providers; and the authority to review formal complaints about NHS bodies that have not been resolved locally. The Commission is chaired by Sir Ian Kennedy and its website may be located at: http://www.healthcare commission. org.uk/ [Accessed February 28, 2008]

The Commission for Social Care Inspection inspects and reviews, principally, all social care services for adults in the public, private and voluntary sectors in England. They also give a "star rating" to councils which become an important part of an annual Comprehensive Performance Assessment (CPA). This Commission is chaired by Dame Denise Platt and the website for CSCI is located at: http://www.csci.org.uk/ [Accessed February 28, 2008]

Whereas it was first proposed in 2005 that the two Commissions should merge, the merger is now scheduled to take place in 2008 under the provisions of the proposed Health and Social Care Act 2008.

Healthcare and Resource Allocation (or rationing)

Key Principle: **The general rule at common law is that the courts have refused to direct how funds should be allocated (rationed) within the NHS if the decision relating to the allocation wasn't unlawful or irrational.**

R. v Secretary of State for Social Services, Ex p. Hincks (1979) 123 S.J. 436

After hospital patients had waited for treatment for periods longer than was advisable because of a shortage of facilities, they sought declarations that the respondent authorities were in breach of their statutory duties under the then prevailing National Health Service Act to provide the necessary facilities and health service.

Held: The application was dismissed as it was not the court's function to direct Parliament what funds to make available and how to allocate them. The court could interfere with the

Secretary of State's conduct only if he had acted so as to frustrate the policy of the Act, or in a manner in which no reasonable minister could have acted.

Commentary
Initially, the refusal of the courts to become involved in the allocation of scarce medical resources continued, even in life-or-death situations:

R. v Central Birmingham HA Ex p. Walker (1987) 3 B.M.L.R. 32
The mother of a premature baby who needed a heart operation sought an order to require the health authority to carry out the operation that had been postponed a number of times because of a shortage of specially trained nurses in the intensive care unit where he would have to go after the operation.

Held: (At first instance) The application was refused, with MacPherson J. saying:

> "... I detect a general criticism of the decisions as to the staffing and financing of the National Health Service and of those who provide its funds and facilities. It has been said before, and I say it again, that this court can no more investigate that on the facts of this case than it could do so in any other case where the balance of available money and its distribution and use are concerned....
>
> I am wholly convinced that this decision of the health authority is not justiciable, that is to say that it is not a matter in which the court should intervene. If it were so, then any question of priority or clinical judgment of which case came first could be subject to review where it may depend on the location of available facilities."

And in the Court of Appeal, Sir John Donaldson M.R. said:

> "This court could only intervene where it was satisfied that there was a *prima facie* case, not only of failing to allocate resources in the way in which others would think that resources should be allocated, but of a failure to allocate resources to an extent which was *Wednesbury* unreasonable ... Even then, of course, the court has to exercise its judicial discretion. It has to take account of all the circumstances of the particular case with which it is concerned."

R. v Cambridge DHA Ex p. B [1995] 1 W.L.R. 898
Doctors who had been treating a 10-year-old girl, B, for acute myeloid leukaemia after she became ill, the year after she had received a bone marrow transplant from her sister, decided that

no further treatment should be given to prolong her life. The proposed treatment consisted of chemotherapy, with an estimated chance of success of 10 to 20 per cent and, if successful, a second bone marrow transplant with the same estimated chance of success. The total cost of treatment would be about £75,000. B's father challenged the decision and, at first instance, an order was granted requiring the Health Authority to reconsider its decision not to treat B. The authority appealed, claiming such further treatment would be "experimental" and, given the limited chance of successful treatment, the cost could not be justified.

Held: The appeal was allowed as the court had to confine itself to ruling only on whether the authority's decision was lawful. To require the authority to make a decision on the basis that only part of the funding might be required if the chemotherapy was unsuccessful was unrealistic. Moreover, the authority's decision was not flawed by the use of the word "experimental" to describe the proposed course of treatment. The treatment had no proven record of success and it was essential to make agonising decisions on the most effective use of limited resources.

Commentary
There is no reason to believe the cases above would not be followed unless, of course, it could be shown that decisions were contrary to guidance from the Department of Health that had been ignored, or were irrational, as in the following cases:

R. v North Derbyshire HA Ex p. Fisher [1997] 8 Med L.R. 327
The health authority disregarded a health circular requesting all health authorities to facilitate the introduction of beta-interferon into the NHS and to continue prescribing it in hospitals for those suffering from multiple sclerosis.

Held: Whereas the circular provided merely guidance and was not mandatory, the health authority had failed in its duty to give serious consideration to the advice contained in the circular and had implemented an unlawful blanket ban on making the drug available. Accordingly, the decision to refuse to fund F's treatment would be quashed and an order was made requiring the health authority to formulate and implement a policy that took full account of the circular.

Commentary
In common with the following case, this case was also applied by the case involving Swindon NHS Primary Care Trust, below.

North West Lancashire HA v A, D and G [2001] 1 W.L.R. 977
Of the three applicants, each of whom suffered from gender identity dysphoria, two had been diagnosed as having a clinical need for gender reassignment surgery and the third was waiting assessment for suitable surgery. However, whereas the initial policy of the health authority was not to pay for such surgery or specialist counselling outside its own area (having the effect that the only specialist clinic in London), a revised policy provided for exceptions based on overriding clinical need but was qualified by stating that "such exceptions will be rare, unpredictable and will usually be based on circumstances that could not have been predicted at the time when the policy was adopted". The health authority then refused requests by the applicants to be referred to the clinic in London.

Held: At first instance, the authority's decisions and policy were quashed and the judgment was upheld on appeal. Whilst it was not improper to have a general policy and to have exceptions to it in circumstances that could be left undefined, it was evident that the authority did not really believe that the condition was an illness that merited anything other than psychiatric reassurance. Moreover, the ostensible provision made for exceptions in individual cases effectively amounted to a blanket policy against funding treatment. Accordingly, the authorities policies were quashed and the matter remitted to the authority for reconsideration of its policies and their decisions on their individual merits.

Commentary
The appellate judiciary were of the opinion that this case could be decided without reference to the provisions of the European Convention on Human Rights and Fundamental Freedoms, arts 3 and 8, degrading treatment and right to respect for a private life, respectively. With regard to devoting resources to a particular treatment, this case was applied by the following:

R. (on the application of Rogers) v Swindon NHS Primary Care Trust [2006] 1 W.L.R. 2649

The applicant, Ann Marie Rogers, was a patient with primary breast cancer who was prescribed by her oncologist a drug (Herceptin) which was licensed for the treatment of late stage breast cancer but not for the earlier stage from which she suffered. However, she came within the eligible group of patients for whom the drug was likely to be effective and to increase her life expectancy. She applied to the defendant primary care trust for her treatment to be funded by the National Health Service. It was the general policy of the trust to fund off-licence drug treatment not approved by the National Institute for Health and Clinical Excellence ("NICE") only where a patient had a special healthcare problem that presented an exceptional need for treatment having regard to the funds available. In the case of the drug in question the trust decided to fund off-licence treatment in exceptional circumstances but without regard to cost. Mrs Rogers was denied funding because she was not considered to be an exceptional case. At first instance, her claim for judicial review of that decision was dismissed on the ground that the trust's policy in relation to the drug was not irrational.

Held: The appeal was allowed. In deciding whether the trust's policy was irrational, the question to be considered was whether there were any relevant exceptional circumstances which could justify the trust refusing treatment to one patient in the eligible group but granting it to another. The only relevant consideration was the clinical needs of the patient and, accordingly, the only reasonable approach was to fund patients who were properly prescribed the drug by their doctor.

Funding Treatment Elsewhere in the EU

Key Principle: **Where a patient may experience "undue delay" in obtaining operative treatment on the NHS in the UK, it may be possible for the NHS to fund that treatment elsewhere in the EU.**

R. (on the application of Watts) v Bedford Primary Care Trust [2004] EWCA Civ 166

Wheelchair-bound Mrs Yvonne Watts applied to her PCT to have her bi-lateral hip-replacement performed in France under a

Community law scheme after she had been told that she would have to wait a year for the operation in England. The PCT refused but reclassified her condition and, as a result, reduced her waiting time to four months. Mrs Watts did not wait, however, and she had the operation performed in France. On her return, Mrs Watts sought reimbursement of her full costs plus a declaration that the trust's decision had been unlawful and contravened the Human Rights Act 1998 Sch.1 Pt I Art.3 (degrading treatment) and Art.8 (right to respect for private life). Mrs Watts failed at first instance as Munby J. found that, although undue delay might be evident even within target waiting times, there was no evidence of undue delay in her case. The appeals of both Mrs Watts and the Department of Health were referred to the ECJ.

Held: In Case C–372/04, the ECJ decided that in determining an acceptable waiting time, Member States had to apply "an objective medical assessment of the clinical needs of the person concerned in the light of all the factors characterising his medical condition". Accordingly, if a patient has to wait for treatment longer than medically advised, the NHS must refund the costs when the patient seeks and obtains treatment elsewhere in the EU, because the patient has a right to receive a service under Art.49 EC. In this case, however, Mrs Watts' rights under Art.49 EC were extinguished when her condition was reclassified and her waiting time was reduced to four months. Moreover, there had been no breach of either Art.3 or Art.8 of the European Convention on Human Rights.

Commentary
In Case C–157/99, *BSM Geraets-Smits*, the ECJ decided that where a patient residing in one Member State of the EU was experiencing "undue delay" in receiving treatment there, his State insurance system had to be prepared to fund the appropriate treatment in another Member State where it could be performed expeditiously.

However, plans to formalise the process of a patient resident in one Member State seeking and receiving treatment in another Member State, via an EU Directive and, perhaps, without prior authorisation from the NHS funding body (usually a PCT, in England), were shelved, at least temporarily, in December 2007, pending finalisation of how a single market in healthcare could function to the satisfaction of all Member States.

The Labour Government and the Conservative opposition expressed very different opinions on the proposal, with Dawn Primorolo, the Health Minister saying:

> "What we cannot allow and will not allow is that a few very wealthy patients choose to go elsewhere and then give the NHS the bill".

By contrast, Andrew Lansley, the Conservative health spokesman said:

> "So long as the EU rules allow us to maintain the principles of NHS care, we can and should accept the implications of maximising patient choice".

Continuing Reform of the NHS

On entering office in June 2007, Prime Minister Gordon Brown appointed Sir Ara Darzi as health minister and charged him with the task of undertaking a major NHS review. In July 2007, just a couple of weeks after his appointment, Sir Ara made his first proposals on the future of healthcare in London. These included the setting up of "polyclinics"—described as "super GP surgeries"—which "would incorporate a GP service alongside diagnostic tests, social care, mental health services and some minor surgery" (BBC News online, July 11, 2007). The polyclinics would be equipped with X-ray and ultrasound machines and it was thought that "by 2017 a network of polyclinics throughout London could provide up to 50% of outpatient treatment currently carried out in hospitals" (*ibid*). The proposals drew a less-than-enthusiastic response both from *Health Emergency*, a union-funded pressure group, and from the chairman of the BMA's consultants committee.

Sir Ara's completed review of the NHS is expected before the 60th anniversary of the NHS, on July 5, 2008. At the end of the review, the Government will consider the case for a new NHS Constitution.

Meanwhile, the latest reforms revolve around the National Programme for IT (NPfIT) which is aimed at helping the NHS to deliver better, safer care to patients via new computer systems and services; and those contained within the proposed Health and Social Care Act 2008 that establishes a Care Quality Commission (CQC) that will be responsible for the registration, review and inspection of certain health and social care services in England. In doing so, the CQC will merge and replace the

Commission for Healthcare Audit and Inspection (the "Health-care Commission") and the Commission for Social Care Inspection (CSCI); and take on the functions previously under-taken by the Mental Health Act Commission (MHAC).

Reforms introduced by the proposed Health and Social Care Act 2008 in relation to the regulation of healthcare professionals are noted in Ch.2.

2. THE DOCTOR-PATIENT RELATIONSHIP

"Doctors" and "Patients"

Key Principle: Provisions relating to "doctors" and "patients" are provided for both in primary legislation and statutory instruments; and the regulation of the doctor-patient relationship and the accountability of the former to the latter is governed likewise.

The General Practitioner: Who is a "Doctor"?

Meaning of "GP": NHS (General Medical Services Contracts) Regulations 2004, SI 2004/291

Interpretation

2.–(1) In these regulations—
"general medical practitioner" means ... a medical practitioner whose name is included in the General Practitioner Register .. [and the] "General Practitioner Register" means the register kept by the General Medical Council under Art.10 of the General and Specialist Medical Practice (Education, Training and Qualifications) Order 2003.

Commentary
The attribution of the title "doctor" to medical graduates is merely a convention. Section 3(1) of the Medical Act 1983 refers, simply, to a "person whose fitness to practise is not impaired ... is entitled to be registered ... as a fully registered *medical practitioner*".

Privileges of Registered Medical Practitioners.
Part VI of the Medical Act 1983 (ss.46–49) provides for the "Privileges of Registered Practitioners". It should be noted, however, that ss.46–48 are subject to minor amendments to be made by SI 2002/3135 (not in force as at February 1, 2008).

Section 46 provides that only a registered person can recover fees in respect of "any medical advice or attendance, or for the performance of any operation unless he proves that he is fully

registered" ["and holds a licence to practise"—amendment
pending, as noted].

Section 47 provides that certain appointments "in any hospital
... [and] ... in any prison ... are not to be held by any person
who is not fully registered" ["and who holds a licence to practise
..."..].

Section 49 provides a sanction in that "any person who wilfully and falsely pretends to be or takes or uses the name or title
of physician, doctor of medicine ... or any name ... or descrip-
tion implying that he is registered under ... this Act ... shall be
liable on summary conviction to a fine ...".

Section 49A (when in force) will provide an additional "Pen-
alty for pretending to hold a licence to practise", viz:
49A

(1) If a person who does not hold a licence to practise—

    (a) holds himself out as having such a licence; or
    (b) engages in conduct calculated to suggest that he has
        such a licence,

    he shall be liable on summary conviction to a fine not
    exceeding level five on the standard scale.

For case law decided by reference to s.40 of the Medical Act
1858 (very similar to s.49 of the 1983 Act), see: *Younghusband v
Luftig* [1949] 2 K.B. 354—respondent did not use the title of
"doctor of medicine" wilfully and falsely; see, also, another case
with a similar outcome: *Wilson v Inyang* [1951] 2 K.B. 799.

Key Principle: **A pre-requisite for a general practitioner's
eligibility to enter into a contract with a Primary Care Trust, so
as to provide services under SI 2004/291, is that he has to be on
the *medical performers list* that is maintained by the Primary
Care Trust.**

The NHS (Performers Lists) Regulations 2004, SI 2004/585
Interpretation and modification

2.–(1) In these Regulations—
"medical performers list" means a list of medical practitioners
prepared and published pursuant to reg.3(1)(a);

Performers lists

(1) A Primary care Trust shall prepare and publish,...

    (a) a medical performers list

(2) Performers lists shall be available for public inspection

Medical performers list

22.–(1) Subject to [exceptions], a medical practitioner may not perform any primary medical services, unless he is a general medical practitioner and his name is included in a medical performers list.

Commentary

Regulation 4 of SI 2004/585 provides the requirements for applying for inclusion on the performers list and reg.9 details the requirements with which a performer in a performers list must comply. Regulation 10 provides the mandatory provisions for the removal of the performer from the PCTs performers list (for reasons of convictions for serious criminal offences and death, for example) after the criteria for a decision on removal, as provided for in reg.11, are discussed.

    N.B. The regulations and PCTs apply to England, only.

Key Principle: **A medical practitioner who wishes to provide general medical services for a PCT must be eligible to be contracted under SI 2004/291.**

Part II, reg.3 of SI 2004/291 provides that: "... a Primary Care Trust may only enter into a contract if the conditions set out in regulations 4 and 5 are met."

Conditions relating solely to medical practitioners

4.–(1) In the case of a contract to be entered into with a medical practitioner, that practitioner must be a general medical practitioner

(2) In the case of a contract to be entered into with two or more individuals practising in partnership—

    (a) at least one partner (who must not be a limited partner) must be a general medical practitioner;...

Commentary

Paragraph 53 of Sch.6 to SI 2004/291 provides, so far as is relevant here:

(1) ... [No] medical practitioner shall perform medical services under the contract unless he is—

    (a) included in a medical performers list for a PCT in England; ....

Moreover, *R. (on the application of Malik) v Waltham Forest Primary Care Trust* [2006] 3 All E.R. 71 confirmed that a doctor had to included on the performers list before he could enter a contract to provide general medical services under SI 2004/291.

Regulation 5, SI 2004/291, which provides for a "general condition relating to all contracts", specifies, inter alia, that whether it be an individual or a partnership that is contracted, (s)he or they must not have been convicted of a serious criminal offence (as provided for in reg.5(2)); nor convicted of a specified offence under the Children and Young Persons Act 1933 on or after March 1, 2004; nor has been adjudged bankrupt.

SI 2004/291, Part V: Contracts; Required Terms

Essential Services

15.–(1) ... the services which must be provided under a general medical services contract ("essential services") are the services described in paragraphs (3), (5), (6) and (8).

(3) The services described in this paragraph are services required for the management of its registered patients and temporary residents who are, or believe themselves to be—

    (a) ill, with conditions from which recovery is generally expected;
    (b) terminally ill; or
    (c) suffering from chronic disease, delivered in the manner determined by the practice in discussion with the patient.

(5) The services described in this paragraph are the provision of appropriate ongoing treatment and care to all registered patients and temporary residents taking account of their specific needs including—

(a) the provision of advice in connection with the patient's health, including relevant health promotion advice; and

(b) the referral of the patient for other services under the Act.

(6) A contractor must provide primary medical services required in core hours for the immediately necessary treatment of any person to whom the contractor has been requested to provide treatment owing to an accident or emergency at any place in its practice area.

(8) [Refer, also, to regulations 9 and 10] A contractor must provide primary medical services required in core hours for the immediately necessary treatment of any person [(a) whose application for inclusion in the contractor's list has been refused / (b) whose application for acceptance as a temporary resident has been rejected / (c) who is present in the contractor's practice area for less than 24 hours]; and the period for providing such treatment may last for 14 days or until that person has been registered elsewhere (a) / accepted elsewhere as a temporary resident (b); or for up to 24 hours (c).

Commentary
Schedule 6, reg.26 provides for "other contractual terms" which include:

- Providing premises suitable for the delivery of the contractor's [GPs] services;

- Invite newly registered patients to participate in a consultation; and

- be prepared to see registered patients aged between 16 years and 75 who have not attended for a consultation within three years prior to making a request; and

- provide consultations for patients aged over 75 years who have not participated in a consultation during the 12 months prior to making a request.

Other parts of Sch.6, reg.26 with which a contractor must comply include:

Part III Prescribing and Dispensing

Excessive Prescribing

46.–(1) The contractor shall not prescribe drugs, medicines or appliances whose cost or quantity, in relation to any patient, is, by reason of the character of the drug, medicine or appliance in question in excess of that which was reasonably necessary for the proper treatment of that patient.

Part IV Persons Who Perform Services
Level of Skill

67. The contractor shall carry out its obligations under the contract with reasonable care and skill.

(For a discussion on the standard of care by which a doctor is judged, see Ch.7 on Medical Negligence).

Part V Records, Information, Notifications and Rights of Entry
Patient Records

73.–(1) In this paragraph, "computerised records" means records created by way of entries on a computer.

(2) The contractor shall keep adequate records of its attendance on and treatment of its patients and shall do so—

  (a) on forms supplied to it for the purpose by the Primary Care Trust; or

  (b) with the written consent of the Primary Care trust, by way of computerised records, or in a combination of those two ways.

Confidentiality of personal data

75. The contractor shall nominate a person with responsibility for practices and procedures relating to the confidentiality of personal data held by it.

(For further discussion of aspects of confidentiality in medical records, see Ch.6 on Confidentiality)

Who is a doctor's (GP's) patient?

Key Principle: **Provisions for applications for inclusion in a list of patients and requests for removal from the list—whether**

at the request of the patient or the contractor [GP]—are contained in SI 2004/291

SI 2004/291, Schedule 6, Part II: Patients

List of Patients

14. The Primary Care Trust shall prepare and keep up to date a list of all the patients—

    (a) who have been accepted by the contractor for inclusion in its list of patients ... and who have not been subsequently removed from that list...

    (b) who have been assigned to the contractor ... and whose assignment has not subsequently been rescinded.

Application for inclusion in a list of patients

15.–(1) The contractor may, if its list of patients is open, accept an application for inclusion in its list of patients made by or on behalf of any person whether or not resident in its practice area or included, at the time of that application, in the list of patients of another contractor or provider of primary medical services.

   (2) The contractor may, if its list of patients is closed, only accept an application for inclusion in its list of patients from a person who is an immediate family member of a registered patient whether or not resident in its practice area or included, at the time of that application, in the list of patients of another contractor or provider of primary medical services.

   (4) An application may be made—

    (a) on behalf of any child—

      (i) by either parent, or in the absence of both parents, the guardian or other adult who has care of the child,

      (ii) by a person duly authorised by a local authority to whose care the child has been committed under the Children Act 1989, or

      (iii) by a person duly authorised by a voluntary organisation by which the child is being accommodated under the provisions of that Act; or

    (b) on behalf of any adult who is incapable of making such an application, or authorising such an application to be made on their behalf, by a relative or the primary carer of that person.

Temporary residents

16.–(1) The contractor may, if its list of patients is open, accept a person as a temporary resident provided it is satisfied that the person is—

    (a) temporarily resident away from his normal place and is not being provided with essential services (or their equivalent) under any other arrangement in the locality where he is temporarily residing; or

    (b) moving from place to place and not for the time being resident in any place.

  (3) A contractor which wishes to terminate its responsibility for a person accepted as a temporary resident before the end of—

    (a) three months; or

    (b) such shorter period for which it agreed to accept him as a patient,

shall notify him either orally or in writing and its responsibility for that patient shall cease 7 days after the date on which the notification was given.

Refusal of applications for inclusion in the list of patients or for acceptance as a temporary resident

17.–(1) The contractor shall only refuse an application made under paragraph 15 or 16 if it has reasonable grounds for doing so which do not relate to the applicant's race, gender, social class, age, religion, sexual orientation, appearance, disability or medical condition.

Removal from the list at the request of the patient

19.–(1) The contractor shall notify the Primary Care Trust in writing of any request for removal from its list of patients received from a registered patient.

Removal from the list at the request of the contractor

20.–(1) Subject to paragraph 21, a contractor which has reasonable grounds for wishing a patient to be removed from its list of patients which do not relate to the applicant's race, gender, social class, age, religion, sexual orientation, appearance, disability or medical condition shall—

(a) notify the Primary Care Trust in writing that it wishes to have the patient removed; and

(b) subject to sub-paragraph (2), notify the patient of its specific reasons for requesting removal.

(2) Where, in the reasonable opinion of the contractor—

(a) the circumstances of the removal are such that it is not appropriate for amore specific reason to be given; and

(b) there has been an irrevocable breakdown in the relationship between the patient and the contractor,

the reason given under sub-paragraph (1) may consist of a statement that there has been such a breakdown.

Removals from the list of patients who are violent

21.–(1) A contractor which wishes a patient to be removed from its list of patients with immediate effect on the grounds that—

(a) the patient has committed an act of violence against any of the persons specified in sub-paragraph (2) or behaved in such a way that any such person has feared for his safety; and

(b) it has reported the incident to the police, shall notify the Primary Care Trust in accordance with sub-paragraph (3)

(2) the persons referred to in sub-paragraph (1) are—

(a) the contractor where it is an individual medical practitioner;

(b) in the case of a contract with two or more individuals practising in partnership, a partner in that partnership,

(c) in the case of a contract with a company, a legal and beneficial owner of shares in that company;

(d) a member of the contractor's staff;

(e) a person engaged by the contractor to perform or assist in the performance of services under the contract; or

(f) any other person present—

    (i) on the practice premises, or

    (ii) in the place where services were provided to the patient under the contract.

(3) Notification under sub-paragraph (1) may be given by any means including telephone or fax but if not given in writing shall subsequently be confirmed in writing within seven days (and for this purpose a faxed notification is not a written one).

Commentary

Probably the most regrettable provision under this Part of the Regulations is reg.21 concerning the need to remove from the list violent patients. It is a sad reflection on society that at the beginning of the new millennium security guards are employed in hospitals and GP and dental surgeries have need to warn patients that no violence towards any member of staff will be tolerated.

Key Principle: **It is a requirement under SI 2004/291 that contractors [GPs] establish, operate and publicise to their patients' details of a complaints procedure to be pursued in matters relating to the services provided under the GPs contract**

SI 2004/291: Part VI; Complaints

Complaints procedure

92.–(1) The contractor shall establish and operate a complaints procedure to deal with any complaints in relation to any matter reasonably connected with the provision of services under the contract...

(2) The contractor shall take reasonable steps to ensure that patients are aware of—

    (a) the complaints procedure;...

(3) The contractor shall take reasonable steps to ensure that the complaints procedure is accessible to all patients.

Making of complaints

93. A complaint may be made by or, with his consent, on behalf of a patient, or former patient, who is receiving or has received services under the contract, or—

(a) where the patient is a child—

(i) by either parent, or ... the guardian or other adult who has care of the child, ...

(b) where the patient is incapable of making a complaint, by a relative or other adult who has an interest in his welfare.

Period of Making Complaints

95.–(1) [The general rule relating to] the period for making a complaint is—

(a) six months from the date on which the matter which is the subject of the complaint occurred; or

(b) six months from the date on which the matter which is the subject of the complaint comes to the complainant's notice provided that the complaint is made no later than 12 months after the date on which the matter which is the subject of the complaint occurred.

(2) where the complaint is not made during the period specified [above] [then, having regard to all the circumstances ..] it is still possible to investigate the complaint properly, ...

Commentary

Further requirements for complaints procedures

Regulation 96 specifies the administrative arrangements that must be adhered to, including the making or recording of complaints in writing and the time (usually within 10 days) to respond to the complainant.

Challenging a Doctor's Fitness to Practise

Key Principle: **Since November 1, 2004 a unified system has operated to hear and determine allegations concerning whether a doctor is fit to practise his profession.**

General Medical Council (Fitness to Practise) Rules, SI 2004/ 2608

2. Interpretation

In these Rules—

"allegation" means an allegation that the fitness to practise of a practitioner is impaired...

"Case Examiners" means the medical and lay Case Examiners to whom an allegation is referred...

"medical", in relation to any person, means a registered medical practitioner;

"FTP Panel" means a Fitness to Practise Panel...

Commentary

Prior to the coming into force of the 2004 Regulations, there was a three-fold division relating to the investigation of why a doctor should not, perhaps, continue to practise, and this was based on matters that could relate to his health, performance or misconduct. Since the new Regulations came into force, "fitness to practise" has been the ultimate criterion by which to judge his suitability to remain in practise.

Regulation 4 SI 2004/2608 provides that if it is considered that an allegation falls within s.35C(2) of the Medical Act 1983, it shall be referred to a medical and a lay Case Examiner for consideration.

Section 35C(2) of the Medical Act 1983

A person's fitness to practise shall be regarded as impaired for the purposes of this Act by reason only of—

(a) misconduct;

(b) deficient professional performance;

(c) conviction or caution ... for a criminal offence..

(d) adverse physical or mental health; or

(e)   determination by a [particular body] ... that [the doctor's] fitness to practise as a member of that profession is impaired, ...

Section 35C(4) provides that the Investigation Committee shall investigate the allegation and decide whether it should be considered by a Fitness to Practise Panel.

Sanctions ranging from a warning up to restrictions being imposed on a doctor's registration may be imposed by the GMC. The ultimate sanction, of course, is erasure from the medical register (i.e. being "struck off").

From its introduction in the Medical Act 1969 up to the end of October 2004, a doctor would have to be found guilty of "serious professional misconduct" for his name to be erased from the register. This concept originated as "infamous conduct in a professional respect" in *Allinson v General Council of Medical Education and Registration* [1894] 1 Q.B. 750. That the professional misconduct conduct had to be deemed *serious* before erasure was sanctioned led to the perception that some doctors escaped the ultimate sanction via the generous interpretation of their misconduct by the medically dominated GMC—at one time barely having 25 per cent lay membership. Now that s.36 Medical Act 1983 has been repealed and, along with it, the concept of serious professional misconduct has been consigned to history, being replaced by "fitness to practise", the focus is on the evolution of the composition of the GMC from its unwieldy membership of 104 in 1983 to its present 35 and, very likely, soon, to all its members being independently appointed by the Appointments Commission.

Where a doctor's fitness to practise has been adjudged to be impaired, and a decision has been made to erase his registration, or suspend him, for example he has a right of appeal to the High Court: s.40 Medical Act 1983. An appeal by Professor Sir Roy Meadow against his erasure from the register was successful on appeal to the High court but on further appeal to the Court of Appeal by the GMC succeeded in overturning the immunity from suit of an expert witness in fitness to practise proceedings: *Meadow v GMC* [2007] Q.B. 462.

If the FTP of the GMC imposes a disciplinary sanction under s.35D Medical Act 1983 that appears "unduly lenient", then to "maintain public confidence in regulation", a body known as the Council for Regulatory Health Excellence (CRHE) also may appeal to the High Court: s.29 National Health Service Reform and Health Care Professions Act 2002.

3. MEDICAL ETHICS

Meanings of "ethics"

Key Principle: "Ethics" is an ambiguous term and its meaning is defined according to context and use.

In the introduction to the second edition of their excellent book,
Healthy Respect: Ethics in Health Care, Downie and Calman (1994)
point out that "the term 'ethics' has various meanings and
associations". In fact, they outline three meanings, viz;

> "*First*, it can refer to that branch of philosophy also called moral
> philosophy. ... Ethics in this sense is a theoretical study of practical
> morality and its aim is to discover, analyse and relate to each other the
> fundamental concepts and principles of ordinary practical morality.
> *Second* [it means] ordinary morality as it is found in a professional
> context. [Here] 'morality' and 'moral decision' [are synonyms for]
> 'ethics' and 'ethical decision'.
> The *third* sense of 'ethics' refers to codes of procedure [which]
> underlie professional activity and ... apply across cultural and
> national boundaries."

For their purposes, Downie and Calman say that "our book
involves 'ethics' in all three senses". In this book, the expression
"medical ethics" is used to encompass, essentially, the second
and third meanings the authors gave to "ethics" and to refer to
the principles which health care professionals (principally
"doctors", see Ch.2) accept as relevant to the practice of medicine, as these provide points of reference to which patients, their
families, society as a whole, and the healthcare professionals
must pay proper regard in decision-making, so as to achieve
appropriate outcomes within the law.

Accordingly, any use of the single term "ethics" is no more
than a crude, shorthand reference to any one of its ambiguous
meanings being used in a way that seems clear, for all practical
purposes, in a particular context.

History of Medical Ethics
In *"A Short History of Medical Ethics"*, Albert Jonsen (2000) traced
the development of the subject from its origins, from about

500BC, and noted that for most of its developmental period it consisted of physicians (i.e. "doctors") defining the proper conduct for their profession. Deontological (i.e. duty-based) theories of behaviour followed. Moreover, he observed the similarities in the acceptance of ethical principles by Western and Eastern cultures, although the current view is that medical ethics are culture-specific.

Jonsen noted the contributions of Thomas Percival, who introduced the term "medical ethics" in 1803, and Richard Cabot, the American physician who founded hospital social work and lobbied for preventive medicine.

Amongst the post-Second World War seminal events reviewed by Jonsen is the Nuremberg War Crimes Tribunal of 1947 in which the 10-point Nuremberg Code (see Ch.12) was enunciated.

The use of the terms "bioethics" or "biomedical ethics" add nothing to any points of discussion in this chapter: they are, in essence, umbrella terms that encompass ethical principles common to the biological sciences, medicine and nursing, for example.

Codes of Ethics

Key Principle: **The Hippocratic Oath is probably by far the oldest and the most famous of the codes of ethics and its principles remain at the heart of modern medicine.**

Hippocratic Oath
Elements of the code include:

I will use my power to help the sick to the best of my ability and judgement; I will abstain from harming or wronging any man by it.

I will not give a fatal draught to anyone if I am asked, nor will I suggest any such thing. Neither will I give a woman means to procure an abortion.

I will be chaste and religious in my life and in my practice.

I will not cut, even for the stone, but I will leave such procedures to the practitioners of that craft.

Whenever I go into a house, I will go to help the sick and never with the intention of doing harm or injury. I will not abuse my position to indulge in sexual contacts with the bodies of women or of men, whether they be freemen or slaves.

Whatever I see or hear, professionally or privately, which ought not to be divulged, I will keep secret and tell no one.

Commentary
Despite the Hippocratic Oath being about 2,500 years old, its values in respect of confidentiality (see Ch.6) and in not indulging in sexual relationships with patients remain fundamentally important.

By contrast, attitudes towards abortion have changed—particularly since the Abortion Act 1967 and the Declaration of Oslo (1970, see below)—and "non-interference" in surgical procedures may be changing as the roles of GPs and their practices continue to be scrutinised following their new contracts in 2004 (see Ch.2)

Other codes of ethics applicable to doctors include:

Declaration of Geneva
In essence, this may be thought of as an "updated" Hippocratic Oath. It was accepted by the General Assembly of the World Medical Association in 1948 and last updated in 2006. Its values include:

- I will practice my profession with conscience and dignity;

- The health of my patient will be my first consideration;

- I will respect the secrets that are confided in me, even after the patient has died;

- I will not permit considerations of age, disease or disability, creed, ethnic origin, gender, nationality, political affiliation, race, sexual orientation, social standing or any other factor to intervene between my duty and my patient;

- I will maintain the utmost respect for human life;

- I will not use my medical knowledge to violate human rights and civil liberties, even under threat;

Note that neither the Hippocratic Oath nor the Declaration of Geneva regards confidentiality as an "absolute" principle—see Ch.6.

Declaration of Oslo
This declaration on therapeutic abortion was adopted by the World Medical Association in 1970 and last updated in 2006. Its provisions include:

1. The WMA requires the physician to maintain respect for human life.

2. Circumstances bringing the interests of a mother into conflict with the interests of her unborn child create a dilemma and raise the question as to whether or not the pregnancy should be deliberately terminated.

3. Diversity of responses to such situations is due in part to the diversity of attitudes towards the life of the unborn child. This is a matter of individual conviction and conscience that must be respected.

5. ... where the law allows therapeutic abortion to be performed, the procedure should be performed by a physician competent to do so in premises approved by the appropriate authority.

6. If the physician's convictions do not allow him or her to advise or perform an abortion, he or she may withdraw while ensuring the continuity of medical care by a qualified colleague.

Commentary
The "diversity of attitudes towards the life of the unborn child" contrasts with the doctor's vow under the Hippocratic Oath that "I [will not] give a woman means to procure an abortion." Whilst the Declaration of Oslo reflects the reality of widespread social acceptance of abortion, many doctors prefer to remain true to the Hippocratic Oath and the Abortion Act 1967, as amended, gives doctors the right not to participate in any abortion or treatment authorised by the Act to which he has a conscientious objection: see Ch.10.

Declaration of Helsinki
This code of ethics on medical research on human subjects is discussed in detail in Ch.12.

Comments on the Codes
There a number of limitations on the scope and effects of the various codes, including:

- The codes were written to be profession specific, whereas modern medical care—particularly in hospitals and increasingly so in GPs surgeries—is best provided by team work.

- Values, such as compassion and an appropriate "bedside manner" are not reducible to codes.

- The codes were written before the economics of health care became an issue of major importance—particularly in relation to the allocation of scarce medical resources: see Ch.2 and below.

- The doctor and each of the other members of the healthcare team brings his/her values into decision-making; particularly so, perhaps, since the study of medical law and ethics became a core subject in medical education following the GMC publication of *Tomorrow's Doctors* in 1993 and the core curriculum was published in 1998.

The Principal Theories Underpinning Medical Ethics

Key Principle: **Whilst there is no single theory of medical ethics that can satisfactorily be applied to the increasing range of contentious issues, theories based on duty, outcome and a case-by-case approach have merit in certain circumstances.**

Deontological Theories
The essence of a deontological theory is that medical decision-making is based on a sense of duty, i.e. there is some feature of an act other than, or in addition to, its consequences which makes it right or wrong. Deontological theories include religious theories and non-religious theories. There is no consensus in the religious theories in that some believe we (human beings) are God's creatures and we must obey his moral laws whilst other theories focus on the laws of nature—universal laws—that bind everyone, including God.

The best known deontological theory, however, is Kant's non-religious theory. Kant believed that as human beings are rational creatures, a theory had to be developed without any reference to God (although, as far as he was concerned, the existence of God could be established and he concluded that there is eternal life).

The essence of Kant's theory was that he sought to answer the question: *What is a moral action as contrasted with a non-moral one?* As far as he was concerned, morality was intimately associated with duties and obligations. Indeed, for Kant, the basis of morality is in the *motive* from which the act is done and a person is moral when he acts from a sense of duty (as opposed to acting from inclination, for example). A moral person who acts from a sense of duty [i.e. performs a "moral action"] is a person of "good will".

With regard to a person knowing what his/her duty is in a particular situation, Kant says that every person ought to behave as if his/her conduct were to become a *universal law*. This means that every action must be judged in the light of how it would appear if it were to be a universal code of behaviour. On this basis, telling lies, even if expedient, could not be accepted as moral under any circumstances because if lying was to be regarded as a universal law to which people ought to conform, morality would be impossible. Thus the claim of therapeutic privilege—the euphemism for lying, in *Hatcher v Black* (1954)— would be rejected. The moral action of a doctor in responding to a patient's questioning would be that stated by Lord Bridge in *Sidaway* where his Lordship said that when questioned by an autonomous patient: "... the doctor's duty must ... be to answer both truthfully and as fully as the questioner requires". (See Ch.4 for case notes on *Hatcher v Black* and *Sidaway*).

The foundation of every universal law is its *categorical imperative*—the duty that denotes an absolute, unconditional requirement that exerts its authority in all similar circumstances, e.g. lying is never acceptable; and don't create a life (via IVF treatment, for example) to save the life of another—the latter example being another way of expressing the categorical imperative, i.e. "... act as to treat humanity, whether in thine own person or in that of any other, in every case as an end withal, never as a means only". Quite simply, this means we should respect other people because they are rational human beings like ourselves. If another person was regarded and treated *only* as a means to an end, or "created" for a primary purpose of saving the life of another, i.e. created as a means to achieving merely what we want, then that would amount to disregarding his/her humanity and, in effect, treat that person as a thing: there would be no respect for his/her status as a rational human being. Such reasoning underpinned the objection to the PGD and tissue-typing procedures in the *Hashmi* case and is behind the proposed amendment to the Human Fertilisation and

Embryology Bill 2007–08 that would prohibit tissue-typing for the purposes of creating a "saviour sibling" (see Ch.9).

Commentary

Kantian absolutism may be appropriate in the Declaration of Tokyo, adopted by the WMA in 1975 and last revised in 2006. This declaration unequivocally instructs a physician not to countenance, condone or participate in the practice of torture or other forms of cruel, inhuman or degrading procedures, whatever the offence of which the victim of such procedures is suspected, accused or guilty.

The absolutism makes the theory unworkable, however, when a doctor accepts both the principle that he should never harm his patient and the principle that he should not lie to his patient, and a case arises where the principles clash. This is illustrated by the case of *Hatcher v Black* where the doctor told a lie to his patient on the eve of an operation because he did not want to worry her and his explanation was accepted by the court on the basis of therapeutic privilege: the duty of never lying to a patient could not be performed as the duty of doing no harm was accorded prime importance. In short, the absolutist approach completely ignores the circumstances of a particular case.

Either Kant's theory could be modified by regarding duties such as never lying to a patient as generalisations—"prima facie obligations", as Sir David Ross referred to them, or the theory could be rejected and other theories, such as consequentialism or casuistry, favoured.

Consequentialist Theories

Key Principle: **The essence of a consequentialist theory is that it is the *consequences* of a given action which determine whether it is right or wrong and not the motive from which it is done.**

The most prominent consequentialist theory is *Utilitarianism*. Utilitarianism is traditionally associated with happiness or pleasure. Accordingly, if the consequence of an act is, for example, an increase of pleasure over pain, then the act is of positive moral value and it is "right" to perform it.

The essence of utilitarianism is that *an action is right in so far as it tends to produce the greatest happiness for the greatest number of people*. To this end, we should always try to produce the greatest possible balance of value over disvalue (or the least possible balance of disvalue, if only undesirable results can be achieved); i.e. "the end justifies the means". This attempt at the maximisation of pleasure over pain, or value over disvalue, leads to the principle that *there is one and only one basic principle in ethics, the principle of utility*. (Crudely, utility = the "greatest happiness" principle).

In an attempting to assess the "rightness" of any action, Bentham (1748–1832), in his *Introduction to the Principles of Morals and Legislation*, referred to fourteen pleasures and twelve pains as a comprehensive account of happiness-relevant consequences. The "value" of each pleasure or pain was then adjudged by reference to seven criteria that were collectively referred to as the Felicific Calculus. The significance of this attempt to calculate the utility of an action via the Felicific Calculus was that Bentham was of the opinion that the felicific calculus was that *"on which the whole fabric of morals and legislation may be seen to rest"*.

That there appears to be both a common basis for law and morals and, frequently, a "special relationship" between law and morals, is an opinion that has found support in law, as expressed by Coleridge L.C.J. in *R. v Instan* (1893), when he said that: "... every legal duty is founded on a moral obligation".

Commentary
The advantages of utilitarianism are that as "pleasure" and "pain" are the poles of a continuum and utilitarianism is a monist theory, no pluralist potential for conflict arises. Of course, the huge disadvantages are associated with the theory begin with the individual, subjective assessment of "measuring happiness" but then expecting a legislator to make laws that achieve the "greatest happiness for the greatest number"—a virtual impossibility, particularly in areas such as abortion, euthanasia and "designer babies". Yet even more damning is that respect for each person's autonomy and values such as honesty may be subordinated to the requirements of science and society whenever the "greatest happiness" principle demands it.

Clearly, an approach to medical ethics other than that exemplified by the very different families of consequentialist and deontological theories may prove beneficial.

Casuistry

Key Principle: **Casuistry is the term applied to case-based reasoning; it is the approach that underpins the development of common law and, in essence, it is an approach that rejects the scientific approach of utilitarianism and the moral absolutism of the Kantian deontological theory.**

Casuistic reasoning does not require a pre-existing theoretical basis nor does it emphasise theoretical issues; instead, for the casuist, the facts and circumstances of the case under consideration must be determined for an appropriate response to be elicited. For example, whilst the Kantian approach would be to reject lying under any circumstance and the utilitarian, by telling a lie, could subordinate the respect for the autonomy of an individual to the demands of science and society if need be, the casuist would attempt to ascertain all the relevant information relating to a case and try to determine how and when lying might be appropriate in one case but not in another: cases could be distinguished. Accordingly, a claim of therapeutic privilege in a case such as *Hatcher v Black*, where the doctor's duty of doing no harm to his patient outweighed the general requirement for truth-telling would not necessarily conflict with the general position expressed by Lord Bridge in *Sidaway* where his Lordship said that when questioned by an autonomous patient: "... the doctor's duty must ... be to answer both truthfully and as fully as the questioner requires": the circumstances would determine which approach was appropriate.

Commentary
Any decision made on a casuistic basis may be unsound as no one can be certain that all the circumstances of a case are known and understood prior to the decision being made and there is no rule by which exceptions to general rules can be adjudged to be sound, e.g. if *Hatcher v Black* is still "good law", what rule would permit the judgment to be an exception to Lord Bridge's dictum in Sidaway?

Principlism

Key Principle: **Currently, the determination of whether an action is moral (or "ethical") is more likely to be discussed by**

reference to a series of inter-acting principles that may be upheld by consequentialists and deontologists, alike.

Since 1994, and the publication by Beauchamp and Childress of the fourth edition of their book, *Principles of Biomedical Ethics*, much reference has been made to their work and decision-making in healthcare via four principles, viz; autonomy, beneficence, non-maleficence and justice. The four principles are sometimes grouped together under the heading "principlism".

Autonomy

In essence, this is the right to self-determination of a competent person. As Mill expressed this principle: "... over himself, over his own body and mind, the individual is sovereign". Suffice it to say that this underpinned Cardozo J.'s dictum in *Schloendorff* (see Ch.4) and that the dictum has been approved in English law: *Bland* (1993), see Ch.4.

However, a note of caution, with regard to what may be seen as the undue emphasis placed on a patient's autonomy, was expressed by Kay J. In *R. v Collins and Ashworth Health Authority Ex p. Brady* (2000), where he said:

> "...it would seem to me a matter of deep regret if the law has developed to a point in this area where the rights of the patient count for everything and other ethical values and institutional integrity count for nothing."

Nevertheless, it has been clear since *St George's Healthcare NHS Trust v S* (1998) that an autonomous woman has the right to refuse a Caesarean section even if her refusal brings about her death and that of her unborn baby: no other principle would prevail to save life; that is the potential impact of an autonomous decision.

Beneficence

In essence, this has been the shorthand expression for "doctor knows best". Clearly, it is subordinated to a conflicting wish of an autonomous patient (see Ch.4) and in "... modern law, paternalism no longer rules", per Lord Steyn in *Chester v Afshar* [2004] UKHL 41 at para.16. Beneficence may also be constrained by the principle of non-maleficence and the requirements of justice.

Non-Maleficence

The principle of non-maleficence imposes on the doctor what is said to be his primary duty of not *doing* his patient any harm. Whereas the translation of the Latin *"Primum non nocere"* as first (or above all) do no harm, appears to give priority to this principle over that of beneficence, the principles are not comparable in that a doctor has a duty not to harm anyone (non-maleficence) but a duty to help only those who are his patients: thus the (invalid) comparison would be between perfect and imperfect duties, respectively.

Justice

The attempt at ascertaining precisely what constitutes justice becomes of the utmost importance in allocating scarce medical resources: how or why should one patient receive a resource but not another? It is easy to accept as a starting point Aristotle's formal principle of justice, expressed as: *"equals should be treated equally and unequals should be treated unequally in proportion to the relevant inequalities"*, but seeing that justice is done is another matter.

Of the criteria that have been suggested for basing the allocation of scarce resources—ranging from "social worth", as put forward in Seattle following the introduction of haemodialysis, to "triage", a concept developed for allocating resources to soldiers injured on a battlefield to return to duty as quickly as possible—the most discussed at present is the QALY—the Quality Adjusted Life Year. Alan Williams, of the University of York, who developed the concept of the QALY in the mid 1980s, said that:

> "The essence of a QALY is that it takes a year of healthy life expectancy to be worth 1, but regards a year of unhealthy life expectancy as worth less than 1. Its precise value is lower the worse the quality of life of the unhealthy person (which is what the 'quality adjusted' bit is all about). If being dead is worth zero, it is, in principle, possible for a QALY to be negative, i.e. for the quality of someone's life to be judged worse than being dead.
>
> The general idea is that a beneficial health care activity is one that generates a positive amount of QALYs, and that an efficient health care activity is one where the cost per QALY is as low as it can be. A high priority health care activity is one where the cost per-QALY is low, and a low priority activity is one where cost-per QALY is high."

Commentary

Criticisms of the use of QALYs include their being "ageist" (operating to the disadvantage of the aged) and considering only the end result of treatment without considering proportional gain or loss of benefit. Moreover, unless patients participate in "point scoring", it seems as if decisions will result from the subjective opinions of clinicians and be no more than beneficence disguised by mathematical formulae. Nevertheless, it seems that NICE (see Ch.1) bases its decisions on what pharmaceutical products to recommend with decisions being associated with a cost of no more than about £30,000 per QALY.

Legal challenges have already been made to some decisions made by NICE and this area of law and ethics is likely to remain volatile for the foreseeable future.

4. CONSENT TO TREATMENT

The Significance of Acquiring Consent to Treatment

Key Principle: A doctor is able to avoid legal liability for the administration of invasive medical treatment by first obtaining the patient's consent.

Re F (Mental Patient: Sterilisation) [1989] 2 F.L.R. 376

Neill L.J. said:

"Treatment or surgery which would otherwise be unlawful as a trespass is made lawful by the consent of the patient."

In *Attorney General's Reference* (No.6 of 1980) [1981] Q.B. 715, it was said that:

"Nothing which we have said is intended to cast doubt upon the accepted legality of properly conducted ... reasonable surgical interference, ... th[is] ... can be justified as ... needed in the *public interest*."

Commentary

The potential legal liability for treatment given in the absence of consent was expressed by Sir Thomas Bingham M.R. in *Airedale NHS Trust v Bland* [1993] 2 W.L.R. 316 at 334G, where he said:

"It is a civil wrong, and may be a crime, to impose medical treatment on a conscious adult of sound mind without his or her consent: *In re F (Mental Patient: Sterilisation)* [1990] 2 A.C. 1"

Of course, it's crucial to note that the consent must be given voluntarily and not given under duress or the undue influence of any other person. As Lord Donaldson M.R. said, in *Re T* [1993] Fam 95, where there's doubt:

"The real question in each case is: does the patient really mean what he says or is he merely saying it for a quiet life, to someone else or because the advice and persuasion to which he has been subjected is such that he can no longer think and decide for himself? In other words, is it a decision expressed in form only, not in reality?"

Consent may be given orally, in writing or even via non-verbal communication such as nodding the head in an affirmative manner or holding out an arm to signify consent to being vaccinated: *O'Brien v Cunard SS Co* (1891) 28 N.E. 266. All forms of consent are equally valid—but for evidential purposes, it may be better for the consent to be in writing.

The Primacy of Patient Choice

Key Principle: **It is well established in law and moral theory that the right of self-determination of an autonomous person prevails over a conflicting medical opinion.**

Schloendorff v Society of New York Hospital (1914) 211 N.Y. at 126:
Cardozo J. said:

> "Every human being of adult years and sound mind has a right to determine what shall be done with his own body; and a surgeon who performs an operation without his patient's consent, commits an assault..."

Commentary
This dictum, which some regard as "the classic expression of civil liberties", has been cited with approval in the House of Lords by Lord Goff in *Airedale NHS Trust v Bland* [1993] 2 W.L.R. 316, 367E-F. His Lordship said:

> "... it is established that the principle of self determination requires that respect must be given to the wishes of the patient, so that if an adult patient of sound mind refuses, however unreasonably, to consent to treatment or care by which his life would or might be prolonged, the doctors responsible for his care must give effect to his wishes, even though they do not consider it to be in his best interests to do so: see *Schloendorff v Society of New York Hospital* (1914) 105 N.E. 92, 93, per Cardozo J."

Other examples of unequivocal judicial dicta championing the sovereignty of the patient were expressed in: (i) the New Jersey case of *Bennan v Parsonnett* (1912) 83 N.J.L. 20, which affirmed that:

"No amount of professional skills can justify the substitution of the will of the surgeon for that of his patient"

Later, in (ii) the Canadian case of *Hopp v Lepp* (1979) 98 D.L.R. 3d 464, Prowse J. said:

"Each patient is entitled to make his own decision even though it may not accord with the decision knowledgeable members of the profession would make. *The patient has a right to be wrong.*"

And, (iii) in the English case of *Re T* [1993] Fam 95, Lord Donaldson M.R. said:

"... the patient's right of choice exists whether the reasons for making that choice are rational, irrational, unknown or even non-existent."

Capacity is Essential for a Patient's Purported Primacy of Choice (i.e. Right to Self-Determination) to be Recognised in Law

Key Principle: **English common law contained a rebuttable presumption that an autonomous person—one of "adult years and sound mind", i.e. one having the right to self-determination—had the capacity to consent to treatment or to refuse treatment.**

Re T (Adult: Refusal of Medical Treatment) [1993] Fam 95

T, who was involved in a road traffic accident when she was 34 weeks pregnant, signed a form refusing consent to a blood transfusion, although the form and contents were not explained to her. The refusal followed a talk with her mother and T. When T went into labour, a Caesarean section was performed but the baby was stillborn. T's condition deteriorated and a declaration was granted stating that, in the emergency then prevailing, it would not be unlawful for the hospital to administer a blood transfusion, and this they did. T appealed.

Held: Where a decision is made in the light of outside influence of family members the court must consider whether the subsequent decision is that of the patient and whether it was intended to apply in a changed situation. Here, the influence of T's mother had vitiated the right to refuse. Moreover, in a life-

threatening situation, if doctors had real doubts as to the validity of a refusal they should seek a declaration from the court that the proposed treatment was lawful.
Lord Donaldson M.R. said:

> "The right to decide one's own fate presupposes a capacity to do so. Every adult is presumed to have that capacity but it is a presumption that can be rebutted."

Key Principle: **The essence of the leading common law case on assessing the capacity of an adult, Re C (Adult: Refusal of Treatment) [1994] 1 W.L.R. 290, has now been enshrined in s.3 Mental Capacity Act 2005.**

Re C (Adult: Refusal of Treatment) [1994] 1 W.L.R. 290
C, who was a 68-year-old paranoid schizophrenic who had been in Broadmoor special hospital for 30 years, developed a gangrenous foot. He objected to an amputation even though he was told there was an 85 per cent chance that he would die if he refused it.

Held: he succeeded in obtaining an injunction restraining the health authority from amputating his gangrenous foot then *or at any time in the future.* C succeeded because the presumption of self-determination *had not been displaced.* The judge, Thorpe J., was of the opinion that C had satisfied a three-stage process of decision-making, viz;

(i)   he had comprehended and retained the treatment information;

(ii)   he had believed that information; and

(iii)   he weighed the information "in the balance to arrive at a choice".

Commentary
The approach to capacity expressed in *Re C* was approved by the Court of Appeal in *Re MB (Medical Treatment)* [1997] 2 F.L.R. 426 and later cases, such as *Re W (Adult: Refusal of Medical Treatment)* [2002] EWHC 901 (Fam Div).

Section 3 Mental Capacity Act 2005: Inability to make decisions

(1) ... a person is unable to make a decision for himself if he is unable—

    (a) to understand the information relevant to the decision,

    (b) to retain that information,

    (c) to use or weigh that information as part of the process of making the decision, or

    (d) To communicate his decision (whether by talking, using sign language or any other means),

(3) The fact that the person is able to retain the information relevant to a decision for a short period only does not prevent him from being regarded as able to make a decision.

A Competent Patient Cannot be Compelled to Undergo Treatment

Key Principle: **A competent patient who refuses life-saving treatment has a legal right to sue if the treatment is administered.**

Malette v Shulman (1990) 72 O.R. (2d) 417

Mrs M, a Jehovah's Witness, was unconscious and bleeding profusely as a result of a road traffic accident. She carried a card requesting that "no blood or blood products be administered to me under any circumstances". Nevertheless, soon after arrival at the hospital the doctor in the emergency department decided that her condition was serious and she needed a transfusion.

Held: Despite the doctor's good motives and his thinking that he was acting in her best interests, the intervention constituted a battery and M was awarded damages of $20,000.

Commentary

Two principal points emerge from a case where refusal is communicated via a card because the patient is temporarily incapacitated. First, providing there was no doubt that the patient had capacity at the time when the directive was recorded, and the decision to do so was made voluntarily, then the right of refusal of consent to medical treatment via an advance directive is acknowledged at common law and in statute. In English law, this was clearly expressed by Lord Keith in *Airedale NHS Trust v Bland* where his Lordship said that the patient's right extended to:

"... the situation where the person, in anticipation of his ... entering into a condition such as PVS, gives clear instructions that in such event he is not to be given medical care, including artificial feeding, designed to keep him alive."

The second point that emerges is the unequivocal common law dicta that protect a patient's "sovereign right" to bodily integrity by respecting his refusal to accept well-intentioned medical interference. In particular, according to Flaherty J. in the American case of *McFall v Shimp* (1978) 10 Pa D & C 3d 90:

"For our law to *compel* [a patient] to submit to an intrusion of his body would change every concept and principle upon which our society is founded."

Indeed, to quote a later American case:

"No right is held more sacred, or is more carefully guarded by the common law, than the right of every individual to the possession and control of his own person, free from the restraint of interference of others, unless by clear and unquestionable authority of law."

(Dictum in the American case of: *In the Matter of Claire Conroy* (1985) 486 A 2d 1209)

Pregnant Women in Labour Refusing Caesarean Sections

Key Principle: **English law upholds the right of a competent, pregnant woman in labour to refuse a Caesarean section even if that refusal threatens her life and that of her unborn baby**

Re MB [1997] 2 F.L.R. 426

MB, a 23-year-old woman, had initially consented to a Caesarean section but then changed her mind because a needle phobia caused her to refuse consent to the anaesthetic. She then also refused inhalational anaesthesia. It was thought that there was a

50 per cent risk of serious injury to the baby if delivered vaginally but little risk to the mother.

Held: The first instance decision to grant a declaration of lawfulness to perform the Caesarean section was upheld on appeal as the needle phobia had rendered MB incompetent. However, Butler-Sloss L.J. expressed the wholly different situation that would have prevailed had MB been competent, saying:

"A competent woman who has the capacity to decide may, for religious reasons, other reasons, rational or irrational reasons or no reasons at all, choose not to have medical intervention even though the consequence may be the death or serious handicap of the child she bears or her own death."

St George's Healthcare NHS Trust v S (No. 2) [1998] 3 W.L.R. 936

Following the safe delivery of her baby, S appealed against the decision that granted a declaration that a non-consensual Caesarean section could be performed on her on the basis that she was incompetent.

Held: As S was not incompetent, the non-consensual Caesarean section was unlawful: it constituted a battery. It was said that:

"... an unborn child is not a separate person from its mother. Its need for medical assistance does not prevail over [the mother's] rights. [The mother] is entitled not to be forced to submit to an invasion of her body against her will, whether her own life or that of her unborn child depends on it. Her right is not reduced or diminished merely because her decision to exercise it may appear morally repugnant."

Commentary

In a series of cases in the 1990s, pregnant women were subjected to non-consensual Caesarean sections. The decisions appeared to result from a dictum of Lord Donaldson M.R. in *Re T (Adult: Refusal of Medical Treatment)* [1993] Fam 95 where he said:

"What matters is that doctors should consider whether at that time [the patient] had a capacity which was commensurate with the gravity of the decision which [she] purported to make. The more serious the decision, the greater the capacity required."

He added that "The only possible qualification [to a competent woman exercising her right to self determination] is a case in which the choice may lead to the death of a viable foetus"—a surprising dictum, given that English law does not attach personality to a foetus.

Nevertheless, a 30-year-old woman who had refused a Caesarean section after being in labour for two days was still subjected to the procedure when the President of the Family division granted a declaration on the basis that the baby's life might be saved: *Re S* (1992) *The Times*, 16 October. A number of other cases were decided on the basis that the pregnant woman was "incompetent". However, in retrospect, the cases have to be viewed as a feeble attempt at introducing a paternalistic judicial policy at the expense of established legal principles.

Minors and Their Capacity to Consent to Treatment

Key Principle: **That a minor over the age of 16 can give an effective consent to treatment is a principle enshrined in statute; and a minor below the age of 16 may have the capacity to consent if (s)he meets the common law criteria of being capable of understanding the nature of the treatment intended and displaying sufficient maturity.**

Statute

Family Law Reform Act 1969, Section 8(1)
The consent of a minor who has attained the age of sixteen years to any surgical, medical or dental treatment which, in the absence of consent, would constitute a trespass to his person, shall be as effective as it would be if he were of full age; and where a minor has ... given an effective consent to any treatment it shall not be necessary to obtain any consent for it from his parent or guardian.

Commentary
The provisions of s.8(1) do NOT mean that a minor under the age of 16 lacks capacity. This is confirmed by s.8(3) of the 1969 Act which provides that:

"Nothing in this section shall be construed as making ineffective any consent which would have been effective if this section had not been enacted."

The rationale for permitting a minor under the age 16 to consent to medical treatment was clearly expressed by Lord Scarman in *Gillick* where his Lordship said that:

"a fixed age limit of 16 ... brings with it an inflexibility and a rigidity which in some branches of the law can obstruct justice, impede the law's development and stamp on the law the mark of obsolescence where what is needed is the capacity for development."

Capacity of a minor at common law

Gillick is the leading case on the determination of a minor's capacity.

Gillick v West Norfolk and Wisbech Area Health Authority [1986] 1 A.C. 112

Mrs Victoria Gillick objected to a 1981 DHSS circular which stated that in certain circumstances a doctor could prescribe contraceptive advice and treatment to a girl under 16 without the knowledge or consent of her parents: i.e. (in effect) Mrs Gillick was contending that girls under the age of 16 did not have capacity to consent to contraceptive treatment. In the High Court she failed to get a declaration that the DHSS guidelines were unlawful; she then succeeded in gaining a unanimous decision in her favour in the Court of Appeal. On appeal:

Held: Mrs Gillick failed by 3—2 to have this decision upheld by the House of Lords.

Commentary

In essence, the capacity of a minor aged under 16 is based on the minor demonstrating a capability of understanding the nature of the advice given together with a sufficient maturity to understand what is involved in the treatment.

Pertinent extracts from their Lordships opinions include:
Lord Fraser:

"... provided the patient, whether a boy or a girl, is capable of understanding what is proposed ... I see no good reason for holding that he or she lacks the capacity to express (his or her wishes) validly and effectively and to authorise the medical man ... to give the treatment."

Lord Scarman:

> "As a matter of law the parental right to *determine* whether or not their minor child below the age of 16 will have medical treatment *terminates* if and when the child achieves sufficient understanding and intelligence to enable him or her to understand fully what is proposed."

From this, we can deduce that a "child [who] achieves sufficient understanding and intelligence to enable him or her to understand fully what is proposed" and who is of sufficient maturity, can consent to treatment without having to worry about the decision being subjected to parental authority—a point already enshrined in statute: s.8(1) FLRA 1969, above. By contrast, it would appear that a child who could not be regarded as having achieved "sufficient understanding and intelligence", perhaps by way of failing to demonstrate a staged development because of a fluctuating competence, could have his / her decisions nullified by parental authority or the courts in wardship.

Minors Refusing Treatment

Key Principle: **A minor who risks death or severe permanent injury by way of refusing treatment may have his decision nullified and overridden by parental authority and / or the courts making a decision in the best interests of the minor in wardship.**

Re R [1991] 3 W.L.R. 592

R, a 15-year-old girl, was admitted to hospital under provisions of the Mental Health Act 1983. The consultant in the specialist adolescent psychiatric unit wished to administer to her anti-psychotic medication by injection. Whereas the local authority at first consented to this, they withdrew the consent after R had made a three hour telephone call to a social worker to whom she sounded lucid and rational. However, the unit was not prepared to keep R unless it was given authority to administer the medication. The local authority then initiated wardship proceedings and sought permission of the court for the doctors at the unit to administer the medication with or without R's consent. At first instance, the judge granted the application for R to be made a

ward of court and for her to be given the medication on the basis
that she was not competent to refuse treatment. He added that if
she was a competent minor, then the wardship jurisdiction
would not entitle him to overrule her refusal. The Official Solicitor appealed and requested guidance on the determination of
whether R was a competent minor in the *Gillick* sense and if so:
(i) whether the parent of a competent minor had the power to
override the minor's decision either by granting consent when
the minor had refused it, or vice versa; and (ii) whether the court
had the power to override the decision of a competent minor
who was a ward.

Held: The staged development of a normal child does not
"fluctuate upon a day to day or week to week basis" (per Lord
Donaldson). No minor who exhibits fluctuating competence i.e.
having the capability of understanding to meet the *Gillick* criteria
one day but not the next can be regarded as *Gillick competent*.
With regard to the two specific questions:

(i) Parents *do* retain their capacity to authorise treatment
    when their Gillick competent minor child objects. This is
    due to consent being:

    "...a key which unlocks a door. Furthermore, whilst in the
    case of an adult of full capacity there will usually be one key
    holder, namely the patient, in the ordinary family unit where
    a young child is the patient there will be two key holders,
    namely the parents, with a several as well as a joint right to
    turn the key and unlock the door."

    In other words, parental consent would provide the doc-
    tor who administered treatment to a non-consenting
    minor with a defence to civil and criminal actions. As to
    Lord Scarman's reference in *Gillick* to "the parental right
    to *determine* whether or not their minor child below the
    age of 16 will have medical treatment *terminates* if and
    when the child achieves sufficient understanding and
    intelligence ...," Lord Donaldson M.R. said that the right
    to determine (i.e. the power both to authorise and veto
    treatment) was wider than the right to consent and that:

    "The parents can only have a right of *determination* if either the
    child has no right to consent, i.e. is not a key holder, or the

parents hold the master key which could nullify the child's consent."

(ii) Since the courts powers in wardship are not derived from parental responsibility and, in theory, they are limitless, then the courts could override the refusal of a *Gillick competent* minor and consent to treatment if they thought it was in the minor's best interests.

Although the initial academic comment on the decision in *Re R* was almost universally hostile, *Re R* was followed in *Re W* (1992).

Re W (Consent to treatment) [1992] 4 All E.R. 627

16-year-old W was an anorexic in the care of the local authority. She refused to consent to treatment for her condition and was made a ward of court. At first instance, Thorpe J. found that although W had sufficient understanding to make a decision, nevertheless, the court had inherent jurisdiction to order her to be taken to hospital and to be treated against her wishes if necessary. On appeal,

Held: Lord Donaldson M.R. said:

"no minor of whatever age has power by refusing consent to treatment to override a consent to treatment by someone who has parental responsibility for the minor and a fortiori a consent by the court."

Furthermore, s.8 of the 1969 Act, which gives minors aged 16 and over the right to consent to surgical, medical or dental treatment and which cannot be overridden by those with parental responsibility, can be overridden by the court. Significantly, Lord Donaldson also observed a feature of anorexia nervosa being that it is capable of destroying the ability to make an informed choice, i.e. it creates a compulsion to refuse treatment or only to accept treatment which is likely to be ineffective. Accordingly, since *"Good parenting involved giving minors as much rope as they could handle without an unacceptable risk that they would hang themselves"* and s.8 of the Family Law Reform Act 1969 did not confer complete autonomy on minors over the age of 16 with regard to their medical treatment, the court would exercise its inherent jurisdiction and authorise the treatment of W.

Commentary
First, Lord Donaldson regretted his use of the "key-holder" analogy in *Re R*. He said this was:

> "because keys can lock as well as unlock. I now prefer the analogy of the legal 'flak jacket' which protects from claims by the litigious whether he acquires it from his patient who may be a minor over the age of 16, or a 'Gillick competent' child under that age or from another person having parental responsibilities which include a right to consent to treatment of the minor."

Secondly, *Re R* and *Re W* were not the only controversial cases involving minors refusing treatment during the 1990s. In *Re M (Child: Refusal of Medical Treatment)* 1999 Johnson J. declared that it would be in the best interests of a 15-year-old girl to authorise a heart transplant despite the girl's statement that:

> "If I had someone else's heart, I would be different from anyone else—being dead would not make me different from anyone else. I would feel different with someone else's heart, that's good enough reason not to have a heart transplant".

Parental Choice May Prevail if Decisions are made in the Best Interests of the Minor

Key Principle: **English law contains a rebuttable presumption that parents act in the best interests of their children.**

Children Act 1989, Section 1(5)
Where a court is considering whether or not to make one or more orders under this Act with respect to a child, it shall not make the order or any of the orders unless it considers that doing so would be better for the child than making no order at all.

Commentary
The court's jurisdiction in wardship is theoretically limitless. Accordingly, it can override any parental decision to consent to or to refuse treatment for their minor children.

See Ch.11 for the contrasting decisions in *Re B (A Minor)(Wardship: Medical Treatment)* [1990] 3 All E.R. 927 and *Re T (A Minor)(Wardship: Medical Treatment)* [1997] 1 All E.R. 906 where, in each case, parents had refused consent for operative treatment.

Three other notable cases of the courts sanctioning treatment for children following parental refusals are in respect of a blood transfusion and an HIV test.

Re S (A Minor)(Medical Treatment) [1993] 1 F.L.R. 376
Here, a local authority sought a court order to override the refusal on religious grounds of Jehovah's Witness parents to consent to a blood transfusion for their child.

Held: The order was granted and Thorpe J. said:

> "...it is difficult to pursue the argument that the religious convictions of the parents should deny the child the chance of treatment."

Commentary
The case and the outcome were factually very similar to the facts and decision in the American case of *Prince v Massachusetts*.

Prince v Massachusetts (1944)
A Jehovah's Witness child was in need of a blood transfusion to which the parents refused their consent.

Held: Holmes J. authorised it saying:

> "Parents may be free to become martyrs themselves, but it does not follow that they are free in identical circumstances to make martyrs of their children before they have reached the age of full and legal discretion when they can make the choices for themselves."

See also: Re C (A Child)(HIV Testing) [2000] 2 W.L.R. 270 where a declaration was granted to test a child for HIV, despite the objection of both parents.

The full and voluntary consent of a patient is obtained only after an appropriate amount of information relating to the proposed treatment is imparted to him in simple, non-technical language.

Key Principle: **In English law, the standard of *how much* information relating to proposed treatment should be given to** a patient, in order to obtain the latter's valid consent to treatment, has been based on a dictum of Bristow J. in *Chatterton v Gerson*:

Chatterton v Gerson [1981] Q.B. 432
Bristow J. said:

> "... once the patient is informed in *broad terms* of the *nature of the procedure which is intended,* and gives her consent, that consent is *real* ... Of course, if information is withheld in bad faith, the consent will be vitiated by fraud."

Commentary

It was the above dictum that gave rise to the term "real consent" as being the expression signifying a valid consent to treatment given by a competent person. This contrasted with the term "informed consent" which originated in American case law in the same year as *Bolam* was decided in England (below).

Key Principle: **The long-established standard of *who decides* what is the appropriate amount information to be imparted to a patient, has been based on the *Bolam* test.**

Bolam v Friern HMC [1957] 2 All E.R. 118
The essence of this case for present purposes is in the direction McNair J. gave to the jury, viz;

> "A doctor is not ... negligen[t] if he *acted in accordance with a practice accepted as proper by a responsible body of medical men skilled in that particular art* ... [and] if a warning had been given, would it have made any difference? The only man who can really tell you the answer to that question is [B], and he was never asked the question."

Commentary

The *Bolam* test (or standard) was a test for negligence. However, it developed into such a wide ranging "test" that the English courts and, for example, the Australian courts, began to restrict its development via decisions in *Rogers v Whitaker* (1993) (Australia), and the English cases of *Bolitho* (1997), *Pearce* (1998) and *Re S* (2000)—all discussed below.

Nature of the liability for failure to impart the appropriate amount of information prior to administering treatment

Chatterton v Gerson [1981] Q.B. 432, per Bristow J.:

"When the claim is based on negligence the plaintiff must prove not only the breach of duty to inform but that had the duty not been broken she would not have chosen to have the operation. Where the claim is based on *trespass to the person*, once it is shown that the consent is unreal, then what the plaintiff would have decided if she had been given the information which would have prevented vitiation of the reality of her consent is irrelevant."

Commentary

Hills v Potter [1984] 3 All E.R. 716 and the Canadian case of *Reibl v Hughes* (1980) 114 DLR (3d)1 agreed that a claim for inadequate pre-treatment information should be pursued in negligence and not battery.

Key Principle: **Whereas American jurisprudence supports the principle that a claim for inadequate pre-treatment information be pursued in negligence, some States' jurisprudence imposed a seemingly different standard of information disclosure, with the standard being set by the law—as opposed to the medical profession setting the standard in English law. This enabled a patient's "informed consent" to treatment to be obtained.**

Canterbury v Spence (1972) 464 F 2d 772
Robinson J.:

"It seems obviously *prohibitive* and *unrealistic* to expect physicians to discuss with their patients *every* risk of proposed treatment—no matter how small or remote—and *generally unnecessary* from the patient's viewpoint as well. [And as to what should be discussed]: ... the test for determining whether a particular peril must be divulged is its materiality to the patient's decision: all risks potentially affecting the decision must be unmasked. ... Furthermore, the standard is not subjective as to either the physician or the patient; it remains *objective* with due regard for the patient's informational needs and with suitable leeway for the physician's situation. In broad outline, we agree that a risk is thus *material* when a *reasonable person*, in what the physician knows or should know to be the patient's position, would be likely to attach significance to the risk or cluster of risks in deciding whether or not to forego the proposed therapy. [By contrast with the *Bolam* standard, however]: Respect for the patient's right of self determination on particular therapy demands a *standard set by law* for physicians rather than one which physicians may or may not impose on themselves. Any definition of scope in terms purely of a professional standard is at odds with the patients prerogative to decide on projected therapy himself."

Commentary

Informed consent thus displayed three differences from "real consent" as expressed in *Chatterton v Gerson*, viz;

- All material risks—as opposed to the broad terms of the nature of the treatment intended—were to be imparted to the patient;

- The law—not the medical profession—set the standard; and

- A risk was material when "a *reasonable person*, in what the physician knows or should know to be the patient's position, would be likely to attach significance to the risk or cluster of risks in deciding whether or not to forego the proposed therapy". This "objective standard" was severely criticised by Lord Bridge in *Sidaway* (1985)—the case in which the House of Lords had the opportunity to import the doctrine of informed consent.

Sidaway v Board of Governors of the Bethlem Royal and the Maudsley Hospital [1985] A.C. 871.

Mrs S consented to an operation to relieve the pain in her arms and shoulders caused by pressure on a nerve root. However, the operation resulted in S becoming severely disabled by partial paralysis. She then sued both F (the doctor who performed the operation) and the Maudsley Hospital. S did not suggest that the operation had been performed otherwise than skilfully and carefully. Her complaint was that the operation to which she agreed involved two specific risks over and above the risk inherent in any surgery under general anaesthesia. These were: (i) damage to a nerve root, assessed as about a 2 per cent risk; and (ii) damage to the spinal cord, assessed as less than a 1 per cent risk. It was this second risk which materialised and she consequently suffered partial paralysis.

Held: The doctor's obligation to advise and warn his patient was part and parcel of his general duty of care owed to each individual patient. Prima facie, providing he conformed to a responsible body of medical opinion in deciding what to tell and what not to tell his patient he discharged his duty properly. Accordingly, (at the time of the judgment, anyway) *there was NO doctrine of informed consent in this country (cf.* say, some States in America) where it is essential that a doctor informs the patient of all *material* risks inherent in the treatment so as not to vitiate the patient's consent.

Lord Bridge expressed several reasons for rejecting the doctrine of informed consent, one of which was:

> "... the objective test [i.e. the patient centred reasonable person standard which] seems to me to be so imprecise as to be almost meaningless."

Lord Templeman seemed to be of the opinion that a patient should take a proactive approach and not merely base a decision on the basis of the information imparted to him, i.e.:

> ... if a patient knows that a major operation may entail serious consequences cannot complain of lack of information unless asks in vain for more information or unless there is some danger which by its nature or magnitude or for some other reason requires to be separately taken into account by in order to reach a balanced judgment in deciding whether or not to submit to the operation, ...

Nevertheless, Lord Templeman still believed it was for the doctor to decide what information was to be given to the patient:

> "At the end of the day, the doctor, bearing in mind the best interests of the patient and bearing in mind the patient's right of information which will enable the patient to make a balanced judgment must decide what information should be given to the patient and in what terms that information should be couched."

Lord Diplock, however, appeared to promote a divisive application of informed consent in that it would be confined to "highly educated men of experience". He said:

> "... when it comes to warning about risks, the kind of training and experience that a judge will have undergone at the bar makes it natural for him to say (correctly): it is my right to decide whether any particular thing is done to my body, and I want to be fully informed of any risks there may be involved of which I am not already aware from my own general knowledge as *a highly educated man of experience,* so that I may form my own judgment whether to refuse the advised treatment or not."

Lord Scarman delivered the only dissenting opinion as far as disclosure of information was concerned: he clearly favoured adoption of the doctrine of informed consent. He said:

"... in a medical negligence case where the issue is as to the advice and information given to the patient as to the treatment proposed, the available options and the risks, the court is concerned primarily with a patient's right. The doctor's duty arises from his patient's rights. If one considers the scope of the doctor's duty by beginning with the right of the patient to make his own decision as to whether he will or will not undergo the treatment proposed, the right to be informed of significant risk and the doctor's corresponding duty are easy to understand, for the proper implementation of the right requires that the doctor be under a duty to inform his patient of the material risks inherent in the treatment."

That Lord Scarman delivered the only dissenting opinion meant that the attempt to introduce the doctrine of informed consent into English law was defeated by four opinions to one. However, as case law below illustrates, the trend in English law has been to move away from the "doctor-knows-best" position in favour of a standard that's getting progressively closer to the standards adopted in some other common law jurisdictions. It is a matter of debate, however, whether the principles gleaned from the later cases are best described as coming within the expression "informed consent".

Key Principle: **Courts are becoming increasingly less reliant on the *Bolam* test as the definitive standard for approving the amount of information that should be imparted to a patient for a legally valid consent to be obtained**

A significant first step in rejecting the *Bolam* standard appeared to have been taken by the High Court of Australia in *Rogers v Whitaker* (1993). Here, it was decided that it is a matter for *the courts* to determine the standard of care owed by a doctor to his patient: medical practice will be no more than a guide to help judges in their decision-making. This does not prevent a doctor from claiming "therapeutic privilege", however, particularly where a patient is "unusually nervous, disturbed or volatile".

In common with the prudent patient standard in America (*Canterbury v Spence*) and Canada (*Reibl v Hughes*), *Rogers v Whitaker* decided that a patient must be informed of all *material risks*. These are risks to which *either* a reasonable person in the patient's situation would attach significance, *or* to which *the patient in question* would attach significance if he was informed of them by a doctor who was aware or should have been aware of his (the patient's) concerns. If the patient can show that he would not have consented if he had been informed of all material risks, then, in essence, the doctor has no defence to a charge of negligence.

In 1994, in the English case of *Smith v Tunbridge Wells Health Authority* [1994] 5 Med L.R. 334 a 28-year-old man succeeded in claiming that he had not adequately been informed of the inherent risk of impotence before having rectal surgery. He succeeded in his claim despite evidence that a responsible body of surgeons did not warn their patients of such a risk. The claimant succeeded because the judge said the failure to warn was neither reasonable nor responsible. The judgment did not specify a requirement for the disclosure of all material risks; it criticised the application of the generally accepted English standard of disclosure.

A further restraint on the *Bolam* standard was imposed by the House of Lords, in *Bolitho v City and Hackney Health Authority* [1998] A.C. Here, the applicability of the *Bolam* test was affirmed *but* it was *subject to the proviso* that in cases involving the weighing of risks against benefits it could be demonstrated that the experts who had formulated their view had directed their minds to the question of comparative risks and benefits and had reached a *defensible* conclusion on the matter. That is, before a practice could be described as being in accordance with the practice accepted as proper by a "responsible" or "reasonable" or "respectable" body of professional opinion the exponents of that opinion could demonstrate that such opinion had a *logical* basis. *If the courts were not convinced that a logical conclusion was reached by the medical profession, then the law would set the standard for them.* However, the principal qualification to this apparent revision of the *Bolam* standard was expressed by Lord Browne-Wilkinson when he said that it would "very seldom" be right for a judge to conclude that the genuine views of a competent medical expert were illogical … though he reserved the right to do so.

Second, a Court of Appeal decision in 1998. In *Pearce v United Bristol Healthcare NHS Trust* (1998) 48 B.M.L.R. 118, Mrs Pearce's child was stillborn two weeks after the due date of her delivery. Mrs Pearce had been warned of the risks of induction and Caesarean section but not of the low risk of a stillbirth associated with non-intervention. Given the low risk, the Court of Appeal held that she had not established negligence in the failure to disclose the risk. However, the case is noteworthy for the surprising ratio expressed by Lord Woolf M.R., viz;

> "In a case where it is being alleged that a plaintiff has been deprived of the opportunity to make a proper decision as to what course of action he or she should take in relation to treatment, it seems to me to be the law ... that *if there is a significant risk* which would *affect the judgment of a reasonable patient*, then in the normal course it is the responsibility of the doctor to inform *the patient* of that risk, if the information is needed so that *the patient* can determine for him or herself as to what course he or she would adopt."

Moreover, given the majority (3–2) decision in *Chester v Afshar* [2005] 1 A.C. 134, where the law set a policy standard on information disclosure where there was "a small, but well established, risk of serious injury as a result of surgery" (per Lord Steyn, para.16), coupled with the requirements of disclosing *"significant risks"* to a *"reasonable patient"*, it seems if English law is certainly moving well-away form the professional-practice *Bolam* standard even if, as yet, there is no express statement of the incorporation of "informed consent" in English medical law. Indeed, given the specific reference to "significant" risk and the Court of Appeal finding in *White v Taylor* (2004) that they did not have to follow the policy decision in *Chester v Afshar*, one should be reluctant to equate the increasing departure from the *Bolam* standard with a corresponding move to incorporate the standard of informed consent espoused in cases such as *Canterbury v Spence*.

The legal basis on which non-consensual treatment may be administered to an adult at common law and under statute

Key Principle: **The legal basis for the administration of non-consensual medical treatment has focused on the "best interests" tests at common law, and / or be provided for in statutory form.**

(a) At Common Law

Re F [1990] 2 A.C. 1

Here, it was decided that non-consensual treatment could be administered if it was in a patient's best interests and it was necessary to do so. The problem was that "best interests" were allowed to be determined by the medical profession on the basis of a *Bolam* standard—of which there may have been several. Clearly, the scope for medical paternalism was very wide.

Commentary

The *Re F* test has been modified by:

Re S (Adult Patient: sterilisation: Patient's best interests) [2001] Fam 15

The principal point here, for the present discussion, is that whereas the medical profession remained responsible for providing the court with the best medical option/presenting the court with a range of options via the *Bolam* standards, the second, or determinative, stage of selecting the single best option— which may entail far more than simply considering medical options—was a decision for the court, alone, to make. (For more on this case, see Ch.8).

This common law basis may remain applicable where, for an example, a patient is rushed to hospital in an emergency and treated in good faith, in a manner deemed to be necessary and appropriate, and to which there is no known objection: contrast *Malette v Shulman* (above).

Non-consensual treatment may be administered to a minor in wardship providing it is in the minor's best interests—see *Re R, Re W, Re M* and *Re S*, above.

(b) Under Statute

Part IV of the Mental Health Act 1983 contains the provisions relating to the administration of non-consensual medical treatment. In particular, there are three sections which apply to non-consensual treatment, viz;

Section 58 provides for consent to treatment *or* a second opinion;

Section 62 provides for treatment which is "immediately necessary"; and

Section 63 provides for treatment not requiring consent (Details are given in Ch. 5, Mental Health Law).

See also ss.4 and 5 of the Mental Capacity Act 2005 for considerations of a patient's best interests (and see ss.24–26 in respect of advance decisions to refuse treatment).

5. MENTAL HEALTH LAW

The distinctive nature of mental health law

Key Principle: Mental Health Law tends to be treated as a distinct area of law given that provisions of the Mental Health Act 1983 may be employed to:

- compulsorily detain a person who has not committed an offence, with the period of detention being potentially indefinite;

- override a detainee's right to self-determination in respect of consenting to treatment; and

- treat the detainee's mental health in order to prevent its deterioration, or to restore it, when there is no established "standard" by which mental health can be judged.

Commentary
The Mental Health Act 1983 is awaiting amendment by the Mental Health Act 2007. Sections 2–4 and 136 of the 1983 Act will continue to provide the legal bases for the compulsory detention of a person; and ss.58, 62 and 63 provide for the non-consensual administration of treatment. There will be no definition of mental illness in the amended Act, however. Moreover, Thomas Szasz (in *"Law, Liberty and Psychiatry"* (1974)) has contended that there is no such thing as mental illness. Indeed, he said:

"... 'mental illness' is not the name of a medical disease or disorder, but is a quasi-medical label whose purpose is to conceal conflict as illness and to justify coercion as treatment".

Szasz asserted that:

"... 'mental illness' is a metaphor which we have come to mistake for a fact. We call people physically ill when their body functioning violates certain anatomical and physiological norms; similarly we call people mentally ill when their personal conduct violates certain ethical, political and social norms....
We should guard against .. the discomfort the mental patient's behaviour may cause us. If intense enough, it may justify intolerance

toward personal idiosyncrasies and so-called aberrations of behaviour. And yet, labelling conduct as sick merely because it differs from our own may be nothing more than discrimination disguised as medical judgment."

Key Principle: **The lack of a definition of mental illness (presuming, of course, that mental illness is not regarded as a myth) does not mean that that unilateral treatment decisions can be imposed, unless the legal authority to do so exists:**

R. v Hallstrom, Ex p. L [1986] 2 All E.R. 306
Here, McCullough J. said that:

"There is ... no canon of construction which presumes that Parliament intended that people should, against their will, be subjected to treatment which others, however professionally competent, perceive, however sincerely and however correctly, to be in their best interests. ... It goes without saying that, unless clear statutory authority to the contrary exists, no one is to be detained in hospital or to undergo medical treatment or even to submit himself to medical examination without his consent. That is as true of a mentally disordered person as of anyone else."

Commentary
First, a significant illustration of a detained patient being able to refuse treatment not only at the time treatment was proposed but also at any time in the future, because the presumption of his having capacity was not rebutted, was demonstrated in *Re C* [1994] 1 W.L.R. 290 which gave rise to the three-stage common law test for capacity—a test now enshrined in s.3 of the Mental Capacity Act 2005: see Ch.4.

Second, a single definition of mental disorder will apply throughout the amended 1983 Act: provisions relating to the other categories of disorder currently contained in the unamended 1983 Act and the expression "mental illness" are omitted.

Defining "Mental Disorder"

Key Principle: **The definitions of categories of mental disorder, as provided for in the Mental Health Act 1983, will be replaced by a single definition that will apply throughout the amended Act.**

[*N.B.*: The term "original" will be used to refer to provisions of the Mental Health Act 1983 as it existed prior to the amendments to be made by the Mental Health Act 2007]

Mental Health Act 1983, Section 1 ("original" Act provisions):
  (2) In this Act—

- "mental disorder" means mental illness, arrested or incomplete development of mind, psychopathic disorder and any other disorder or disability of mind and "mentally disordered" shall be construed accordingly;
- "severe mental impairment" means a state of arrested or incomplete development of mind which includes severe impairment of intelligence and social functioning and is associated with abnormally aggressive or seriously irresponsible conduct on the part of the person concerned and "severely mentally impaired" shall be construed accordingly;
- "mental impairment" means a state of arrested or incomplete development of mind (not amounting to severe mental impairment) which includes significant impairment of intelligence and social functioning and is associated with abnormally aggressive or seriously irresponsible conduct on the part of the person concerned and "mentally impaired" shall be construed accordingly;
- "psychopathic disorder" means a persistent disorder or disability of mind (whether or not including significant impairment of intelligence) which results in abnormally aggressive or seriously irresponsible conduct on the part of the person concerned;

  (3) Nothing in subsection (2) above shall be construed as implying that a person may be dealt with under this Act as suffering from mental disorder or from any form of mental disorder described in this section, by reason only of promiscuity or other immoral conduct, sexual deviancy or dependence on alcohol or drugs (and see below).

Commentary
Whereas "severe mental impairment", "mental impairment" and "psychopathic disorder" were all associated with abnormally aggressive or seriously irresponsible conduct, a person did not have to behave abnormally to come within the scope of MHA

1982, s.1(2) since it also applied to those with arrested or incomplete development of mind and any other disorder or disability of mind.

In *W v L* [1974] a man who had perpetrated many acts of cruelty to animals, killing several, was diagnosed as having a psychopathic disorder. The question arose as to whether he was also suffering from a "mental illness". Lawton L.J. thought that the ordinary sensible person would say "Well, the fellow is obviously mentally ill". Brenda Hoggett (now Baroness Hale, having been elevated to the House of Lords in 2004) criticised this "man-must-be-mad" test for mental illness saying:

> "It draws no recognisable distinction between illness and personality disorder. It tells us nothing about why some people who are cruel to animals should be regarded as responsible for their actions and some should not .. ".

The amended definition in s.1(2) (when in force) provides that: " 'mental disorder' means any disorder or disability of the mind; and 'mentally disordered' shall be construed accordingly". Moreover, s.1(3) of the 2007 Act provides that the other three definitions in the current 1983 Act, viz; severe mental impairment, mental impairment and psychopathic disorder, will be omitted.

The removal of the categories of mental disorder (when in force) provides just one of the amendments to the 1983 Act—an Act that has been described by Lord Steyn as "out of date in its approach": *R. (on the application of Munjaz) v Ashworth Hospital Authority* [2006] 2 A.C. 148.

As for s.1(3) of the original Act, this is to be amended to read: "Dependence on alcohol or drugs is not considered to be a disorder or disability of the mind for the purposes of subsection (2)". The abridged provision makes no practical difference since neither "promiscuity nor other immoral conduct" is, per se, regarded as a mental disorder.

Compulsory Admission to Hospital

Key Principle:	Sections 2–4 of the MHA 1983 provide the legal bases for patients' compulsory admission to hospital. Section 2 will remain unaffected by the Mental Health Act 2007 and s.4 is subjected to a relatively minor amendment. The major amendment is in respect of the deletion of the categories of mental disorder and the replacement of the "treatability" test in the current s.3 with an "appropriate treatment" test.

Compulsory admission to hospital

Section 2: admission for assessment

An application for admission for assessment may be made in respect of a patient on the grounds that—

(a) he is suffering from mental disorder of a nature or degree which warrants the detention of the patient in hospital for assessment (or for assessment followed by medical treatment) for at least a limited period; and

(b) he ought to be so detained in the interests of his own health or safety or with a view to the protection of other persons.

Commentary

The statutory provision for detaining a patient "in the interests of his own health or safety" contrasts with moral theory and Mill's assertion in his essay *"On Liberty"* that:

> "the only purpose for which power can be rightfully exercised over any member of a civilized community, against his will, is to prevent harm to others. His own good, either physical or moral, is not a sufficient warrant."

The maximum period of detention for assessment under s.2 is 28 days. A patient's detention under s.2 for a longer period was challenged in the House of Lords in *R. (on the application of MH) v Secretary of State* [2006] 1 A.C. 441 as being incompatible with Art.5(4) of the European Convention on Human Rights. The claim was rejected, however, as: there was no authority that Art.5(4) required every detention to be subject to judicial review; every hospital manager was under a statutory duty to take steps to ensure that patients understood their rights under the provisions of their detention; and there were ways in which a case could be referred to a Mental Health Review Tribunal (MHRT). Accordingly, the protective measures associated with s.2 were effective and not incompatible with the Convention.

The amended section 3

Section 3(2) will provide that:

An application for admission for treatment may be made in respect of a patient on the grounds that—

(a) he is suffering from mental disorder of a nature or degree which makes it appropriate to receive medical treatment in a hospital; and

[(b) will be repealed]

(c) it is necessary for the health or safety of the patient or for the protection of other persons that he should receive treatment and it cannot be provided unless he is detained under this section; and

(d) appropriate medical treatment is available for him

Admission for treatment under s.3 is for a period of up to six months, in the first instance. This can be extended for a further six months and then, if necessary, for up to a year at a time with no limit to the number of times the detention can be extended.

Commentary
The original "treatability" test

Under the original, or unamended, 1983 Act, s.3(2)(b) provides for:

"... such treatment [that] is likely to alleviate or prevent deterioration of [the patient's] condition."

In the *Cannons Park* case, the "treatability" test in s.3(2)(b) was satisfied when treatment prevented the deterioration of the detained patient:

R. v Canons Park MHRT Ex p. A [1995] Q.B. 60

The MHRT had rejected A's application for discharge on grounds of safety, finding that her condition was not being alleviated by the treatment she was receiving. The appropriate treatment for her was deemed to be group therapy with which she refused to co-operate. The MHRT appealed the decision of the Divisional Court that there was no power to detain her if she could not be properly treated.

Held: The appeal was allowed, since the tribunal had to have regard only to the "appropriateness" and "safety" tests referred to in the 1983 Act. The tribunal had to have regard to the "treatability" test, only when exercising its discretion as to whether to discharge or not. For the purposes of the "treatability" test medical treatment should not be narrowly construed; a patient was not to be considered untreatable merely because she refused to co-operate.

Lord Roch said:

"... treatment in hospital will satisfy the treatability test although it will not immediately alleviate or prevent deterioration in the patient's condition provided that alleviation or stabilisation is likely in due course. [Moreover], the treatability test can still be met although initially there may be some deterioration in the patient's condition due, for example, to the patient's initial anger at being detained. [Also], the treatability test is satisfied if nursing care, etc, is/are likely to lead to an alleviation of the patient's condition in that the patient is likely to gain an insight into his problem or cease to be uncooperative in his attitude towards treatment which would potentially have a lasting benefit."

Key Principle: **If treatment under s.3 is unlikely to alleviate or prevent the deterioration of a *restricted* patient's (i.e. a criminal's) condition (and see ss.41–43 MHA 1983 for restriction orders), then s.73 may provide for the patient's discharge:**

Reid v Secretary of State for Scotland [1999] 2 A.C. 512
In 1967, following a conviction of culpable homicide and a finding that he was suffering from mental deficiency, R was made subject to a detention order and a restriction order without limit of time. R was subsequently found not to be suffering from mental deficiency but was instead described as having a specified category of mental disorder. He applied for discharge from hospital on the ground that it was no longer appropriate for him to be detained for treatment as he suffered from a persistent mental disorder "manifested only by abnormally aggressive or serious irresponsible conduct" which was not treatable. He succeeded on appeal on the basis that there was no evidence which enabled a conclusion that his continued detention was likely to "alleviate or prevent a deterioration of his condition". The Secretary of State appealed.

Held: Appeal allowed. The treatability of a patient was an inherent part of the "appropriateness" test. Whereas, in the instant case, there was agreement among experts that medical treatment was not likely to alleviate R's condition, the treatability test was wide enough to include things other than medication and psychiatric treatment. The fact that the structured and controlled environment of the hospital resulted in an improvement in R's anger management could be considered in relation to the treatability test. Accordingly, it was wrong to depart from the initial finding that R's condition was being alleviated by the treatment he was receiving in hospital.

Some Treatments must abide by certain procedural requirements

Key Principle: **Two procedures within Pt IV of the MHA 1983 (ss.56–64), viz. those in ss.57 and 58, are markedly different from their common law counterparts. At common law, the consent of a competent patient is sufficient to authorise the administration of treatment; and a refusal will mean that administration of such treatment will be a civil wrong and may be a crime. By contrast, s.57 requires both consent *and* a second opinion; and one procedure under s.58 permits the administration of treatment *even if the patient has refused it*.**

Section 57(1) [pre-amendment]
The patient must consent and a second opinion is required for the following more serious types of treatment:

(a)   any *surgical operation for destroying brain tissue or for destroying the functioning of brain tissue*; and

(b)   *any surgical* implantation of hormones for the purpose of reducing male sex drive.

Commentary
The significance of s.57 is summed up by Gostin who comments:

"A s.57 treatment thus requires both the patient's consent *and* a second opinion: it is virtually the only provision in English law which stipulates that, even if the patient consents, treatment cannot be administered unless there is *independent* verification that the patient is competent to give his consent and that the treatment is effective. The state therefore has the right to intervene in cases where the doctor and patient agree on the need for a medically recognised treatment.)"

Section 58: Treatment requiring consent or a second opinion [pre-amendment]

(1) This section applies to the following forms of medical treatment for mental disorder—[including]

    (b) the administration of medicine to a patient by any means (...) at any time during a period for which he is liable to be detained as a patient to whom this part of this Act applies if three months or more have elapsed since the first occasion in that period when medicine was administered to him by any means for his mental disorder.

Commentary

Whereas treatment may be administered without consent during the first three months of detention, the patient's consent to continuing treatment after this period must be sought and noted, if obtained; or a second opinion appointed doctor (SOAD) must provide adequate reasons why treatment should be continued and these should be communicated to the patient unless the communication would cause serious harm to the physical or mental health of the patient or any other person: *R. (on the application of Wooder) v Feggetter* [2003] Q.B. 219.

Gostin comments on s.58:

> "s.58 represents a fundamental departure from traditional common law assumptions in that it specifies circumstances in which treatment can be imposed upon a patient who is competent to understand the nature and purpose of the treatment, but refuses to give his consent."

The administration of treatment under s.58 will be sanctioned by the courts if it is "convincingly" shown that the proposed treatment is a medical necessity: *Herczegfalvy v Austria* (1993) 15 E.H.R.R. 437 applied; and even if a responsible body of medical practitioners were of the opinion that the treatment was medically unnecessary, that, alone, would not be conclusive in favour of the patient.

N.B.: The provisions of Pt IV of the current MHA 1983 will be amended to incorporate "appropriate treatment" provisions.

Sections 57 and 58 have no application in the event of treatment being immediately necessary under s.62. In practice, s.62 has little significance; s.63 is far more important.

Key Principle: **Under s.63 of the MHA 1983, treatment can be imposed on patient who is competent but who has refused consent.**

Commentary

The treatment must be for the mental disorder as s.63 does not sanction treatment for a physical condition unrelated to the mental disorder. Nevertheless, the range of treatments sanctioned by common law in respect of a patient's mental condition is wide and includes tube-feeding, intervention to prevent a stillbirth and the treatment of a disorder that was not specified when the patient was detained.

B v Croydon Health Authority [1995] Fam 133

B suffered from a psychopathic disorder and one of her symptoms was a compulsion to harm herself. While she was compulsorily detained in hospital under s.3 of the MHA 1983, she stopped eating and her weight fell to a dangerous level. Nevertheless, she sought to restrain the health authority from tube feeding her without her consent. Whereas an injunction was granted and it remained in force pending a court hearing, in the High Court Thorpe J. held that tube feeding constituted medical treatment for the mental disorder from which B was suffering and that her consent was not required by virtue of the provisions of s.63 of the MHA 1983. B appealed.

Held: B's appeal was dismissed. On its proper construction, the term "medical treatment" in s.63 of the Act of 1983 referred to treatment which, taken as a whole, was calculated to alleviate or prevent a deterioration of the mental disorder from which the patient was suffering; that a range of acts ancillary to the core treatment including those which prevented the patient from harming herself or those which alleviated the symptoms of the disorder fell within s.63; and that, accordingly, tube feeding constituted medical treatment for the purposes of s.63 and could be carried out lawfully without the consent of B. Accordingly, the decision of Thorpe J. was affirmed.

Commentary

See also:

Re KB (Adult) (Mental Patient: Medical Treatment) (1994) 19 B.M.L.R. 144 where, in respect of tube-feeding an anorexic patient, Ewbank J. said that: "... relieving symptoms is just as much part of treatment as relieving the underlying cause."

Tameside and Glossop Acute Services Trust v CH [1996] 1 F.L.R. 762

Tests carried out at the 38th week of the pregnancy of the patient, who was detained under s.3 of the MHA 1983, indicated that unless labour was induced very shortly the foetus was likely to die *in utero*. Her doctor's opinion was that it was in her interests to give her a live baby, but the patient was delusional and believed that the medical staff were a threat to her child. It was thought that as a still-birth would have a deleterious effect on her health, then it was in her best interests to give birth to a healthy child. In turn, the optimum treatment of her physical condition that would follow such a birth would lead to optimum treatment of her mental state and, eventually, to the outcome of her psychiatric recovery.

Held: The patient had failed to satisfy the three-stage test in *Re C (Adult: Refusal of Treatment)* [1994] 1 W.L.R. 290 in that she failed to comprehend, believe and weigh the information about the prospective treatment. The medical evidence was clear that it was in the best interests of the patient for her to give birth to a live child and achievement of a successful pregnancy was a necessary part of the treatment for her psychiatric condition. The proposed treatment was within the broad interpretation of s.63 of the 1983 Act (as approved in *B v Croydon*, above). Accordingly, it followed that the patient's consent was not required and that the doctor was entitled, if he considered it clinically necessary, to use restraint to the extent reasonably required to achieve the birth of a healthy baby.

Commentary

Section 4 of the Mental Capacity Act 2005 now provides that a patient who is not competent to consent to treatment must be treated in a way that is considered to be in his / her best interests. The essence of the *Re C* test is enshrined in s.3 of the Act.

R. (on the application of B) v Ashworth Hospital Authority [2005] 2 A.C. 278

B was detained in a hospital as a restricted patient under ss.37 and 41 of the MHA 1983. On the basis of a diagnosis by clinicians that he also suffered from psychopathic disorder he was transferred by the hospital authority to a personality disorder ward so as to be treated compulsorily for that disorder under s.63 of the Act. At first instance, the judge refused B judicial review of the decision to detain him on that ward. However, the Court of Appeal concluded that s.63 did not permit compulsory medical treatment of a disorder which was not specified in the hospital order under which the patient was detained and so allowed B's appeal, granting declaratory relief that treatment without his consent for a psychopathic disorder was unlawful unless and until he was classified as suffering from that disorder by a mental health review tribunal under the 1983 Act. The hospital authority appealed to the House of Lords.

Held: The appeal was allowed. Section 63 of the MHA 1983 authorised the treatment of any disorder from which a patient suffered, even if this did not fall within the form of disorder from which he was classified as suffering when the detention order was made. Moreover, s.63 so construed, was not in breach of the protection afforded to a patient by his Convention rights, and so he could be treated compulsorily under s.63 for his psychopathic disorder in a personality disorder ward without the need for reclassification.

Key Principle: **The imposition of non-consensual treatment on a detained patient does not necessarily violate Art.3 ECHR, although "the more drastic the treatment, the more the doctor must be satisfied of the need for it" per Collins J. in** *R. (on the application of B) v Haddock* **[2005] All E.R. (D) 309.**

R. (on the application of N) v M [2003] 1 W.L.R. 562
Here, N appealed against the dismissal of her application to quash decisions by two consultant psychiatrists, M and O, that she required treatment involving the injection of anti psychotic medication. Since N did not consent to that treatment, M asked O to be appointed as a second opinion appointed doctor by the Mental Health Commission. O issued a certificate under s.58(3)(b) of the MHA 1983 in which he stated that N was suffering from paranoid psychosis or severe personality disorder and required anti psychotic drugs. N contended that she was suffering from an untreatable personality disorder and that there was a body of responsible medical opinion to the effect that the

proposed treatment was not in N's best interests and was not medically necessary.

Held: N's appeal was dismissed as: (1) the judge had applied the correct standard of proof, namely that it had to be "convincingly" shown that the proposed treatment was a medical necessity, in that N was suffering from a psychotic illness for which medication by injection was medically necessary; and (2) the fact that a body of responsible medical opinion viewed the proposed treatment as medically unnecessary did not conclusively determine in favour of the patient the issue of whether the treatment should be permitted. The court's duty was to consider whether, in the light of all the evidence, the treatment should be permitted, and the judge had been right to apply the best interests test *and* the medical necessity test in accordance with *Herczegfalvy* and *not* the *Bolam* test.

Commentary

The Court of Appeal said that relevant factors requiring consideration before deciding to administer treatment under s.63 included:

(a)   how certain is it that the patient does suffer from a treatable mental disorder,

(b)   how serious a disorder is it,

(c)   how serious a risk is presented to others,

(d)   how likely is it that, if the patient does suffer from such a disorder, the proposed treatment will alleviate the condition,

(e)   how much alleviation is there likely to be,

(f)   how likely is it that the treatment will have adverse consequences for the patient and

(g)   how severe may they be?

Moreover, the court of Appeal decided that

- It was necessary, though not sufficient, for a *Bolam* test to be satisfied before a treatment decision could be reached;

- It had to be convincingly shown that the claimant suffered from a treatable illness; and

- The proposed medical treatment was necessary—and, to ensure that Art.3 ECHR would not be invoked, the standard would be that as laid down in *Herczegfalvy v Austria*

Codes of Practice and Treatment

Key Principle: **Patients detained under the MHA 1983 should be treated in accordance with guidelines provided in Codes of Practice issued under s.118 of the Act. However, it must be noted that Codes of Practice provide guidelines not instructions:**

R. (on the application of Munjaz) v Ashworth Hospital Authority [2006] 2 A.C. 148
The NHS trust appealed against the decision that its policy governing the frequency of medical review of the seclusion of psychiatric patients detained at its high security mental hospital departed from the code of practice issued by the secretary of state under s.118(1) MHA 1983 and was unlawful. The code provided, inter alia, that hospitals should have clear guidelines on the use of seclusion, including the frequency of reviews of the need to continue the procedure. The central issues were (i) whether the trust's policy was unlawful under domestic law, and (ii) whether the policy had failed to comply with Arts 3, 5 and 8 of the ECHR, as given the force of law by the Human Rights Act 1998. M, a patient detained under the 1983 Act, at the trust's hospital, contended that the policy was unlawful under domestic law as it provided for less frequent medical review of seclusion, particularly after day seven, than was laid down in the code.

Held: (By a majority) the appeal was allowed. The reasons included: (1) the code provided guidance and not instruction. Where the policy had departed from the code in providing for less frequent medical review after day seven, the trust had explained the justification for the policy in very considerable detail. (2) The policy, properly operated, would be sufficient to prevent any possible breach of the Art. 3 rights of a patient secluded for more than seven days, and there was no evidence that the frequency of medical review provided in the policy risked any breach of those rights. With regard to Art. 5, the policy, properly applied, did not permit a patient to be deprived of any residual liberty to which he was properly entitled. Moreover, it was difficult to see why the policy would be incompatible with Art. 8, as its purpose was to define standards to be followed and to prevent abuse and arbitrariness. In any event, the policy was justified under Art. 8(2) as it was necessary for the prevention of disorder or crime, for the protection of health or morals, or for the protection of the rights and freedoms of others.

Treatment of Informal Patients: Section 131 of the Mental Health Act 1983; Article 5 ECHR; and the subsequent amendment of the Mental Capacity Act 2005 by the Mental Health Act 2007

Voluntary Patients admitted under section 131

Key Principle: About 90 per cent of the quarter-of-a-million people who require treatment for mental disorder and who are admitted to the mental health system each year, are admitted informally under s.131 of the Mental Health Act 1983.

Commentary

Section 131 appears to be confined to admission for treatment as it has no provision for assessment as distinct from treatment. However, in *R. v Kirklees MBC, Ex p. C* [1993] 2 F.L.R. 187, Lloyd L.J. had no doubt that "an adult patient may be lawfully admitted to hospital for assessment, provided he or she consents, just as he or she may be lawfully admitted to hospital for an operation".

The most significant issue here, however, is in respect of an informal adult patient where a House of Lords judgment on this provision was criticised by the European Court of Human Rights and, ultimately, this prompted a review that led to the amendment of the Mental Health Act 1983 and the Mental Capacity Act 2005:

R. v Bournewood Community and Mental Health NHS Trust, Ex p. L [1999] 1 A.C. 458

Here, L, a former long-term adult inpatient at B's hospital, had been re-admitted to hospital where a consultant took the view that L required inpatient treatment but that it was not necessary to detain him compulsorily under the Mental Health Act 1983 as he had not resisted admission. The result of legal arguments over the lawfulness of his detention over a two-year period by B, who were responsible for his care and treatment, was that the Court of Appeal held that L had been unlawfully detained as the Act left no room for the application of the common law doctrine of necessity. Patients incapable of consenting could only be admitted under the provisions of the Act dealing with compulsory detention, since informal admissions under s.131(1) of the Act were limited to patients who could and did consent to admission. This decision was appealed to the House of Lords.

Held: Their Lordships reversed the decision and allowed the appeal, stating that the 1983 Act s.131(1) was in identical terms to the Mental Health Act 1959 s.5(1). A hospital was entitled to treat and care for patients admitted under s.131(1) who were incapable of consenting on the basis of the common law doctrine of necessity. B's actions, which had been carried out in the discharge of its responsibility for L's treatment, had been in L's best interests and, to the extent that they might otherwise be regarded as infringing L's civil rights, were justified by the doctrine of necessity. L's re-admission to hospital under s.131(1) did not amount to the tort of false imprisonment, as he had not been deprived of his liberty, since he was not kept on a locked ward and had not made any attempt to leave.

Commentary
This case was referred to the European Court of Human Rights and the decision was reported in: *HL v UK* (2005) 40 E.H.R.R. 32. The House of Lords had considered L's detention from the point of view of the tort of false imprisonment, whereas the European Court of Human Rights considered it from the Convention concept of "deprivation of liberty" in Art.5(1). The Convention concepts are considered next before considering the judgment in *HL's* case (p.94, below).

Deprivation of Liberty and Persons of Unsound Mind—Article 5 ECHR

Key Principle: **Article 5(1) of the European Convention on Human Rights and Fundamental Freedoms, as given the force** of law by the Human Rights act 1998, provides that "No one shall be deprived of his liberty save in the following cases and in accordance with a procedure prescribed by law".

A permissible instance of deprivation of liberty

A permissible instance of deprivation of liberty is contained in Art.5(1)(e) of the Convention which provides for "the lawful detention of ... persons of unsound mind, alcoholics or drug addicts or vagrants".

Commentary

The criteria to be satisfied for a lawful detention on the grounds of "unsoundness of mind" are those specified by the European Court of Human Rights in *Winterwerp*:

Winterwerp v Netherlands (1979) 2 E.H.R.R. 387

Here, the European Curt of Human Rights decided that:

> "In the court's opinion, except in emergency cases, the individual concerned should not be deprived of his liberty unless he has been reliably shown to be of 'unsound mind'. The very nature of what has to be established before the competent national authority—that is, a true mental disorder—calls for objective medical expertise. Further, the mental disorder must be of a kind or degree warranting compulsory confinement. What is more, the validity of continued confinement depends upon the persistence of such a disorder."

In essence, *Winterwerp* requires that three conditions have to be satisfied if a person is to be detained on the grounds of unsoundness of mind, viz;

- Except in an emergency, a "true" mental disorder has to be established via objective medical expertise; secondly,

- The mental disorder must be of a kind or degree that warrants compulsory confinement; and

- the validity of continued confinement depends upon the persistence of such a disorder.

In *Aerts v Belgium* (2000) 29 E.H.R.R. 50, it was decided that a lawful detention is dependent upon the person receiving treatment for his condition and that that treatment be administered in a hospital, clinic or other appropriate institution. Accordingly, detention in a prison that offered no treatment was unlawful.

That the mental disorder must "of a kind *or* degree"

warranting compulsory confinement has been criticised by Bartlett and Sandland (2003) as being too wide: their argument is that any compulsory confinement should be based on "the kind *and* degree" of mental disorder.

Moreover, "Everyone who is deprived of his liberty by arrest or detention shall be entitled to take proceedings by which the lawfulness of his detention shall be decided speedily by a court and his release ordered if the detention is not lawful": Art.5(4). So, in *R. (on the application of C) v MHRT* [2002] 1 W.L.R. 176, the applicant succeeded in his contention that a uniform policy for tribunal hearings requested by patients detained under s.3 of the MHA 1983 would be fixed at eight weeks after the date of the application did not comply with the requirement of Art.5(4) of the Convention for the detention to be decided speedily. By contrast, neither a *target date* of eight weeks maximum for the listing of hearings or cases requiring eight weeks preparation would be inconsistent with the Convention rights.

Key Principle: **Interpretation of Art.5 by the European Court of Human Rights is being incorporated into English law as the "Bournewood safeguards" by way of amending the Mental Capacity Act 2005.**

HL v UK (2005) 40 E.H.R.R. 32 (The "Bournewood" judgment)

Held: HL was deprived of his liberty when he was admitted informally to B's hospital. In particular: the manner in which he was deprived of his liberty was not in accordance with "a procedure prescribed by law", thus it breached Art.5(1) ECHR; and Art.5(4) had been breached as he was not able to have the lawfulness of his detention decided speedily by a court. Because HL's assessment, care, treatment, movement and residence were under the complete and effective control of the health care professionals, he was not free to leave B's hospital as and when he wished. Accordingly, this amounted to a "deprivation of liberty" requiring safeguards satisfying Arts 5(1) and 5(4) which would not have been required had there been only a restriction (not a deprivation) of his liberty.

Commentary

The 44-page document, *"The Bournewood safeguards: Draft illustrative guidance"*, for England and Wales, published in December 2006, are being issued as a Code of Practice under s.42 of the Mental Capacity Act 2005. As the Draft illustrative Code of Practice made clear:

6.   The Bournewood safeguards make it clear that a person may only be deprived of their liberty in their own best interests and when there is no less restrictive alternative.

10. A Bournewood authorisation relates solely to the issue of deprivation of liberty. It does not give authority to treat people, nor to do anything else that would normally require their consent.

See also: ss.49–51 and Schs 7–9 of the Mental Health Act 2007.

Discharge of Detained Patients

Key Principle: **The provisions for the discharge of detained patients are principally contained in s.23 of the MHA 1983 as amended by the (now repealed) Health and Social Care (Community Health and Standards) Act 2003.**

R. (on the application of von Brandenburg) v East London and the City Mental Health NHS Trust [2004] 2 A.C. 280

A mental Health Review Tribunal had ordered the release of B, who had been detained under s.2 of the MHA 1983. However, before B had left the hospital, he was readmitted under s.3. B contended that there had been no change of circumstances since the tribunal hearing. This was challenged by the approved social worker, who contended that B had declined to continue taking his medication, with the result that his condition had significantly deteriorated. The issue of law was whether it was lawful to readmit a patient under s.2 or s.3 when a mental health review tribunal had ordered his discharge, and when it could not be demonstrated that there had been a relevant change of circumstances.

Held: B's appeal was dismissed. The test was not whether there had been a relevant change of circumstances. Rather, an approved social worker could not lawfully apply for the admission of a patient whose discharge had been ordered by the decision of a mental health review tribunal of which the approved social worker was aware, unless he had formed the reasonable and bona fide opinion that he had information not known to the tribunal which put a significantly different complexion on the case. An application could not be made simply because the approved social worker disagreed with the tribunal's decision to discharge. There was a limited duty on the approved social worker to give reasons for his decision to seek readmission where that was inconsistent with the effect of an earlier tribunal decision, but he could not be required to make any disclosure which was potentially harmful to the patient or others, and reasons could be given in very general terms. The factual dispute between the parties was untested but there had been no challenge to the bona fides of the judgment of the approved social worker in reaching his decision to apply for B's admission, and it would be hard to regard it as anything other than reasonable.

Commentary

The principal provisions relating to discharge in s.23(2) of the MHA 1983 are powers, not duties. Accordingly, a finding that the mental disorder which justified the patient's detention no longer exists, does not mean that the patient is entitled to immediate and unconditional release into the community: *Johnson v UK* (1999) 27 E.H.R.R. 440; it means that the discharge can be delayed until appropriate after-care arrangements have been made.

Challenging detention

Key Principle: **A patient's detention under s.3 may be challenged via habeas corpus or judicial review.**

Re S-C (Mental Patient: Habeas Corpus) [1996] Q.B. 599

S, a mental patient, appealed against the dismissal of his application for a writ of habeas corpus following his admission to and detention in hospital under s.3 of the Mental Health Act 1983. He argued that the admission and detention were unlawful as the approved social worker had not completed the required application form correctly in accordance with the Act, s.11(4), which provided that on making an application for treatment an approved social worker had to consult with the nearest relative and could not proceed if that relative objected to the making of the application. Here, the social worker had stated that she had consulted S's mother believing her to be the nearest relative, when in fact the nearest relative was his father who objected to the application.

Held: Adjourning the appeal, that (1) the detention was unlawful, as the approved social worker's statement was false since on the date of admission she knew that S's nearest relative was his father and that he objected to the admission. Any delegation of his role to the mother had to be in writing pursuant to Regulations made under the 1983 Act, but no such authorisation had been given and therefore there was no authority to detain; and (2) S had not sought to overturn an administrative decision, but to show that the hospital lacked jurisdiction to detain him. Therefore an appropriate remedy was not by way of judicial review but by a writ of habeas corpus, as it was not for the court to rule that an apparently valid application was lawful when the statutory safeguards to protect mental patients had clearly been violated. The matter was adjourned to enable the health authority to give reasons why S should continue to be detained.

Commentary
The decision in *Re S-C (Mental Patient: Habeas Corpus)* should be contrasted with that in the *Barking Havering and Brentwood* case that follows.

B v Barking Havering and Brentwood Community Healthcare NHS Trust [1999] 1 F.L.R. 106
B, a patient detained under s.3 of the 1983 Act, appealed against the dismissal of her applications for habeas corpus and judicial review against BHB in relation to the renewal of her detention under s.20 of the Act. At the time of renewal B had been granted weekly leaves of absence under s.17 of the Act for five days per week and part of the other two days, although B had subsequently returned to the hospital full time following a change in circumstances. Following the decision in *R. v Hallstrom Ex p. W (No.2)* [1986] Q.B. 1090, where it was held that a patient on leave under s.17 could not have his detention renewed under s.20, the medical profession had adopted the practice of ensuring that a patient was not on leave when the renewal procedures were instigated. B contended that it followed from the reasoning in Ex p. W, that the in-patient treatment that she received during the period she had been granted leaves of absence could not be

regarded as anything other than an assessment, which, since it would not be sufficient to justify detention under s.3, should not be sufficient to justify renewal under s.20.

Held: Appeal dismissed. The interpretation of s.20 espoused in Ex p. W was incorrect and would lead to results contrary to Parliament's intentions. Furthermore, B's submission had to be rejected as the treatment received by a patient granted a leave of absence had to be viewed as a whole. The requirement for the patient to return to hospital for monitoring as an in patient was an essential part of such a patient's treatment and one which it might not be possible to provide if the patient did not continue to be detained. Taking that approach, the requirements of s.20 could be satisfied provided that the treatment involved an element of in patient therapy. Moreover, in cases such as the present, applications for habeas corpus were to be discouraged unless no other form of relief was required, as judicial review was the more appropriate procedure: *Re S-C (Mental Patient: Habeas Corpus)* [1996] Q.B. 599 was not followed (although it was approved on the facts of the case). Where applications were made both for judicial review and habeas corpus, the proceedings should be harmonised if at all possible.

Supervised Community Treatment

Key Principle: **Sections 32–36 of the Mental Health Act 2007 contain the provisions on Supervised Community Treatment.**

After the s.17 current 1983 Act provisions on "leave of absence from hospital" in the 1983 Act, s.32 of the 2007 Act makes new provisions—destined, principally, to be ss.17A to 17G—to be inserted to deal with Community Treatment Orders and the effect of their revocation, and the power to recall a community patient to hospital.

The supervised community treatment provisions replace the after-care supervision provisions in ss.25A–25J that were inserted into the 1983 Act by the Mental Health (Patients in the Community) Act 1995 which are to be repealed under s.36 of the 2007 Act.

It is hoped that the new provisions will at least reduce, if not eliminate, the small number of patients (the "revolving-door" patients) who have left hospital to live in the community where they have failed to comply with a care plan, resulting in deterioration of their mental health and, ultimately, re-admission to hospital.

The other principal provisions of Ch.4 of the 2007 Act, i.e. ss.34 and 35, provide for the following amendments to Pt 4 of the 1983 Act: Consent to Treatment, under s.34; and a new Pt 4A—Treatment of Community Patients Not Recalled to Hospital—is to be inserted under the provisions of s.35.

Summary of the Amendments to the 1983 Act made by the 2007 Act.

The amending measures of the Mental Health Act 2007 include:

- A single definition of mental disorder will replace the four categories of mental disorder in s.1(2) of the curent Act;

- The "treatability test" in s.3 will be replaced by a new "appropriate treatment" test;

- A broader group of persons will be able to fulfil the functions of "approved social worker" and "responsible medical officer";

- The provisions for determining "nearest relative" will be amended to include civil partners;

- The concept of supervised community treatment (SCT) will be introduced to enable a small number of patients to live in the community whilst remaining subject to provisions of the 1983 Act (as amended);

- There will be a single Mental Health Tribunal for England and one for Wales.

Of course, it should not be forgotten that the Mental Capacity Act 2005 (ss.4 and 16, in particular) also will be amended (by s.50 of the Mental Health Act 2007) to give effect to the *Bournewood* safeguards. Other sections in the 2005 Act that make specific provisions about the deprivation of liberty—ss.6(5), 11(6) and 20(13)—will also be amended.

It has not yet (January 2008) been announced when the amendments will be in force.

6. CONFIDENTIALITY

Statement of the Law

Key Principle: Whilst "it is well settled that there is an abiding obligation of confidentiality as between doctor and patient", a duty of confidence may arise in the absence of a pre-existing relationship.

Att-Gen v Guardian Newspapers (No.2) [1990] 1 A.C. 109, 281
Lord Goff said:

> "... a duty of confidence arises when confidential information comes to the knowledge of a person (the confidant) in circumstances where he has notice, or is held to have agreed, that the information is confidential, with the effect that it would be just in all the circumstances that he should be precluded from disclosing the information to others."

Commentary

In the same report (at pp.281–282), Lord Goff explained that "the principle of confidentiality only applies to information to the extent that it is confidential", i.e. for information to be regarded as confidential, it must not be in the "public domain" nor must it be "useless information" or "trivia". Most importantly, however, according to his Lordship, was that whether a confidence was protected or disclosed was a matter of balancing countervailing public interests. Another Law Lord, Lord Keith, cited the doctor-patient relationship as a well established relationship that gives rise to the duty of confidence and so tacitly affirmed the existing common law rule expressed by Boreham J. in Hunter v Mann [1974] Q.B. 767 at 772 that:

> "... the doctor is under a duty not to disclose, without the consent of the patient, information which he, the doctor, has gained from his professional capacity."

That parties did not have to be in a confidential relationship before a breach of the duty of confidence arose, so affirming Lord Goff's opinion (above), was a point made also by Lord Hoffman in *Wainwright v Home Office* [2003] 3 W.L.R. 1337, para.29.

Key Principle: The duty of confidentiality is not confined to protecting the rights of competent adults: it extends to mentally incapacitated adults and, in respect of children, particularly, though not exclusively, "Gillick competent" children. Moreover, it may be a professional and/or legal requirement to maintain the confidences of a deceased patient.

Incompetent Adult Patients

An incompetent adult patient has the right to have his interests in privacy considered and for a balance to be struck between privacy and disclosure in the same way as they are for a competent patient:

R. (S) v Plymouth City Council [2002] 1 W.L.R. 2583

Hale L.J. expressed the view that:

"Both at common law and under the Human Rights Act, a balance must be struck between the public and private interests in maintaining the confidentiality of this information and the public and private interests in permitting, indeed requiring, its disclosure for certain purposes."

Children

Venables v NGN [2001] Fam 430, 469

Here, Dame Elizabeth Butler Sloss said:

"Children, like adults, are entitled to confidentiality in respect of certain areas of information. Medical records are the obvious example."

R. (on the application of Axon) v Secretary of State for Health [2006] Q.B. 539

Mrs Sue Axon sought judicial review of a Department of Health document entitled *"Best Practice Guidance for Doctors and other Health Professionals on the Provision of Advice and Treatment to Young People under Sixteen on Contraception, Sexual and Reproductive Health"*. The document noted that: "The duty of confidentiality owed to a person under 16, in any setting, is the same as that owed to any other person. This is enshrined in professional codes ... All services providing advice and treatment on contraception, sexual and reproductive health should produce an explicit confidentiality policy which reflects this guidance and makes clear that young people under 16 have the same right to confidentiality as adults."

Mrs Axon had had an abortion twenty years earlier and, as she had regretted it ever since, she wanted to ensure that her young daughters could not experience such a situation without her knowledge. Amongst the relief sought by Mrs Axon, was a declaration that the guidance was unlawful as it misrepresented the law as expressed by the House of Lords in *Gillick* [see Ch.4] and it infringed her rights under Art.8 ECHR (the right to respect for family life).

Held: Silber J. dismissed the application. There was nothing in the advice that contravened parents' rights to respect for family life under Art.8 ECHR: accordingly, the advice was lawful. Moreover, he referred to the opinions of Lords Fraser and Scarman in *Gillick*, which remained good law, and decided that young girls would not seek advice and treatment unless they could be assured of confidentiality. Advice and treatment for the relevant matters could be given if the following criteria were met:

(1)   that the young person understands the advice;

(2)   that the young person cannot be persuaded to inform his or her parents or to allow the health professional to inform them that their child was seeking advice or treatment on sexual matters;

(3)   that the young person is very likely to begin or to continue having sexual intercourse with or without advice or treatment on such matters;

(4)   that unless the young person receives advice and treatment on the relevant sexual matters, his or her physical or mental health or both are likely to suffer; and

(5)   it is in the best interests of the young person to receive such advice and treatment without parental consent.

Commentary
It is important to note that there is no direct link between competence and confidentiality. Confidentiality attaches to the nature of the information: it is independent of a person's capacity—indeed, it may prevail even after death—and, generally, is based

in equity, although as is noted below (p.5) Arts.8 and 10 ECHR now play an integral part in the law of confidence.

For the authority that a duty of confidentiality may be owed to a baby, see the judgments of the appellate bench in *Re C* [1999] Fam 39 (CA).

Deceased Patients
In essence, the principal means of maintaining a deceased patient's confidential information arise from professional guidance and at common law. The guidance given by the GMC in para.30 is noted, below

Re C (Adult Patient: Restriction of Publicity after Death) [1996] 2 F.L.R. 251
Accompanying a court order granting a declaration that life support treatment could be withdrawn from a young man in the persistent vegetative state, was the grant of another order preventing the identification of the man and his family. The Official Solicitor sought guidance as whether the order would persist following the man's death.

Held: The order would remain in force throughout the currency of valid reasons. The reasons were expressed to include: the detrimental effect on the medical staff that might occur on revocation of the order; consideration of the man's family; the issue of medical confidentiality; and the public interest in allowing applications for withdrawal of treatment orders to be made without fear of publicity.

Legal Basis

Key Principle: **Whereas a breach of confidence may found an action in (say) contract or the tort of negligence, the principal legal basis underpinning the duty of confidence, whether at common law or under statute, is in equity.**

Fraser v Evans [1969] 1 Q.B. 349
Lord Denning M.R.:

> "The jurisdiction for [confidentiality] is based not so much on property or on contract as on the duty to be of good faith. No person is permitted to divulge to the world information which he has received in confidence, unless he has just cause for doing so."

Stephens v Avery [1988] Ch 449
Sir Nicolas Browne Wilkinson V.C. said:

> "The basis of equitable intervention to protect confidentiality is that it
> is unconscionable for a person who has received information on the
> basis that it is confidential subsequently to reveal that information."

Commentary
The recognition of equity as the principal legal basis underpinning the duty of confidentiality is not a late twentieth-century
phenomenon: it may be traced back at least to the mid-nine-
teenth century; but what is of significance, now, are the opinions
of the House of Lords in cases such as *Att-Gen v Guardian
Newspapers* (No.2) (1990) and, particularly, *Campbell v MGN*
(2004) (below).

At the end of the twentieth century, the essence of the law of
confidentiality and its legal basis could be summarised by
reference to *Att-Gen v Guardian Newspapers* (1990) and *Ashworth
Security Hospital v MGN* (2000). In summary, the impact of *Att-
Gen v Guardian Newspapers* (the "Spycatcher" case) may be
expressed in terms of the decision that there was a public interest
in giving legal protection to confidences imparted under explicit
or implicit notices of confidentiality and that the opinion of Lord
Goff above effectively encapsulates the common law test for
breach of confidentiality developed in the 1960s and expressed in
Stephens v Avery [1988] Ch 449, viz, there must be:

1. the necessary quality of confidence attached to the infor-
    mation imparted (i.e., must not be in the public domain);

2. the information must have been imparted in circum-
    stances importing an obligation of confidence; and

3. there must be an unauthorised use of that information to
    the detriment of the party communicating it.

By the beginning of the new millennium, then, in *Ashworth
Security Hospital v MGN* [2001] 1 W.L.R. 515, at 627, Lord Phillips
M.R. was under no doubt that:

> "It is well settled that there is an abiding obligation of confidentiality
> as between doctor and patient and, in my view [the patient] is entitled
> to be confident that details about his condition and treatment remain
> between himself and those who treat him."

Continuing development of the legal basis

(a) At Common Law

Key Principle: **Since the incorporation of the European Convention on Human Rights and Fundamental Freedom via the Human Rights Act 1998 became part of English law in 2000, the House of Lords has further recognized and emphasised Arts 8 and 10 of the Convention to be an integral part of the law of confidence.**

Campbell v MGN [2004] 2 A.C. 457

The fashion model Naomi Campbell had been photographed leaving a meeting of Narcotics Anonymous. The photographs accompanied an article in the Daily Mirror that praised her fight against drug addiction and gave details about her treatment. In hearing the claim for breach of confidence, it fell to be decided by the House of Lords if her attendances at meetings of Narcotics Anonymous were confidential and, if so, was there a greater (public) interest in protecting the freedom of the press so sanctioning the breach?

Held: The majority of the House decided that the time, place and nature of the drug therapy were confidential, hence the taking of the photographs and the publication of the article constituted a breach of confidence. The public interest element involved a "balancing exercise" between the right to a private life, as provided for in Art.8 ECHR and the right to freedom of expression under Art.10 ECHR. First, as Campbell had made public statements proclaiming she did not take drugs, either she had waived confidentiality or, in the alternative, the public interest justified the press in publishing an article to correct Campbell's misleading statements. However, as there was little public interest in the story, her private life prevailed over the right to freedom of expression. In essence, the breach of confidence occurred because of the publication of the *nature* of the information as opposed to any pre-existing relationship between Naomi Campbell and the newspaper. The relatively small sums she was awarded in damages and aggravated damages came as no surprise given that Baroness Hale had said the case was, in essence, "a prima Donna celebrity against a celebrity-exploiting newspaper".

Commentary

The more significant aspects of the case focus on some of the opinions expressed in the House. For example, in para. 17 of the report, Lord Nicholls stated:

> "The time has come to recognize that the values enshrined in Arts.8 and 10 are now part of the cause of action for breach of confidence."

Moreover, Lord Nicholls was of the opinion that the "essence of the tort is better encapsulated now as misuse of private information". However, if this is equivalent to a breach of an equitable obligation of confidence, it adds nothing.

Baroness Hale sought to answer the question of: "... the nature of the freedom of expression which was being asserted by [MGN]". As part of the balancing act (between Arts.8 and 10 ECHR), Baroness Hale continued (at para.157):

> "The weight to be attached to the[] various considerations is a matter of fact and degree. Not every statement about a person's health will carry the badge of confidentiality or risk doing harm to that person's physical or moral integrity. The privacy interest in the fact that a public figure has a cold or a broken leg is unlikely to be strong enough to justify restricting the press's freedom to report it. What harm could it possibly do? ... in this case there was, as the judge found, a risk that publication would do harm. The risk of harm is what matters at this stage, rather than the proof that actual harm has occurred. Blundering in when matters are acknowledged to be at a 'fragile' stage may do great harm."

Article 8(1) ECHR, which recognizes a right to respect for "private and family life" has been interpreted as "the ability to conduct one's life in a manner of one's own choosing": *Pretty v UK* (2002) 35 E.H.R.R. 1, para.62

Of course, the rights may be overridden by the provisions of Art.8(2) providing they are "in accordance with the law and .. necessary in a democratic society ...". This limited infringement is in line with proportionality being recognized as a well-established general principle of European Community (hence English) law. It would seem that this provision also supports the decision in *W v Egdell* (1990) (below)

Prior to the coming into force of the Human rights Act 1998, one of the few cases that focused on the interpretation of Art.8 ECHR was *Z v Finland* (1998).

Z v Finland (1998) 25 E.H.R.R. 371

Z was married to a man who had raped other women. The prosecuting authorities wanted to know when the man became aware of his HIV+ status. The wife's medical records were accessed to determine this and the contents were disclosed in court. The wife complained that her human rights had been infringed.

Held: That while accessing her medical records was justified in the pursuit of the serious criminal offences being tried, it did not justify making them public: her identity and HIV status did not have to be disclosed; this was disproportionate to the aim. The Court expressed the view that:

> "The protection of personal data, not least *medical data*, is of funda-mental importance to a person's enjoyment of his or her right to respect for private and family life as guaranteed by Article 8 of the Convention ... Without such protection, those in need of medical assistance may be deterred from revealing such information of a personal and intimate nature as may be necessary in order to receive appropriate treatment and, even, from seeking such assistance, thereby endangering their own health and, in the case of transmissible diseases, that of the community."

Key Principle: **The incorporation of Arts. 8 and 10 ECHR into English law has not meant that the English law has developed a tort of infringement of privacy.**

Wainwright v Home Office [2004] 2 A.C. 406

Mrs Wainwright (W) and her son, who were both strip searched before visiting another son of hers in prison, appealed against the setting aside of a county court judgment that they had suf-fered a form of trespass to the person. Moreover, W now con-tended that the prison officers were liable, inter alia, for the invasion of privacy, the tort existing due to the European Con-vention on Human Rights 1950 Art.8, even though the Human Rights Act 1998 had not been in force at the time of the events.

Held: The appeal was dismissed. While privacy was a value underlying the common law of breach of confidence, it was not in itself a principle of law and there was no tort of invasion of privacy. Moreover, the jurisprudence of the European Court of

Human Rights did not indicate that a principle of privacy was necessary to comply with Art.8.

(b) Under Statute
Key Principle: **An action for breach of confidentiality may be expressly provided for under statute: it is not confined to being a part of the equitable jurisdiction of the English courts.**

Section 171(1) Copyright, Designs and Patents Act 1988
"Nothing [in this part of the Act] affects ... the operation of any rule of equity relating to breaches of trust or confidence."

Commentary
Clearly, the most important statutory provisions for present purposes are those contained in the *European Convention of Human Rights and Fundamental Freedoms*, Arts. 8 and 10, as given the force of law by the Human Rights Act 1998.

Confidentiality as expressed in Codes of Ethics

Key Principle: **Whilst the duty of confidence is expressed in several codes of ethics, the codes are not consistent in their proclamations.**

Hippocratic Oath
All that may come to my knowledge in the exercise of my profession or outside of my profession or in daily commerce with me, *which ought not to* be spread abroad, I will keep secret and never reveal.

Declaration of Geneva (as amended in 1994)
I will *respect* the secrets which are confided in me, even after the patient has died.

World Medical Association's International Code of Medical Ethics (1949)
Here it is stated that:

> "A doctor *shall* preserve absolute secrecy on all he knows about his patient because of the confidence entrusted to him."

Commentary

The absolutist position contained in the International Code of Medical Ethics is not shared by the Hippocratic Oath or the Declaration of Geneva. Indeed, the absolutist approach is unsustainable when a patient requires the input from a team of healthcare professionals for the management of, and recovery from, his illness (see below). Moreover, information "which ought not to be spread abroad" (Hippocratic Oath) is not necessarily synonymous with the "respect" required by the Declaration of Geneva.

It should also be noted that the principal theories of ethics that underpin the codes all support confidentiality, albeit for different reasons. For example, Utilitarianism sees the respect for confidentiality as a means to maximise the principle of utility by way of encouraging patients to seek medical assistance while deontologists draw attention to protecting privacy and enhancing an individual's autonomy.

Given that the GMC has the legal power to discipline doctors, including erasing their registrations ("striking off"), considerable weight should be given to its guidance on confidentiality.

GMC

Confidentiality: Protecting and Providing Information

April 2004

Patients' right to confidentiality

Principles

1. Patients have a right to expect that information about them will be held in confidence by their doctors. Confidentiality is central to trust between doctors and patients. Without assurances about confidentiality, patients may be reluctant to give doctors the information they need in order to provide good care. If you are asked to provide information about patients you must:

    - inform patients about the disclosure, or check that they have already received information about it;

- anonymise data where unidentifiable data will serve the purpose;
- be satisfied that patients know about disclosures necessary to provide their care, or for local clinical audit of that care, that they can object to these disclosures but have not done so;
- seek patients' express consent to disclosure of information, where identifiable data is needed for any purpose other than the provision of care or for clinical audit—save in the exceptional circumstances described in this booklet;
- keep disclosures to the minimum necessary; and
- keep up to date with and observe the requirements of statute and common law, including data protection legislation.

2.   You must always be prepared to justify your decisions in accordance with this guidance.

9.   You must respect patients' confidentiality. Seeking patients' consent to disclosure of information is part of good communication between doctors and patients. When asked to provide information you must follow the guidance in paragraph 1 [above].

10. ... You should make sure that the patients are aware that personal information about them will be shared within the health care team, unless they object, and of the reasons for this. ... You must respect the wishes of any patient who objects to particular information being shared with others providing care, except where this would put others at risk of death or serious harm.

22. Personal information may be disclosed in the public interest, without the patient's consent, and in exceptional cases where patients have withheld consent, where the benefits to an individual or society of the disclosure outweigh the public and the patient's interest in keeping the information confidential. In all cases where you consider disclosing information without consent from the patient, you must weigh the possible harm (both to the patient, and the overall trust between doctors and patients) against the benefits which are likely to arise from the release of information.

26. Ultimately, the "public interest" can be determined only by the courts; but the GMC may also require you to justify your actions if a complaint is made about the disclosure of identifiable information without a patient's consent. The potential benefits and harms of disclosures made without consent are also considered by the Patient Information Advisory Group in considering applications for Regulations made under the Health and Social Care Act 2001.

Disclosure after a patient's death

30. You still have an obligation to keep personal information confidential after a patient dies. The extent to which confidential information may be disclosed after a patient's death will depend on the circumstances. If the patient had asked for information to remain confidential, his or her views should be respected. Where you are unaware of any directions from the patient, you should consider requests for information taking into account:

- whether the disclosure of information may cause distress to, or be of benefit to, the patient's partner or family;
- whether disclosure of information about the patient will in effect disclose information about the patient's family or other people;
- whether the information is already public knowledge or can be anonymised;
- the purpose of the disclosure.

If you decide to disclose confidential information you must be prepared to explain and justify your decision.

Corporate responsibility of NHS bodies to protect data

Key Principle: **Responsibility for the protection of a patient's data is not confined to health professionals: the employing body also has a responsibility as the data controller—a "Caldicott guardian"—named after the author of the Report (Dame Fiona Caldicott) that detailed six "Caldicott" principles (that are additional to the eight principles of data protection).**

The six Caldicott Principles are:

- The use or transfer of information should be justified;

- Patient information should not be used unless it is absolutely necessary;

- Use the minimum necessary patient information;

- Access to patient information should be on a strict "need to know" basis;

- All staff must be aware of their responsibilities;

- All staff must understand and comply with the law.

Commentary
Implementation of the Caldicott principles and the nomination of a Caldicott Guardian is necessary for purposes such as protecting patient confidentiality whilst, at the same time, complying with a duty under s.19 of the Freedom of Information Act 2000 to adopt and maintain a Publication Scheme for promoting greater openness by public authorities. See, for example, the "Freedom of Information" page on the NHS blood and Transplant site at: http://www.nhsbt.nhs.uk/about/freedom_of_information/part1.html [Accessed February 28, 2008].

Disclosures that do not incur sanctions (Permissible breaches / "Defences")

Key Principles:　Statutes, common law and professional guidance have given rise to a number of situations where it has been deemed permissible (even a requirement) to disclose information without incurring liability for breach of confidence. Where a patient has consented to the release of information, the release cannot constitute a breach or even a "relaxation" of the rule: the information is, by definition, no longer confidential.

Consent to publish

C v C [1946] 1 All E.R. 562
Both the petitioner and the respondent in proceedings for a decree of nullity requested that the doctor release details of the venereal disease that the respondent was suffering. The doctor, who had been treating the respondent, refused unless he was

subpoenaed. This duly ensued and a direction was sought so as to avoid the recurrence of a similar issue. Lewis J. said the question to be answered was:

> "Is a doctor, when asked by a patient to give him or her particulars of his or her condition and illness to be used in a court of law, when those particulars are vital to the success or failure of the case, entitled to refuse and in effect to say: 'Go on with your case in the dark and I will tell you in court when I am subpoenaed what my conclusions are?'...
>
> ...It is, of course, of the greatest importance ... that proper secrecy should be observed in connection with ... the confidential relationship existing between doctor and patient. But, in my opinion, those considerations *do not* justify a doctor in refusing to divulge confidential information to a patient or to any named person or persons when asked by the patient so to do. ... and in *all cases* where the circumstances are similar the doctor is not guilty of any breach of confidence in giving the information asked for."

Commentary

There is no breach of confidence when there is consent to publish: there is no longer any "secrecy" or confidentiality attaching to the information to be breached. Equally, "straightforward descriptions of everyday life are not normally thought confidential": *R. (S) v Plymouth City Council* [2002] 1 W.L.R. 2583 at 2594, per Hale L.J.

Sharing information

Recent guidance from both the GMC and the Department of Health stresses the importance of informing the patient of the importance of disclosing information for the benefit of their healthcare and that they are aware of the implications of this sharing of information.

Confidentiality: NHS code of Practice (Department of Health 2003)

12. It is extremely important that patients are made aware of information disclosures which must take place in order to provide them with high quality care. ... the efforts made to inform them should reflect the breadth of the required disclosure. This is particularly important where disclosure extends to non-NHS bodies ...

14. Patients generally have the right to object to the use and disclosure of confidential information that identifies them,

and need to be made aware of this right. .... Patients must be informed if their decisions about disclosure have implications for the provision of care or treatment...

15. Where patients have been informed [of the use and disclosure of their information and of their choices] then explicit consent is not usually required for information disclosures needed to provide that healthcare. Even so, opportunities to check that patients understand what may happen and are content should be taken...

Commentary
The result of an American survey at the beginning of the 1980s was that a Dr Siegler was

"astonished to learn that at least 25 and possibly as many as 100 health professionals and administrative personnel ... had access to the patient's record and all of them had a legitimate need, indeed a professional responsibility, to open and use that chart".

This led to his describing confidentiality as a "decrepit concept". When this finding was reported to the patient whose concern had prompted the enquiry, the patient asked Dr Siegler "just what you people mean by confidentiality".

Disclosure is required by statute or court order

See, for example:

- Public Health (Control of Disease) Act 1984 s.10 provides a list of notifiable diseases and s.11(1)(a) and (b) provides for a registered medical, practitioner to send to the proper officer of the local authority for that district a certificate stating—(a) the name, age and sex of the patient and the address of the premises where the patient is; (b) the disease or, as the case may be, particulars of the poisoning from which the patient is, or is suspected to be suffering and the date, or approximate date, of its onset...

- Road Traffic Act 1988, s.172(2) provides that where the driver of a vehicle is alleged to be guilty of an offence ... (b) any ... person shall if required ... give any information which it is in his power to give and may lead to identification of the driver;

Commentary

This sub-section is identical to that in the forerunner of this Act, the Road Traffic Act 1972, and in *Hunter v Mann* [1974] 1 Q.B. 766, Boreham J. said of this provision:

> "I am driven to the conclusion that a doctor acting within his professional capacity, and carrying out his professional duties and responsibilities, is within the words 'any other person' in [this subsection]".

- Human Fertilisation and Embryology Act 1990, s.31(5) provides that:
  Regulations cannot require the Authority to give any information as to the identity of a person whose gametes have been used or from whom an embryo has been taken if a person to whom a licence applied was provided with the information at a time when the Authority could not have been required to give information of the kind in question.

- Abortion Regulations 1991, SI 1991/499—Reg.5: ... any information furnished to a Chief Medical Officer in pursuance of these Regulations shall not be disclosed except that disclosure may be made—

  (d) pursuant to a court order, for the purposes of proceedings which have begun; or
  (e) for the purposes of bona fide scientific research; or
  (f) to the practitioner who terminated the pregnancy; or
  (g) to a practitioner, with the consent in writing of the woman whose pregnancy was terminated;...

Disclosure in "the Public Interest"

Key Principle: **For disclosure of confidential information in the public interest to be lawful, there must be compelling circumstances in which the public interest in disclosure substantially outweighs the interest in maintaining patient confidentiality.**

X v Y [1988] 2 All E.R. 648

Two doctors were being treated in hospital for AIDS. Their names were passed to a newspaper by a health authority employee. The health authority succeeded in obtaining an

injunction to prevent the newspaper publishing details of the
doctors. Rose J. said:

> "I keep in the forefront of my mind the very important public interest
> in freedom of the press. And I accept there is some public interest in
> knowing that which the defendants seek to publish ... But in my
> judgment those public interests are substantially outweighed when
> measured against the public interests in relation to loyalty and con-
> fidentiality both generally and with particular reference to AIDS
> patients' hospital records ... The deprivation of the public of the
> information sought to be published will be of minimal significance if
> the injunction is granted."

The public, in general, and patients, in particular, are entitled to
expect hospital records to be confidential and it is not for any
individual to take it upon himself or herself to breach that confidence whether induced by a journalist or otherwise:

H (A Healthcare Worker) v Associated Newspapers Ltd and N (A Health Authority) [2002] Ll Rep Med 210

H, a healthcare worker, was HIV positive. He obtained an order
in the Court of Appeal preventing a newspaper disclosing the
identification of the health authority, by whom he was
employed, but not of his (H's) speciality, since the risk that such
information would reveal his identity was so low as not to
warrant a fetter on the freedom of expression enjoyed by the
newspaper.

W v Egdell [1990] Ch 359

The legal advisers to a prisoner in a secure hospital did not
pursue his application for a transfer to a regional secure unit
when a medical report, prepared by Dr Egdell, proved unfa-
vourable. However, when the prisoner's routine review of his
detention was due and Dr Egdell became aware that his report
would not be included in the prisoner's notes, he sent copies to
the medical director of the hospital and to the Home Office. W
sought an injunction in contract and equity alleging that Dr
Egdell had breached his duty of confidence.

Held: The Court of Appeal unanimously upheld the decision
of the trial judge (Scott J.) to dismiss the action. According to
Bingham L.J.:

> "The parties .. agreed .. that the crucial question was how ... the
> balance should be struck between the public interest in maintaining

professional confidences and the public interest in protecting the public against possible violence ... Only the most compelling circumstances could justify the doctor acting in a way which would injure the immediate interests of his patient, as the patient perceived them, without obtaining his consent."

Commentary

The decision to uphold the "public interest in protecting the public against possible violence" would now find support in Art.8(2) ECHR.

Where data is anonymised

R. v Department of Health Ex p Source Informatics [2000] 2 W.L.R. 940

In this case, the Court of Appeal unanimously reversed the decision at first instance and decided that anonymised patient data that had been obtained by pharmacists and doctors from prescription forms for the purpose of being used in the creation of a database for pharmaceutical companies, did not breach any patient's confidentiality.

Simon Brown L.J. at para. 31;

"The confidant is placed under a duty of good faith to the confider and the touchstone by which to judge the scope of his duty and whether or not it has been fulfilled or breached is his own conscience, no more and no less. One asks, therefore, on the facts of this case: would a reasonable pharmacist's conscience be troubled by the proposed use to be made of patients' prescriptions? Would he think that by entering Source's scheme he was breaking his customers' confidence, making unconscientious use of the information they provide?"

Commentary

Whereas some commentators have contended that the decision in *Source Informatics* shifts the focus from the protection of confidentiality to fairness of use, it is not a contention that is easy to support given that there was no confidential information to protect. To suggest otherwise in a fact-specific case is to attempt to equate imparting anonymised data with breaching patient confidentiality. By definition, there is no confidentiality in anonymised data.

Research

Key Principle: The GMC publication: *Research: The Role and Responsibility of Doctors* (February 2002), paragraphs 30–42 provide ethical guidance and, in particular, para.34 specifically draws the attention of doctors to the possibility of breaking the law if they do not act in accordance with the guidelines:

Where consent cannot be obtained
34. Where it is not practicable to contact participants to seek their consent to the anonymisation of data or use of identifiable data in research, this fact should be drawn to the attention of a research ethics committee so that it can consider whether the likely benefits of the research outweigh the loss of confidentiality to the patient. Disclosures may otherwise be improper, even if the recipients of the information are registered medical practitioners. The decision of a research ethics committee would be taken into account by a court if a claim for breach of confidentiality were made, but the court's judgment would be based on its own assessment of whether the public interest was served.

A duty in negligence

Key Principle: No clear authority exists in English law for negligence being a basis on which to bring an action for breach of confidentiality. The authorities that exist are outside the English legal system, e.g. *Furniss v Fitchett* [1958] N.Z.L.R. 396, and the Californian case of:

Tarasoff v Regents of the University of California (1974) 529 P 2d 55
The student medical centre at the University of California was sued in negligence by the parents of a murdered girl, T, for failing to warn T of the risk posed to her by one of their patients, P. P had confided his intention to kill T in a psychologist employed at the centre. The staff informed the campus police who briefly detained P but then released him when he appeared rational. The medical centre passed no information to T who was murdered by P soon afterwards.

Held: There was a breach of duty to exercise reasonable care to protect T.

Patients' Access to Medical Records

At common law

Key Principle: **The patient's consent to the release of confidential information in a court of law is no indication of a common law right to access medical records.**

C v C [1946] 1 All E.R. 562

Held: There was no breach of the duty of confidentiality when the patient had specifically requested that her records be disclosed in court.

A more recent case has affirmed that there is no right at common law that permits a patient to have access to his records; and it has also stated that this does not amount to a deprivation of his human rights:

R. v Mid Glamorgan FHSA, Ex p. Martin, [1995] 1 All E.R. 356 (CA)

The applicant, who had a history of psychological problems, had been refused access to his health records on the grounds that it would be detrimental to him. However, access was offered to the applicant's medical advisor so that he could decide if disclosure would be harmful to him.

Held: in deciding that the health authority could deny a patient access to his records on the basis that it would be harmful to him, Nourse L.J. said:

> "A doctor, likewise a health authority, as the owner of a patient's medical records, may deny the patient access to them if it is in his best interests to do so, ... the doctor's general duty, likewise the health authority's, is to act at all times in the best interests of the patient. Those interests would usually require that a patient's records should not be disclosed to third parties; conversely, that they should usually be handed on by one doctor to the next or made available to the patient's legal advisers if they are reasonably required for the purposes of legal proceedings in which he is involved."

Commentary
Even where a court order is obtained for the discovery of
documents, it may confine the disclosure to the patient's legal
adviser. As patients' records become computerized and accessible to relevant personnel in NHS bodies throughout the
country, it becomes closer to being an anomalous anachronism
that denies the autonomous patient access to "his" records.

Under Statute

Key Principle: **There is no statutory provision that gives a
patient an absolute right to access the information in his
medical records.**

Access to Medical Reports Act 1988

This Act came into force on January 1st 1989 and applies to both
private and NHS patients. It does *not* give a patient a *general right*
to *access* to medical records but provides that in certain circumstances (s)he has a right of access to an individual medical report
sought from a particular doctor in connection with *employment* or
insurance purposes.

Section 1: Right of access
It shall be the right of an individual to have access ... to any
medical report relating to the individual which is to be, or has
been, supplied by a medical practitioner for employment purposes or insurance purposes.

Commentary
The first limitation of the Act is that if the doctor does *not* have
"responsib[ility] for the clinical care of the individual" (s.2(1)),
because he is not the individual's GP, then the provisions of the
Act *do not* apply.

However, it has be noted that a potential employer or insurance company seeking a medical report on an individual must
obtain that individual's consent to seek the report: i.e. the patient
has, it appears, some control over the dissemination of information on his medical records; s.3(1). As a condition to granting
consent the individual may require that he be given access to the
medical report prior to its supply to the employer/insurance
company: s.4(1). (Where this condition has not been imposed the

individual still has potential right of access up to six months thereafter: s.5)

"Access" means inspection of a copy of the medical report or obtaining such a copy: s.6(4) & (3). In the latter case, the individual may be charged a reasonable fee: ss.4(4) & 6(3).

N.B.: The Individual's right of access is *not* absolute. Section.7 provides for three situations where a doctor will be excused from granting access, viz;

(i) where, in the doctor's opinion, disclosure would be "likely to cause serious harm to the physical or mental health of the individual *or others"*;

(ii) where disclosure would indicate the intentions of the doctor in respect of the individual; and

(iii) where disclosure would be likely to reveal information about another or identify another who had supplied information to the doctor unless that other had consented or was a doctor in whose care the individual had been.

Each of the above situations may prevent the individual from obtaining access to the whole or part of the medical record.

If a doctor wishes to deny access to the whole of a report then he *cannot* supply that report to the potential employer or insurance company without the individual's consent.

It is usual practice to send extracts or copies of notes to doctors outside the hospital service for bona fide use in treatment but not for purposes connected with litigation. (As previously noted, "Information shared with other doctors, nurses or health professionals participating in caring for a patient" is regarded as a permissible breach of confidence by the GMC.)

Access to Health Records Act 1990

In essence, the only significant provision remaining in force of the Access to Health Records Act 1990 (given that it was largely repealed by the Data Protection Act 1998) is s.3(1)(f):

(1) An application for access to a health record, or to any part of a health record, may be made to the holder of the record

(f) Where the patient has died, [by] the patient's personal representative and any person who may have a claim arising out of the patient's death.

Commentary

As will be noted from the above, the provisions now relate, in essence, only to those pursuing claims in intestate succession.

Data Protection Act 1998

Key Principle: **The limited rights of access to personal data of individuals are provided for in Pt II of the Data Protection Act 1998.**

In essence, s.7 DPA 1998 provides that the individual has a right to have communicated to him in an intelligible form "information constituting any personal data of which that individual is the data subject" upon written request and payment of a regulated fee.

Commentary

This prima facie right to access all records—manual or computerized—is subject to the Secretary of State's power in s.30(1) to exempt or modify a patient's access to records—see: SI 2000/413. If the patient is to be denied access, the decision is made only after consulting the health professionals responsible for the patient's care. An aggrieved patient has the right of appeal to the Information Commissioner's Office.

Section 13 provides for compensation for an individual who suffers damage by reason of any contravention or any of the requirements of the 1998 Act.

Section 14 provides for, inter alia, the rectification and erasure of data which appears to the court to be based on inaccurate data.

Commentary

Requests for access to personal data are governed by the Data Protection Act 1998: the Freedom of Information Act 2000 has no application as is made clear in s.40 of the 2000 Act which provides that:

Any information to which a request for information relates is *exempt information* if it constitutes personal data of which the applicant is the data subject.

Reform of Access to Medical Records

It was announced in December 2006 that the Government would pursue its plans for a national computerised medical record system as part of its 10-year £20 billion upgrade of NHS computer systems, supposedly in the interests of patient care. It will not be compulsory for patients to have their records uploaded to a national database, however.

Allegedly, the system will be "security–protected" to prevent unauthorized access and any person who accesses medical records without good reason may be prosecuted. More importantly, perhaps, is that every patient will be able to check his records before they are uploaded to the national database.

Commentary
Given that thousands of health care professionals have the potential right to access the computerised records, the potential for breach of confidence is significant and Siegler's expression of astonishment (above) over the observation:

"... that at least 25 and possibly as many as 100 health professionals and administrative personnel ... had access to the patient's record and all of them had a legitimate need, indeed a professional responsibility, to open and use that chart", pales into relative insignificance.

More seriously, perhaps, were the reports at the end of 2007 of the HM Revenue and Customs (HMRC) losing computer disks containing confidential details of 25 million child benefit recipients. This was followed by the DVLA admitting the loss of driving test data, and this, in turn, was followed by revelations of finding medical records and then police files in the street. Such carelessness hardly inspires confidence in those of us who have a legitimate expectation that our confidential data will be respected by others.

7. MEDICAL NEGLIGENCE

Negligence

Key Principle: The definition of negligence and the burden of proof to be discharged by the claimant applies equally in medical negligence cases as in any other action for a claim in negligence.

> "In strict legal analysis, negligence means more than heedless or careless conduct, whether in omission or commission: it properly connotes the complex concept of duty, breach, and damage thereby suffered by the person to whom the duty was owing: on all this liability depends, …".

(per Lord Wright in: *Lochgelly Iron Co v M'Mullan* [1934] A.C. 1, 25).

Commentary
The ingredients to be proved to establish liability in medical negligence are the same as for negligence in any other situation, viz;

- Duty of care;
- breach of that duty (which, of course, means that the requisite standard has first to be established in order to determine whether the conduct or omission complained of has fallen below it) and that
- the claimant's damage has been caused by the defendant's breach of duty.

(1) Duty of Care
Following the House of Lords decision in *Caparo v Dickman* [1990] 2 A.C. 605, three criteria have to be established to impose a duty of care on the defendant, viz;

- proximity of relationship;
- foreseeability of damage; and
- it must be reasonable to impose such a duty of care.

With reference to the relationship of proximity, the House of Lords in *Caparo* adopted the dictum of Brennan J. in *Sutherland Shire Council v Heyman* (1985) 60 A.L.R. 1 and said that the Court, guided by situations in which the existence, scope and limits of a duty of care had previously been held to exist, rather than a single general principle, would determine whether the particular damage suffered was the kind of damage which the defendant was under a duty to prevent and whether there were circumstances from which the court could pragmatically conclude that a duty of care existed.

Duty of Care in the Doctor—Patient Relationship

In *Sidaway*, Lord Templeman said at [1985] 2 W.L.R. 480, 508E: "The relationship between doctor and patient is contractual in origin, the doctor performing services in consideration for fees payable by the patient." Indeed, where a medical practitioner is privately engaged the contractual duty he owes to his patient is to be undertaken with reasonable skill and care: i.e. in the absence of express terms in a contract, the contractual duty is identical to the duty of care imposed in tort. As Tucker J. said in *Morris v Winsbury-White* [1937] 4 All E.R. 494 [such a case imposes] "... no duty other than that which exists in the ordinary normal case ...".

To the benefit of the majority of patients, however, the common law has long recognised a doctor as having a duty of care towards his patients independent of contract. In *Pippin v Sheppard* (1822) 11 Price 400, it was said that: "To hold to the contrary would be to leave such persons in a remedyless state"; and in *Gladwell v Steggall* (1839) 5 Bing N.C. 733, Tindal C.J. said that in spite of the absence of a contract between a 10 year old girl and a clergyman who "practised as a medical man" "... this is an action *ex delicto*".

Currently, a doctor (GP) has a duty of care to his patients who, principally, are those on his list or those who require emergency treatment in his practice area when he is able to render it (see Ch.2). By contrast,

"The 'doctor in the house' who volunteers to assist a lady in the audience who, overcome by the drama or by the heat in the theatre, has fainted away is impelled to act by no greater duty than that imposed by his own Hippocratic Oath",

per Lord Goff, in *F v West Berkshire Health Authority* [1989] 2 All
E.R. 545 at 567.

Duty of Care owed by NHS Bodies
Given that there is no contract between an NHS patient and his/
her GP, any legal action alleging negligence will be pursued in
tort. An NHS body may also be responsible for (say) the negligence of one of its doctors via vicarious liability:

Barnett v Chelsea & Kensington HMC [1969] 1 Q.B. 428
Three night-watchmen presented themselves at the casualty
department of a hospital early on New Years Day 1966. They told
a nurse that they had all been vomiting since drinking tea about
three hours earlier. However, when the nurse telephoned the
casualty officer he, too, said he felt unwell. He said to the nurse
"Tell them to go home and go to bed and call in their own
doctors." Shortly afterwards one of the night watchmen, Mr
Barnett, died. His widow sued for damages.

Held: The defendants were vicariously liable for the negligence
of the casualty officer who did not see and examine the deceased
and did not admit him to the wards and treat him. However, as a
post mortem revealed that the deceased died of arsenical poisoning then there would have been no reasonable prospect of
administering a suitable antidote before death. Accordingly, the
defendant's negligence was not the cause of Mr Barnett's death.
(See, also, "Causation", below)

Commentary
That an NHS Body may incur direct liability for negligent acts
has been mooted by the courts. In the Court of Appeal decision
in *Wilsher v Essex AHA* [1987] Q.B. 730, Mustill L.J. stated that:

> "... counsel for the plaintiff explicitly disclaimed on the plaintiff's
> behalf any intention to put forward a case of direct liability. The trial
> had been conducted throughout, he made clear, exclusively on the
> basis of vicarious liability. It is therefore unnecessary to express any
> opinion on the validity in law of a claim on the alternative basis."

However, both Glidewell L.J. and Browne-Wilkinson V.C.
thought that the case could not be properly analysed without
deciding the point. Glidewell L.J. agreed with Browne-Wilkinson
V.C. who had stated that:

"... a health authority which so conducts its hospital that if fails to provide doctors of sufficient skill and experience to give the treatment offered at the hospital may be directly liable in negligence to the patient. ... I can see no reason why, in principle, the health authority should not be so liable if its organisation is at fault."

Browne-Wilkinson V.C. acknowledged that the imposition of direct liability on a health authority raised four particularly awkward questions, viz;

[1] To what extent should the authority be held liable if (e.g. in the use of junior housemen) it is only adopting a practice hallowed by tradition?

[2] Should the authority be liable if it demonstrates that, due to the financial stringency under which it operates, it cannot afford to fill the posts with those possessing the necessary experience? ...

[3] ... is it sensible to persist in making compensation for those who suffer from shortcomings in technologically advanced treatment depend on proof of fault...

[And

4] Given limited resources, what balance is to be struck in the allocation of such resources between compensating those whose treatment is not wholly successful and the provision of required treatment for the world at large?

Browne-Wilkinson V.C. concluded that: "These are questions for Parliament, not the courts".

Notwithstanding the reservations of Browne-Wilkinson V.C., a health authority was found liable under *res ipsa loquitur* in *Bull v Devon* (1993), see below.

Extending the Duty of Care to Ambulance Services

A major extension to the duty of care, post-*Caparo*, was the imposition on the ambulance service of a duty of care to transport a patient to hospital in reasonable time:

Kent v Griffiths [2001] Q.B. 36

A GP telephoned for an ambulance from a patient's home giving details of the patient's condition and requested that an ambulance be sent immediately. A second 'phone call was made by the patient's spouse about a quarter of an hour later and, when the ambulance had still not arrived after another quarter of an hour, the GP made a third call. The ambulance arrived about 10 minutes after the third call / 40 minutes after the first call. On the way to hospital, however, the patient suffered a respiratory arrest, which led to brain damage, and suffered a miscarriage. In the proceedings that ensued, the patient alleged that the ambulance service acted negligently in unreasonably delaying her transportation to hospital; that had the ambulance service acted reasonably, the hospital could have dealt with the respiratory arrest and prevented her brain damage.

Held: That once a call for assistance had been accepted by the ambulance service it could owe a duty of care to members of the public if it was shown that sufficient information was given to the ambulance service for it to understand the nature of the call; that it was made clear that time was of the essence; that the service accepted the call by allocating an ambulance to deal with it; and having regard to all the circumstances, the ambulance failed to arrive at the hospital within a reasonable time. In this case, the claimant was successful in establishing the criteria.

(2) The standard against which doctors are judged

Key Principle: **The common law has insisted on a higher standard of care than the "man on top of a Clapham omnibus" standard from doctors; and doctors who profess to exercise specialist skills must do so with a corresponding standard of care.**

Bolam v Friern Hospital Management Committee [1957] 1 W.L.R. 582, 586
McNair J. said:

> "... where you get a situation which involves the use of some special skill or competence, then the test whether there has been negligence or not is not the test of the man on top of a Clapham omnibus, because he has not got this special skill. The test is the standard of the ordinary skilled man exercising and professing to have that special skill. A man need not possess the highest expert skill; it is well established law that it is sufficient if he exercises the ordinary skill of an ordinary competent man exercising that particular art".

Commentary

McNair J. quoted Lord President Clyde's dictum from the Scottish case of *Hunter v Hanley* (1955) S.L.T. 213, where, in part, it was said that:

> "In the realm of diagnosis and treatment there is ample scope for genuine difference of opinion and one man clearly is not negligent merely because his conclusion differs from that of other professional men, . . .".

That standards could be based on "genuine differences of opinion", meant that there could be a multiplicity of *Bolam* standards and the adoption of one to the exclusion of, perhaps, the majority opinion, would be no indicator of negligence: even a small number of practitioners in a particular speciality (less than 3 per cent) could constitute such a standard, as was the case in *De Freitas v O'Brien* [1993] 4 Med L.R. 281; and when a *Bolam* standard was adjudged appropriate to determine whether a non-consensual operation was necessary in the best interests of a patient, it was rightly condemned as "medical paternalism run amok". See Ch.8 and the case of *Re F* (1989).

Moreover, attempting to justify "genuine differences of opinion" on a single—"Bolam"—standard, and make them all applicable to diagnosis, disclosure of risk and treatment, becomes problematic. Yet acceptance of this indivisibility was affirmed by Lord Diplock in *Sidaway* [1985] A.C. 871 at 895 where his Lordship said:

> "In English jurisprudence, the doctor's relationship with his patient which gives rise to the normal duty of care to exercise his skill and judgment to improve the patient's health . . . has hitherto been treated as a single comprehensive duty . . . This general duty is not subject to dissection into a number of component parts to which different criteria . . . apply . . .".

Given the developments in the requirements of the amount of information to be imparted by doctors to patients before the patients can be said to have given a valid (or "real" or "informed" or "appropriate") consent, and the gradual but discernible move away from reliance on the *Bolam* standard in English law, Lord Diplock's opinion must now be seen as no longer accurate. See Ch.4 for a discussion of post-*Sidaway* case law.

Furthermore, Lord Scarman had said in *Maynard* [1984] 1 W.L.R. 634 at 639 that:

"... a judge's 'preference' for one body of distinguished professional opinion to another also professionally distinguished is not sufficient to establish negligence in a practitioner whose actions have received the approval of those whose opinions, truthfully expressed, honestly held, were not preferred".

However, in an article entitled *"Brushes with Bolam. Where will it lead?"*, (2004) 72 Medico-Legal Journal 127 at 136, Badenoch said he would re-write Lord Scarman's dictum to read:

"In the realm of diagnosis and treatment, negligence may be established by preferring one respectable body of opinion to another ... because, while the body of medical men may be responsible and respectable, it is possible that their practices or their opinions, judged objectively, are not. For there will be occasions, which the judge must be ready to identify, when two opposing contentions cannot both be right".

Indeed, application of the *Bolam* standard has now both been "reigned in" in certain circumstances (*Re S* [2000] 3 W.L.R. 1288—see Ch.4) and "qualified" by *Bolitho* [1998] A.C. 232 (see below).

Key Principle: **The standard of care expected of inexperienced, junior doctors in a specialist hospital unit is determined by the level of the post they occupy in the unit, as inexperience is no defence to an action in medical negligence; whereas, for skilled surgeons, the more skilled they are the higher is the standard of care expected of them.**

Junior Doctors

Wilsher v Essex A H A [1987] Q.B. 730
(See case notes under causation)

Here, the standard of care expected of a junior doctor was said to be determined in the context of the particular post he occupied in the specialist unit. In this case, the junior doctor was found to be not negligent as he had consulted a superior who, himself, had been negligent and for which the health authority was vicariously liable.

Jones v Manchester Corpn [1952] 2 Q.B. 852 at 871
Denning L.J. said:

> "Errors due to inexperience or lack of supervision are no defence as against the injured person ...".

Skilled Surgeons

Maynard v West Midlands RHA [1984] 1 W.L.R. 634 at 638:
Lord Scarman said:

> "... a doctor who professes to exercise a special skill must exercise the ordinary skill of his speciality".

Commentary
The Court of Appeal has been consistent in enforcing standards of care and rejecting allowance for inexperience in cases relating to road safety (*Nettleship v Weston* [1971] 3 All E.R. 581) and patient safety in hospitals (*Jones* and *Wilsher*, above).

Breaching the Duty of Care

In *Sidaway*, Lord Bridge made it clear that the court reserves the right to condemn an accepted practice as negligent ([1985] 1 All E.R. at 663a–c); [1985] 2 W.L.R. at 505c). This accords with the Australian view expressed in *F v R* (1983) where King C.J. said:

> "... professions may adopt unreasonable practices ... not because they serve the interests of the clients, but because they protect the interests or convenience of members of the profession. The court has an obligation to scrutinise professional practices to ensure that they accord with the standard of reasonableness imposed by the law."

Accordingly, and notwithstanding attempted defences based on a *Bolam* standard, the English courts have been prepared to condemn practices as sub-standard in:

Hucks v Cole, a 1968 case but reported in [1993] 4 Med L.R. 393 where Sachs L.J. said, at 397 that if it was not reasonable for a professional practice to contain risks, particularly if they "can be easily and inexpensively avoided" and that "in the light of current professional knowledge" there is no basis for it, then it is the function of the courts to "state that fact, and where necessary to state that it constitutes negligence".

In *Smith v Tunbridge Wells HA* [1994] 5 Med L.R. 334 it was declared "neither reasonable nor responsible" that a 28-year-old man was not warned of the risk of impotence inherent in rectal surgery.

Key Principle: **As an examination of what constitutes responsible medical practice, it may be contended that the Bolitho case qualifies, rather than replaces, or permits an extension of,** *Bolam.*

Bolitho v City & Hackney Health Authority [1998] A.C. 232 at 242
Lord Browne-Wilkinson said:

> "... the court has to be satisfied that the exponents of the body of opinion relied on can demonstrate that such opinion has a *logical basis.* In particular, in cases involving, as they often do, the weighing up of risks against benefits, the judge before accepting a body of opinion as being reasonable, responsible or respectable, will need to be satisfied that, in forming their views, the experts have directed their minds to the questions of comparative risks and benefits and have reached a *defensible conclusion* on the matter".

Commentary
Post-Bolitho case law hasn't been consistent in its application of the requirement for a logical basis and defensible conclusion—perhaps because of the caveat attached by Lord Browne-Wilkinson who said (at p.243) that: "... it will very seldom be right for a judge to reach the conclusion that views genuinely held by a competent medical expert are unreasonable".

Indeed, in one of the first post-Bolitho cases, *Wisniewski v Central Manchester Health Authority* [1998] PIQR P324, Brooke L.J. concluded that this was a case that did not fall into the category of "rare cases" that could not be logically supported or held by responsible doctors.

By contrast, the Court of Appeal in *Marriott v West Midlands RHA* [1999] Lloyd's Rep Med 23 upheld the judgment at first instance that a professional opinion that would have supported a GP's decision not to refer a discharged patient with head injuries back to hospital was not reasonably prudent. Mason and Laurie (2005) say that this decision "moves the Bolitho test from one of logic to one of reasonableness", even though the Court of Appeal "still retained the language of 'logic'".

Lord Woolf, in the Court of Appeal decision in *Penney v East Kent Health Authority* (2000) 55 BMLR 63, at p.70, made it clear that "the Bolam test has no application where what the judge is required to do is to make findings of fact" but he went on to agree that observable abnormalities on slides of cervical smears should not have been labelled "negative". Accordingly, the judgment at first instance, that labelling the slides as "negative" was inconsistent with the principle of "absolute confidence", and thus illogical.

Key Principle: **Whilst it has been said that the general duty of care "is not subject to dissection into a number of component parts to which different criteria apply", the following cases provide a useful illustration of what does / does not constitute a breach of the duty of care in negligence.**

Diagnosis

Failures in diagnosis
Newton v Newton's New Model Laundry (1959) The Times, November 3rd

Inappropriate Treatment
Collins v Hertfordshire Corporation [1947] 1 K.B. 598;
Jones v Manchester Corporation [1952] 2 Q.B. 852;
Contrast: *Roe v Ministry of Health*—a case denying *res ipsa loquitur*; with *Bull v Devon*—both noted below).

Prescription errors
Prendergast v Sam & Dee [1989] 1 Med LR 36 (See below, under "Remoteness")

Disclosing risks
See Ch.4 for discussion of inadequate risk disclosure / the appropriate amount of information to impart prior to operative treatment, failure of which led to actions in negligence in the following cases:

Bolam v Friern HMC [1957] 1 W.L.R. 582;
Sidaway v Board of Governors of the Bethlem Royal Hospital and the Maudsley Hospital [1985] A.C. 871;
Rogers v Whittaker [1993] 4 Med L.R. 79;

Smith v Tunbridge Wells HA [1994] 5 Med L.R. 334
Pearce v United Bristol Healthcare NHS Trust [1998] 48 B.M.L.R. 118
Chester v Afshar [2005] 1 A.C. 134 (An unwarranted modification of the "but for" principle, perhaps? See below).

Res Ipsa Loquitur

Key Principle: **Res ipsa loquitur is a rule of evidence by which C, who is unable to prove how an injury occurred, seeks a prima facie finding of negligence which is then for D to rebut, if he can; but this does NOT shift the burden of proof from C.**

Roe v MoH [1954] 2 Q.B. 66
Two patients who received spinal anaesthetics by injections of nupercaine on the same day developed spastic paraplegia. The nupercaine had been stored in glass ampoules immersed in a solution of phenol. Evidence was adduced that phenol had percolated into the ampoules through invisible cracks and this had contaminated the nupercaine. The plaintiffs contended that the doctrine *res ipsa loquitur* applied.

Held: The contention was rebutted by a full explanation of what had happened in 1947 (the year of the operations). Once the risk of contamination had been identified via a 1951 publication it would have been negligent to have stored the ampoules in phenol thereafter. However, "We must not look at the 1947 accident with 1954 spectacles", per Lord Denning.

Bull v Devon Area Health Authority [1993] 4 Med L.R. 117
Here, a health authority was found to be in breach of its duty of care to a patient when the second of twins, who was born more than an hour after the first twin, suffered mental disability and spastic quadriplegia due to birth asphyxia resulting from the prolonged delay between the deliveries. The health authority's hospital operated a twin-site and the consultant obstetrician who delivered the second twin had to travel from a unit on the other site. It was accepted that the consultant carried out the delivery promptly and efficiently, but the delay had proved catastrophic.

Held: that *res ipsa loquitur* applied in this case: that the hospital's system for summoning an obstetrician on call must either have been inefficient or have been negligently operated. The inefficiency in getting an appropriately qualified person to attend had placed on the authority an evidential burden for it to justify. As it had failed to do so, the breach of duty had been established.

(3) Causation

(i) Factual Causation
The general rule: the "but for" test.

> "If the damage would not have happened *but for* a particular fault then that fault is the cause of the damage; if it would have happened just the same, fault or no fault, the fault is not the cause of the damage." per Denning L.J., *Cork v Kirby Maclean Ltd.* (1952).

In essence, then, the "but for" test acts as a preliminary filter to eliminate those acts or omissions which have no bearing on the ultimate injury.

Barnett v Chelsea & Kensington HMC [1969] 1 Q.B. 428
(See above for the facts of this case).

Held: The defendant's negligence was not the cause of Mr Barnett's death.

Kay v Ayrshire and Arran Health Board [1987] 2 All E.R. 417

Held: There was no medical evidence which proved a causal link between a massive overdose (x30) of penicillin and the child's deafness. The evidence strongly indicated that the deafness was caused by meningitis.

Wilsher v Essex A H A [1986] 3 All E.R. 801
Martin Wilsher, who had been born three months prematurely, was provided with extra oxygen to help him breathe more effectively. The oxygen was meant to have been administered via a catheter into an artery. However, the catheter was inserted into a vein. Neither the (relatively) junior doctor who inserted the catheter nor the more experienced registrar realised that such an error had been made until some 30 hours later, by which time the catheter was changed; the old one having been removed by the

junior doctor and the new one being inserted by the registrar. This catheter was also inserted into a vein. By the time the junior doctor had recognised that an error had been made, Martin Wilsher (MW) had been subjected to an excessive partial pressure of oxygen for about eight to twelve hours. MW contracted retrolental fibroplasia (RLF) and was nearly blind. Unsurprisingly, it was held both by the trial judge and the court of appeal that there was negligence within the aforementioned period of 30 hours. The Court of Appeal, who suggested that a hospital doctor's duty of care is to be assessed in relation to the post he occupies, did not suggest that inserting the catheter into a vein instead of an artery amounted to negligence. What they did find was that the registrar was negligent in failing to appreciate that the junior doctor had not inserted the catheter into the artery; and that the junior doctor was entitled to rely on his work being checked by the registrar. Accordingly, the junior doctor was not negligent, whereas the registrar was liable in negligence. The health authority then appealed to the House of Lords, not on the issue of the registrar's negligence—there was no dispute about that—but on *causation*, the sole issue on which the case was to be decided.

Held: MW lost his case. The mere fact that excess oxygen was one of a number of different factors which could have caused the RLF raised no presumption that it caused or contributed to it in this case.

Commentary
A death, deafness and near-blindness, each following a negligent act or omission, went uncompensated because of the failure to establish causation. A damning indictment of the tort system for recovering damages, perhaps?

Failure to warn and a departure from established principles of causation

Chester v Afshar [2005] 1 A.C. 134
Miss Chester was not warned of the 1–2 per cent risk of nerve damage in the course of recommended surgery nor did she contend that had she been warned that she never would have consented to the surgery or that, had she been warned, she would have looked for a different surgeon to perform the

operation. Her claim was that had she been warned, she would have not consented to surgery *at that time*.

Held: (By a majority of 3–2) that the "but for" test had been satisfied in that it established that the injury would not have occurred *on that day* but for Mr Afshar's failure to warn of the risks.

Commentary

The majority invoked unmeritorious policy issues for "departing from established principles of causation" (per Lord Steyn). Whereas the majority opinions seem to protect patient autonomy, Lord Bingham, in his dissenting opinion, said:

> "I do not … think that the law should seek to reinforce that right by providing for the payment of potentially very large damages by a defendant whose violation of that right is not shown to have worsened the physical condition of the claimant."

The particular focus on the duty to disclose risks has undeniably fractured Lord Diplock's assertion that the normal duty of care "is not subject to dissection into a number of component parts to which different criteria apply". Moreover, the decision in *Chester* is incompatible with the failure of diagnosis in *Gregg v Scott* (below).

(ii) Causation as a matter of law

Remoteness
Key Principle: **In addition to proving causation, the claimant must also prove that the bodily harm he has suffered is of a type the law recognises as being recoverable. In essence, recoverability is based on the harm being a reasonably foreseeable consequence of the breach of duty.**

"There is no duty of care owed to a person when you could not reasonably foresee that he might be injured by your conduct", per Lord Denning, *Roe v MoH* (1954) (above).

Prendergast v Sam and Dee Ltd [1989] 1 Med L.R. 36

Held: The claim of causation was not broken by the pharmacist negligently dispensing daonil instead of amoxil. The doctor's handwriting was so poor (virtually illegible) that it was reasonably foreseeable that daonil would be prescribed. Negligence was apportioned at 25 per cent to the doctor and 75 per cent to the pharmacist.

Loss of a Chance

Key Principle: **Attempts at recovering damages for patients who have lost a chance of effective treatment following negligent diagnoses have proved ineffective, to date.**

Hotson v East Berkshire Health Authority [1987] A.C. 750
P was 13 years old when he fell from a rope he had been swinging on at school. He fell 12 feet to the ground and sustained a serious hip injury. This was not diagnosed when he was first taken to hospital. It was only when he made a second visit to the same hospital and after five days of severe pain that the correct diagnosis was made. It was discovered that his injuries caused disability of the hip joint with a virtual certainty of osteoarthritis. The health authority admitted negligence in failing to diagnose the injury on the first visit to hospital. At first instance the trial judge found that P's condition was 75 per cent likely to have occurred even if the D's had diagnosed and treated the injury promptly. On this basis, P was awarded a quarter of the total damages for the 25 per cent loss of a chance of recovering without the serious complications that had developed. P was awarded £150 damages for his pain and suffering for the five day period (uncontested on appeal) and 25 per cent of the £46,000 damages attributable to his permanent injury (avascular necrosis) as compensation for loss of the 25 per cent chance of recovery. The Court of Appeal dismissed D's appeal against the latter element.

Held: It was for P to establish on the balance of probabilities that the delay in treating him at least materially contributed to the development of his avascular necrosis. Since the trial judge had found as a fact that it was more likely than not (i.e. 75 per cent likely) that the avascular necrosis would have occurred in any event, there had been a manifest failure to prove causation on the question of liability. As Lord Bridge observed, the trial judge had found that

"... on the balance of probabilities the injury caused by [P's] fall left insufficient blood vessels intact to keep the epiphysis alive. This amounts to a finding of fact that the fall was the sole cause of the avascular necrosis".

Commentary

The appeal in *Hotson* was allowed on the narrow basis of "the fall [being] the sole cause of the avascular necrosis". This means that *Hotson* did **NOT** establish "that in no circumstances can evidence of a loss of a chance resulting from a breach of duty of care found a successful claim of damage", per Lord MacKay (unless, that is, the House of Lords overruled the earlier case of *McGhee v NCB* (1973), a case in which the defendants were found liable for their working conditions materially increasing the risk of their employees contracting dermatitis).

Thus, where P sues in respect of "loss of chance", he has to establish that there was a prospect of more than 50 per cent of the injury not occurring but for the tort. If P establishes that the chance was over 50 per cent, he will be entitled to the whole of his damages.

Gregg v Scott [2005] 2 A.C. 176

A year after the claimant had been told by his GP that a lump under his arm was a benign collection of fatty tissue and that no further action was called for, a hospital examination revealed he had non-Hodgkin's lymphoma. By that time, the tumour had spread into his chest. Whilst treatment led to a remission for a while, he was left with a poor prospect of survival. Accordingly, he brought an action against the defendant for damages for negligence, claiming that had he been referred to hospital when seen by the GP there would have been a high likelihood of cure whereas by the time treatment commenced his chances of recovery, defined as surviving for a period of 10 years, had fallen to below 50 per cent. In fact, by the time of the trial, statistical evidence had emerged which was accepted by the judge that the particular sub-type of the disease from which the claimant suffered gave only a 42 per cent chance of survival for ten years even if treated promptly. Moreover, his chances of surviving for the remainder of the ten-year period were now assessed at 25 per cent. The GP was found to be negligent but as his negligence wasn't the cause of the claimant being unlikely to survive ten years, the claimant failed in his claim. He appealed to the Court of Appeal and then the House of Lords.

Held: By a majority, it was decided that a claim for damages for clinical negligence required proof on a balance of probability that the negligence was the cause of the adverse consequences complained of; and, as he could not demonstrate this, it precluded an award of damages.

Commentary

Scott v Gregg differed from *Hotson* in that the final outcome was still prospective in *Scott v Gregg* whereas the permanent injury in *Hotson* was established. Nevertheless, it is, perhaps, a matter of regret that a doctor can make a negligent misdiagnosis and escape liability while the patient suffers a reduced quality of life (and, almost certainly, a reduction in his projected life span) yet receive no compensation.

Moreover, if the decision in *Gregg v Scott* is correct on conventional causation principles, it is submitted that *Chester v Afshar* (above) was wrongly decided.

Gross Medical Negligence and Criminal Liability

Key Principle: **Doctors may be indicted on charges of manslaughter when their actions result in the deaths of their patients.**

R. v Prentice and Sullman; and R. v Adomako [1994] Q.B. 302
Suffice it to say that in these conjoined appeals (heard together with another "non-medical" case), it was determined that the ingredients required to secure convictions for involuntary manslaughter by breach of duty were:

- The existence of a duty;

- A breach of duty causing death; and

- Gross negligence which a jury considers justifying a criminal conviction

The states of mind of defendants that might lead a jury to a finding of gross negligence included:

- Indifference to an obvious risk of injury to health;

- Actual foresight of the risk coupled with the determination nevertheless to proceed with it; and

- Inattention or failure to advert to a serious risk which went beyond "mere inadvertence" in respect of an obvious and important matter which the defendant's duty demanded he should address.

Commentary

The inexperience of Prentice and the misunderstanding of Sullman as to what he was actually required to do, led to their convictions being quashed, but Adomako's conviction was affirmed both by the Court of Appeal, in this case, and by the House of Lords, as reported in: [1995] 1 A.C. 171.

In a later case, *R. v Misra and Srivastava* [2005] 1 Cr.App.R 21, two doctors appealed against their convictions for manslaughter by gross negligence with part of the appeal being directed at whether the crime of gross negligence manslaughter lacked clarity and thus contravened Art.7 of the European Convention on Human Rights. The appeals were dismissed, however, as the principles outlined in Adomako involved no uncertainty.

8. CONTRACEPTION AND STERILISATION

(1) Contraception

Key Principle: **Members of the judiciary were hostile to the reception, in English law, of the practice and promotion of pioneering family planning issues.**

Sutherland v Stopes [1925] A.C. 47

Ms Marie Stopes had published several books promoting family planning. She brought an action in libel against the authors and publishers of a work exposing the dangers alleged to be involved in artificial birth control. Extracts from the work included:

> "... the poor are the natural victims of those who seek to make experiments on their fellows. ... working women are instructed in a method of contraception described [by a professor] as 'the most harmful method of which I have had experience'. ... When we remember that millions [of pounds] are being spent .. on pure milk for necessitous expectant and nursing mothers, on maternity clinics to guard the health of mothers before and after childbirth, for the provision of skilled midwives, and on infant welfare centres—all for the single purpose of bringing healthy children into our midst, it is truly amazing that this monstrous campaign of birth control should be tolerated by the Home Secretary."

Held: It was fair comment. Ms Stopes was liable for the costs in the Court of Appeal and the House of Lords.

Commentary

In 1999, Marie Stopes (1880–1958) was voted "Woman of the Millennium" by readers of the Guardian newspaper in recognition of her work promoting birth control. Her book, *Married Love*, sold more than 750,000 copies from the time of its publication in 1918 up to the printing of the 19th edition in 1931. Ms Stopes also opened a clinic in Holloway, North London, offering free contraceptive advice to poor mothers. In this venture, she had the full support of her wealthy, second husband. Their success enabled the founding of the National Birth Control Association which became the Family Planning Association in

1931. Marie Stopes International is now an organisation promoting birth control in a number of countries. An extract from
the homepage of the organisation's web site reads:

> "Contraception services are still at the heart of the modern-day Marie
> Stopes International (MSI) organisation, in fact, it was Dr Marie Stopes
> herself who founded the UK's first family planning clinic in 1921.
> Back then, finding out about contraception was difficult and many
> women were unable to prevent pregnancy. Nowadays, both women
> and men can make informed choices and have easy access to
> contraception."

For the current range of services provided by Marie Stopes
International, go to: http://www.mariestopes.org.uk/index.shtml
[Accessed February 28, 2008].

Key Principle: **Contraceptive medical treatment is now
acknowledged and accepted as "a legitimate and beneficial
treatment" both under statute and at common law.**

Under Statute
Schedule 1 para.8 of the NHS Act 2006 (formerly s.5(1)(b) NHS
Act 1977) imposes a duty upon the Secretary of State:

> "To arrange, to such extent as he considers necessary to meet all
> reasonable requirements in England and Wales, for the giving of
> advice on contraception, the medical examination of persons seeking
> advice on contraception, the treatment of such persons and the supply
> of contraceptive substances and appliances".

Commentary
Note the four elements of duty encompassed within this section,
viz;

- The giving of advice;
- The medical examination;
- Treatment; and
- Supply of contraceptives

These points are particularly noteworthy when the patient is a
minor.

At Common Law
Gillick v West Norfolk & Wisbech A.H.A. [1986] A.C. 112
For the facts of the case, see below.
Lord Scarman said:

"[contraceptive treatment is] Recognized as a legitimate and beneficial treatment in cases where it is medically indicated".

Commentary
See also: *R. (on the application of Smeaton) v Secretary of State for
Health and Others* [2002] 2 F.L.R. 146 (below) where Munby J. said
that: ... "respect for the personal autonomy which our law has
now come to recognise demands that the choice be left to the
individual".

Minors and Contraception

Key Principle: **A minor of sufficient maturity and understanding has the capacity to consent to contraceptive treatment;
and a doctor who acts for the purposes specified in s.73 Sexual
Offences Act 2003, when prescribing the treatment, does not
commit a criminal offence.**

Gillick v West Norfolk & Wisbech A.H.A. [1986] A.C. 112
Mrs Victoria Gillick objected to a 1981 DHSS circular which
stated that in certain circumstances a doctor could prescribe
contraceptive devices and treatment to a girl under 16 without
knowledge or consent of her parents: i.e. (in effect) Mrs Gillick
was contending that girls under the age of 16 did not have
capacity to consent to contraceptive treatment. In the High Court
she failed to get a declaration that the DHSS guidelines were
unlawful; and whereas she succeeded in gaining a unanimous
decision in her favour in the Court of Appeal, the case was then
further appealed to the House of Lords.

Held: By a majority (3–2), Mrs Gillick failed to have the Court
of Appeal decision upheld by the House of Lords. A "mature
minor" displaying sufficient understanding formed the basis of
the Lords decision to permit a girl under 16 to consent to contraceptive advice and treatment.

Commentary
First, Lord Frazer specified five criteria with which the doctor must satisfy himself he has complied before he may regard the girl's consent as effective, viz;

(1) that the girl ... will understand his advice;

(2) that he cannot persuade her to inform her parents or to allow him to inform the parents that she is seeking contraceptive advice;

(3) that she is very likely to begin or continue having sexual intercourse with or without contraceptive treatment;

(4) that unless she receives contraceptive treatment or advice her physical or mental health or both are likely to suffer;

(5) that her best interests require him to give her contraceptive advice, treatment or both without the parental consent.

Secondly, legislation has made it clear that a doctor who prescribes contraceptive treatment to a minor of sufficient maturity and understanding does not commit a criminal offence if he acts for specified purposes, viz;

Sexual Offences Act 2003

Section 73 Exceptions to aiding, abetting and counselling
(1) A person is not guilty of aiding, abetting or counselling the commission against a child of an offence to which this section applies if he acts for the purpose of—

   (a) protecting the child from sexually transmitted infection,
   (b) protecting the physical safety of the child,
   (c) preventing the child from becoming pregnant, or
   (d) promoting the child's emotional well-being by the giving of advice,

   and not for the purpose of obtaining sexual gratification or for the purpose of causing or encouraging the activity constituting the offence or the child's participation in it.

Commentary

The academic debate that ensued following the *Gillick* case that centred on whether a doctor who prescribed the "pill" to a girl under the age of 16 would be aiding, abetting or counselling a criminal act is now very likely confined to history, thanks to the explicit provisions of s.73 of the 2003 Act.

Post-Coital Birth Control: Contraception or Abortion?

Key Principle: The "morning after" pill prevents implantation of a fertilised egg. Accordingly, it is used as a contraceptive measure: it is not an abortifacient.

R. (on the application of Smeaton) v Secretary of State for Health and Others [2002] 2 F.L.R. 146

John Smeaton, on behalf of SPUC (Society for the Protection for the Unborn Child), sought to challenge the legality of the Prescription Only Medicines (Human Use) Amendment (No.3) Order, 2000, SI 2000/3231, which permitted the sale of the morning after pill without prescription. In essence, the claim was that the morning after pill was an abortifacient, not a contraceptive. The claimants argued that the meaning of "miscarriage" in the Offences Against the Person Act 1861 included the prevention of implantation. If this was accepted, then post-coital contraception could amount to a criminal offence under ss.58 and 59 of the 1861 Act as, to be permissive (lawful) under the Abortion Act 1967 (as amended), any substance that caused miscarriage or abortion would require two doctors acting in good faith to certify that the requirements laid down in the 1967 Act were satisfied. If the morning after pill was ruled to be an abortifacient, then, in the absence of compliance with provisions of the 1967 Act, it could be a criminal offence for a pharmacist to supply the pill and for the woman to take it.

Held:

Munby J. did not accept SPUC's case as to the meaning of the word "miscarriage" in 1861. Some of the leading and most authoritative medical works of the time strongly supported the idea that miscarriage becomes possible only after implantation. Accordingly, SPUC's application was dismissed.

Munby J. said:

"On the logic of its own case, SPUC's challenge, and the allegations of serious criminality *inter alia* by the woman concerned, are not simply to the morning after pill. They extend to *any* chemical or device which operates, or may operate, by impeding, discouraging or preventing the natural process at any time after fertilisation has started, alternatively has completed. They extend to *any* drug or device which may operate in that way, even if it may also operate in a way which impedes, discourages or prevents the process of fertilisation. The medical profession and female members of the public have for years been operating on the basis that the use, prescription and supply of such chemicals and devices is legal and involves no potential criminality. The pill has been available since the 1960s and the morning after pill since the early 1980s. The position has remained unchallenged until sought to be reopened in these proceedings.

. . .

There would ... be something ... grievously wrong with our system ... if a judge in 2002 were to be compelled by a statute 141 years old to hold that what ... millions, of ordinary honest, decent, law abiding citizens have been doing day in day out for so many years is and always has been criminal. I am glad to be spared so unattractive a duty...

. . .

...in this as in other areas of medical ethics, respect for the personal autonomy which our law has now come to recognise demands that the choice be left to the individual."

Commentary

The view that the "morning after pill" and the IUD are not unlawful was expressed by Professor Glanville Williams more than 20 years ago and echoed by the then Attorney General in 1983 who concluded that:

"... the phrase 'procure a miscarriage' cannot be construed to include the prevention of implantation. Whatever the state of medical knowledge in the 19th century, the ordinary use of the word 'miscarriage' related to interference at a stage of pre-natal development later than implantation. [Thus, 'the morning after' pill] does not constitute a criminal offence within either sections 58 or 59 of the Offences Against the Person Act 1861."

(2) Sterilisation

Imposing Liability for failed sterilisation

Key Principle: **Liability will not be imposed unless it can be established that the failure to achieve sterility was due to medical negligence either in the performance of the operation** or in imparting the requisite quantum of information, or to breach of contract, rather than to the inherent possibility that conception might still occur after the attempt purely as a result of the vagaries of nature.

Gold v Haringey Health Authority [1998] Q.B. 481

In 1979, when Mrs G was pregnant and in hospital awaiting birth of her third child, she and her husband were discussing his having a vasectomy. However, a consultant at the hospital suggested that Mrs G be sterilised. This was agreed and was undertaken the day after Mrs G gave birth to a daughter. No mention was made of a sterilisation failure rate of up to six per thousand when carried out immediately after childbirth. The operation did not succeed and Mrs G gave birth to a fourth child three years later. She alleged negligence both in performance of the operation and in non-disclosure of the failure rate contending, on the latter point, that knowledge of this would have been a deciding factor in Mr G being vasectomised.

Held: Mrs G failed in her claims. With regard to the non-disclosure of the failure rate, it was established that in 1979 a substantial body of doctors would *not* have given any warning as to the failure of female sterilisation, the defendants were not liable.

Commentary

Compare the "failure to inform" in this case with the "negligent advice" in *Greenfield v Irwin* (below). Note, also, from the following case, that in the absence of a contractual term specifying otherwise, a private patient may have no more right to the disclosure of information than an NHS patient:

Eyre v Measday [1986] 1 All E.R. 488

In 1978, P, a 35 year old woman, was a private patient of M, a gynaecological surgeon, and she contracted with him to have a laparoscopic sterilisation. This was performed competently, but M did not inform P that there was a chance of between two and six per thousand of her becoming pregnant again. P did conceive, and gave birth to a healthy boy. She sued M for breach of contract.

Held: The contract was for a laparoscopic sterilisation: it was not a guarantee of absolute sterility.

Key Principle: **A doctor who has obtained the patient's consent to an operation may still be liable in negligence if he fails to discuss properly with the patient the implications of sterilisation in a manner consistent with good medical practice or if he sterilises her for reasons of "convenience", rather than necessity.**

Wells v Surrey AHA (1978) *The Times*, July 29

A 35 year old Roman Catholic was about to undergo a Caesarean section for the birth of her second child when she signed a consent form. During the course of the operation she was sterilised.

Held: Although she had in fact consented to such additional surgery as was necessary and she understood the physical implications, she was inadequately counselled as to the mental anguish she would suffer as a result of the sterilisation: getting her consent as she was being wheeled into the operating theatre fell below acceptable medical practice; it was negligent.

Commentary

A coercive force (such as pain) may negate the validity of a patient's consent. By contrast, a patient in pain who refuses to accept treatment may have the right to have that refusal respected—even at the risk of death—if the refusal constitutes a valid advance directive made when the patient was competent: see *Re MB* (1997) and *St George's NHS Trust v S* (1998) in Ch.4.

Devi v West Midlands AHA [1980] CLY 687

A married woman who was the mother of four children went into hospital for a minor gynaecological operation. During the course of the operation, the surgeon sterilised her when he discovered her womb was ruptured. The operation was not immediately necessary and Mrs Devi's religion didn't allow sterilisation or contraception.

Held: Mrs Devi's inability to conceive again, coupled with the neurosis of what had been done to her, was to be compensated for by an award of damages of £6,750.

Commentary
Devi's case is factually very similar to the earlier Canadian case of *Murray v McMurchy* (1949) 2 D.L.R. 442 where it was held that the surgeon was wrong to perform a sterilisation that was not immediately necessary, even if it was convenient to do so following a Caesarean section.

Key Principle: **The courts will not entertain a claim for compensatory damages for the upbringing of a healthy child conceived and born after a negligent sterilisation.**

McFarlane v Tayside Health Board [2000] 2 A.C. 59
Six months after Mr McFarlane had undergone a vasectomy, he was negligently informed that his sperm count was negative and that he no longer need to take contraceptive precautions. However, sometime later his wife conceived and gave birth to their fifth child, a healthy girl, Catherine. Mrs McFarlane sued the Health Board and, amongst the claims, was one for Catherine's upbringing.

Held: Whereas Mrs McFarlane succeeded in claiming damages for the pain, suffering and inconvenience of the birth, she failed in the claim for compensation for the costs of Catherine's upbringing. This claim was regarded as one of pure economic loss and was unanimously rejected. The reasons were not consistent, however.
Lord Millet said:

"There is something morally distasteful, if not morally offensive, in treating the birth of a normal, healthy child as a matter of compensation...
...the law must take the birth of a normal, healthy baby to be a blessing, not a detriment. [The birth] brings joy and sorrow, blessing and responsibility. The advantages and disadvantages are inseparable. ... Nature herself does not permit parents to enjoy the advantages and dispense with the disadvantages.
In other contexts the law adopts the same principle. It insists that he who takes the benefit must accept the burden."

Lord Slynn said:

"Whereas I have no doubt that there should be compensation for the physical effects of the pregnancy and birth, ... I consider that it is not fair, just or reasonable to impose on the doctor or his employer liability for the consequential responsibilities, imposed on or accepted by the parents to bring up a child. ... If a client wants to be able to recover such costs he or she must do so by an appropriate contract."

Lord Steyn had opined that:

"Relying on principles of distributive justice I am persuaded that our tort law does not permit parents of a healthy unwanted child to claim the costs of bringing up the child from a health authority or a doctor. If it were necessary to do so, I should say that the claim does not satisfy the requirement of being fair, just and reasonable."

Commentary
The case law prior to McFarlane had been inconsistent. Damages in respect of bringing up a child born after a failed sterilisation were refused in *Udale v Bloomsbury AHA* [1983] 2 All E.R. 522, because "the coming of a child into the world is an occasion for rejoicing". However, this policy decision was rejected and an award for damages for the cost of rearing the child was made in *Emeh v Kensington and Chelsea and Westminster AHA* [1985] Q.B. 1012, *in respect of a child who suffered from congenital abnormalities*. In this case, it was held that Mrs Emeh's failure to have an abortion on discovering that she was pregnant again did not constitute a novus actus interveniens. The relaxed policy was then extended in *Thake v Maurice* [1985] 2 W.L.R 337 and in *Benarr v Kettering Health Authority* [1988] NLJR 179 to include the cost of rearing *healthy* children.

Inconsistency returned in *Pickett's* case, (1999) *The Times*, February 19, where a claim for damages for a second "late-failure" vasectomy was dismissed despite Judge John Altman finding that St James' University Hospital in Leeds had breached its duty by not warning the couple of possible failure of the second vasectomy. The couple had been told of a 3000–1 risk of a failure of the first vasectomy but received no warning in respect of the second vasectomy. Daughters had been born after both vasectomies. However, the judge decided that the couple had taken a gamble and had lost. That is:

"The reality is they knew of the risks. It was a human decision that, in effect, it couldn't happen to them twice. There was a negligent act, but I also find that negligent act made no difference whatsoever to their state of mind."

In English law, McFarlane's case has been followed in, inter alia, *Greenfield v Irwin, Parkinson v St James and Seacroft University Hospital NHS Trust* and *Rees v Darlington memorial Hospital NHS Trust*. There was a significant departure in Australia's highest Federal Court (the High Court) but this decision—in *Cattenach v Melchior*—will no longer be followed given statutory amendments—see below.

Greenfield v Irwin [2001] 1 W.L.R. 1279

Ms Greenfield (G) had been prescribed a course of contraceptive treatment via injection. However, the practice nurse who administered the treatment had not confirmed that G was not pregnant at the commencement of the treatment. G maintained that had she not been negligently advised, she would have terminated the pregnancy, and would therefore have continued to work outside the home. Accordingly, she sought to claim compensatory damages for the loss of her employment arising from the need to care for the child. Moreover, G argued that all the costs of the child's upbringing should be recoverable as they were consequential to the physical injury of the pregnancy, rather than as a result of negligent advice.

Held: The distinction between advice and physical harm was irrelevant. As a healthy child was an incalculable benefit, any compensation for lost employment was beyond the duty of care. Furthermore, right to family life set out in the Human Rights Act 1998 did not require the court to provide a remedy for G. Appeal dismissed.

However, the *McFarlane* reasoning was rejected in the High Court of Australia in:

Cattanach v Melchior [2003] HCA 38

Mrs Melchior underwent a sterilisation operation, performed by Dr Cattanach, in 1992 after she and her husband had decided to limit their family to the two children they already had. However, in 1997, Mrs Melchior gave birth to the couple's third child. Consequently, the Melchior's sued for damages which included the costs of raising and maintaining the third child until he reached 18-years-of-age.

Held: By a majority (4–3), the High Court of Australia upheld the decision to award damages which included more than A\$100,000 to compensate for Mrs Melchior's pain and suffering in respect of her pregnancy and the birth of her child, the effect on her health and lost earning capacity; plus more than A$105,000 for the costs of raising and maintaining the third child until he reached 18-years-of-age.

Commentary

There will be no repetition of this decision: legislation in Australia now provides that if a child is born following a negligent sterilisation then: "A court can not award damages for economic loss arising out of the costs *ordinarily associated* with rearing or maintaining a child" (s.49A Queensland Civil Liability Act 2003). A similar provision is contained in s.71 New South Wales Civil liability Act 2002.

The reference to the costs "ordinarily associated" is a reference to the costs of rearing or maintaining a healthy child. Of course, if the child is born disabled, the flexibility of this rule may be brought into play. Indeed, s.71(2) of the New South Wales Act explicitly states that it: "does not preclude the recovery of any additional costs associated with rearing or maintaining a child who suffers from a disability that arise by reason of the disability".

Key Principle: **The courts will award compensatory damages for the additional expenses associated with the upbringing of a child that has a "significant disability" and was born following a negligent sterilisation.**

Parkinson v St James and Seacroft University Hospital NHS Trust [2002] Q.B. 266

Mrs Parkinson wished to be sterilised after having given birth to four children. However, her operation was carried out negligently and ten months later she conceived her fifth child. She was warned by a consultant at the hospital that the child might be born with a disability but she declined to have her pregnancy terminated. Thereafter her marriage broke down and her husband left the family home three months before she gave birth to her fifth child, Scott, who was born with severe disabilities. At the trial of a preliminary issue, the judge ruled that she was entitled to recover damages for the costs of providing for her child's special needs relating to his disabilities but not for the basic costs of his maintenance. Ms Parkinson appealed and the defendants cross-appealed.

Held: The appeal and the cross appeal were dismissed. Following *McFarlane*, whereas Ms Parkinson would not be entitled to compensation for the rearing of a healthy child, she was entitled to an award of compensation for the *extra* expenses associated with bringing up Scott, a child with a significant disability, given that the birth of a child with congenital abnormalities was a foreseeable consequence of the surgeon's negligence. As for the meaning of disability, Hale L.J. referred to s.17(11) in Pt III of the Children Act 1989 and said that:

> "A child is disabled if he is blind, deaf or dumb or suffers from mental disorder of any kind or is substantially and permanently handicapped by illness, injury or congenital deformity or such other disability as may be prescribed."

Moreover, Hale L.J. had no doubt about specifying the source of the disability, viz:

> "I conclude that any disability arising from genetic causes or foreseeable events during pregnancy (such as rubella, spina bifida, or oxygen deprivation during pregnancy or childbirth) up until the child is born alive, and which are not *novus actus interveniens*, will suffice to found a claim."

Key Principle: **The wrongful conception and birth of a healthy child might result in the award of a "conventional sum" to** *a parent who is disabled.*

Rees v Darlington Memorial Hospital NHS Trust [2004] 1 A.C. 309

Mrs Rees (R) suffered from a severe, progressive visual disability and had undergone a sterilisation operation as she considered that she would be unable to fulfil the ordinary duties of a mother. The sterilisation had been negligently performed and R gave birth to a healthy son. In the Court of Appeal, the decision, by a majority, was that although damages could not be recovered in respect of costs arising from the birth of a healthy child it was, just as in the case of a child born with a disability, fair, just and reasonable for the *parent* who was disabled to recover by way of damages the additional costs attributable to her disability in bringing up the child. The Trust appealed and argued that the decision was inconsistent with *McFarlane's* case, whereas R invited reconsideration of McFarlane. Indeed, R sought to uphold the decision and cross appealed, claiming the whole cost of raising the child.

Held (By a majority of 4–3): The Trust's appeal was allowed. Considerations of what was fair, just and reasonable and principles of distributive justice precluded an award of damages against a doctor or health authority in respect of the costs of bringing up a normal healthy child. Moreover, the claimant could not recover any extra costs which might be referable to her disability. However, as she was the victim of a legal wrong which had denied her the opportunity to live in the way she had planned, it was unjust that she should be denied any recompense, apart from an award relating to the pregnancy and birth only. Accordingly, a measure of recognition for that wrong would be afforded by a "conventional award" in the sum of £15,000.

Commentary

In *Rees*, the House of Lords added a "gloss" to the legal policy decisions in *McFarlane* by allowing a "conventional sum" of £15,000 to represent the parents' loss of opportunity for living their lives as they wished. Whereas this sum was in addition to damages awarded for the pregnancy and its immediate aftermath, Lord hope said (in para.77) that he was

> "left with the uneasy feeling that the figure [of £15,000] which is to be established by the new rule will in many cases, and especially this one, fall well short ... of compensating the parents for the wrong that has been done to them".

Moreover, it remains to be seen under what circumstances, if any, this "conventional sum" becomes "unconventional" and so may be amended. Moreover, the continuing status of the decision in *Parkinson* remains unclear with opinions in *Rees* ranging from *Parkinson* being correctly decided (Lords Hope and Hutton) to an observation that the case may be inconsistent with McFarlane and so, perhaps, having to be overruled: Lord Steyn, para.40.

Non-consensual Sterilisation

Key Principle: **The practice of sterilising mentally incompetent persons has ranged from promoting eugenic theory, to protecting minors and to sterilising them via the wardship principle and to has been extended by way of a legal basis based on "best interests" for the sterilisation of an adult incompetent.**

Buck v Bell (1927) 274 U.S. 200

Carrie Buck was the "feeble-minded" daughter of a "feeble-minded" mother. Her proposed sterilisation was challenged on the basis that it was "cruel and unusual punishment" under the United States constitution.

Held: the sterilisation was not going to be a punishment but a means to facilitate Carrie Buck's freedom within the community. Oliver Wendell Holmes J. (at p.207):

> "It is better for all the world, if instead of waiting to execute degenerate offspring for crime, or to let them starve for their imbecility, society can prevent those who are manifestly unfit from continuing their kind ... Three generations of imbeciles are enough."

Commentary

Whilst the most notorious examples of non-consensual sterilisations under "racial hygiene laws" are associated with Nazi Germany, other European States (such as Switzerland, Austria and Sweden) have employed similar measures. More than 60,000 persons were forcibly sterilised in Sweden over, approximately, a forty year period, 1935–1975.

By contrast, English and Canadian courts were initially much more protective of their incompetent citizens.

Re D [1976] 1 All E.R. 326

D was an 11-year-old girl suffering from Sotos syndrome. Sotos syndrome may include some or all of the following: accelerated growth during infancy, epilepsy, generalised clumsiness, an unusual facial appearance, behaviour problems including certain aggressive tendencies, and some impairment of mental function which could result in dull intelligence or possibly more serious mental retardation. D's mother, who was described by the judge as "an excellent, caring and devoted mother" had requested that

D be sterilised because she (the mother) recalled that in the past she lived near a family who had the misfortune to have three mentally retarded children, and their plight and their troubled lives had deeply affected her. D's mother was very worried that D might be seduced and possibly give birth to a baby, which might be abnormal. She had always believed that D would not, or should not, marry and in any event would not be capable of bringing up a child. However, the social and behavioural reasons put forward by the consultant paediatrician for performing the sterilisation were seriously challenged by an experienced educational psychologist.

Held: Heilbron J. cited with approval Lord Eldon's dicta in *Wellesley's* case (1827) that: *"It has always been the principle of this Court, not to risk the incurring of damage to children which it cannot repair, but rather to prevent the damage being done."* Heilbron J. continued by noting that:

> "A review of the whole of the evidence leads me to the conclusion that in a case of a child of 11 years of age, where the evidence shows that her mental and physical condition and attainments have already improved, and where her future prospects are as yet unpredictable, where the evidence also shows that she is unable as yet to understand and appreciate the implications of this operation and could not give valid or informed consent, that the likelihood is that in later years she will be able to make her own choice, where, I believe, the frustration and resentment of realising (as she would one day) what happened could be devastating, an operation of this nature is, in my view, contra-indicated".

Accordingly, D remained a ward of Court because the operation was neither medically indicated nor necessary, and it would not be in D's best interest for it to be performed.

Re Eve [1986] 2 S.C.R. 388

Eve, who was 24 years old, attended a school for retarded adults. "She was attracted and attractive to men and Mrs E feared she might quite possibly and innocently become pregnant". Mrs E was a widow approaching 60 years of age. She decided Eve should be sterilised. It was said in Court that Eve would have "no concept of the idea of marriage, or indeed, the consequential relationship between, intercourse, pregnancy and birth".

Held: La Forest J., who also approved Lord Eldon's dicta in *Wellesley's* case, said:

"The grave intrusion on a person's rights and the certain physical damage that ensues from non-therapeutic sterilization without consent, when compared to the highly questionable advantages that can result from it, have persuaded me that it can *never* safely be determined that such a procedure is for the benefit of that person. Accordingly, the procedure should *never* be authorised for non-therapeutic purposes under *parens patriae* jurisdiction."

Commentary
The unqualified approach taken by La Forest J. was given short shrift by Lord Bridge in *Re B* (1988). Indeed, the House of Lords had no difficulty in taking an entirely different view.

Re B [(A minor) (Wardship: Sterilisation) [1988] A.C. 199

Jeanette was a 17-year-old girl with a mental age of five or six. Although she was described as mentally handicapped and epileptic she was exhibiting the normal sexual drive and inclinations for someone of her age. However, it was said that she would not be able to cope with birth or care for a child.

Held: The House of Lords approved the application for sterilisation. The "basic human right" of reproduction argument was rejected. Lord Hailsham said:

"To talk of the 'basic right' to reproduce of an individual who, is not capable of knowing the causal connection between intercourse and childbirth, the nature of pregnancy, what is involved in delivery, unable to form maternal instincts or to care for a child appears ... wholly to part company with reality."

Commentary
According to Lord Oliver, sterilisation would only be approved if it was a "last resort". The cases involving minors that soon followed *Re B* did not seem to focus on this opinion, however.

Re M (A Minor) (Wardship: Sterilisation) [1988] 2 F.L.R. 497

M was a 17-year-old girl with a mental age of five or six. Two factors were cited as "evidence" with regard to the sterilisation proposed for her, viz; that with the improvements in tubal surgery there was a 50 to 75 per cent chance of successfully reversing sterilisation should M's condition ever improve; and that there was a 50 per cent chance that any child born to M might suffer from some degree of mental retardation.

Held: The sterilisation was approved. Bush J. said that the eugenic considerations (that any baby might be born with a degree of mental handicap) were irrelevant—but, (according to Brazier) he did appear to take into account evidence that if M should become pregnant, an abortion on the ground of foetal handicap might be recommended.

Re P (A Minor) (Wardship: Sterilisation) [1989] 1 F.L.R. 182

P was a 17-year-old girl with a mental age of 6 and the communication skills of an average 6-year-old. As she was of normal and attractive appearance, not only did her mother think she was vulnerable to seduction [apparently she had already had sexual intercourse which she described as "painful"], but that if she became pregnant and understood what was happening she might refuse an abortion. It would be better to sterilise her than risk the trauma of separating her from her child at birth.

Held: Allowing the sterilisation, Eastham J. based his decision on, inter alia, Professor Robert Winston's evidence that reversal of female sterilisation carried out by clips on the Fallopian Tubes now has a 95 per cent success rate!

Commentary

"A clear distinction is to be made between an operation to be performed for a genuine therapeutic reason and one to achieve sterilisation", per Sir Stephen Brown P, *In re E (a Minor) (medical treatment)* [1991] 2 F.L.R. 585 where he held that parents were able to give a valid consent to the proposed hysterectomy to be performed on their 17-year-old mentally handicapped daughter. The operation would be carried out for "a genuine therapeutic reason" and the incidental result of sterilisation did not invalidate the consent. Yet this decision appeared wholly to ignore Lord Hailsham's opinion in *Re B* that "[the] distinction ... between 'therapeutic' and 'non-therapeutic' purposes of this operation ... [is] irrelevant...".

Key Principle: At common law, the legal basis of a non-consensual sterilisation performed on an incompetent adult has been based on the best interests of the patient.

Re F [1990] 2 A.C. 1

F, a 36 year old woman had been a voluntary in-patient in a mental hospital for more than 20 years. It was said that she had the verbal capacity of a child of two and the mental capacity of a child of four or five. F had formed a sexual relationship with a male patient and it was said that it would have been "disastrous for her to conceive a child". The psychiatric evidence to reinforce this assertion was that F would not understand the meaning of pregnancy, labour or delivery, and would be unable to care for a baby if she had one. Sterilisation was recommended as other forms of contraception were rejected for various reasons. With regard to the procedure, wardship did not apply as F was over the age of 18: there was no equivalent jurisdiction by which the court could exercise a power to consent on behalf of an incompetent adult. Nor was there jurisdiction under Pt VII of the MHA 1983, "Property and Affairs of Persons Under Disability" as the provisions were limited to business matters, legal transactions and other dealings of a similar kind.

Held: The House of Lords sanctioned the sterilisation and said that it *could be* justified by the principle of *necessity* if it was in the patient's *best interests*. Lord Brandon said that treatment would be in the best interests of a patient "... if, but only if, it is carried out in order to either to save [her life] or to ensure improvement or prevent deterioration in   physical or mental health". The patient's best interests were to be decided by the medical profession on the *Bolam* standard of acting in accordance with a responsible body of medical practitioners.

Commentary

It was remarkable that a test for establishing negligence should apply to decisions relating to the sterilisation of an adult with learning disabilities. Moreover, that any one of a number of indeterminate *Bolam* standards could apply was described by one commentator as "medical paternalism run amok". Also, it was, perhaps, surprising that "necessity" had been chosen as part of the legal basis justifying non-consensual sterilisation for an adult with learning disabilities as this had been rejected the previous year in: *T v T* [1988] Fam 52. Here, Wood J. permitted sterilisation on "the demands of good medical practice". He had rejected the defence of "necessity" on account of its ill-defined limits (though what is more specific about "good medical practice" is problematical!). The fact that the *parens patriae* jurisdiction had been abolished by the Mental Health Act of 1959 (now 1983) without being replaced meant that no one could authorise or prevent a non-consensual sterilisation of an adult. Accordingly, Wood J. acknowledged that if (say) the medical profession sought an anticipatory declaration of the lawfulness of the procedure in pursuit of the demands of good medical practice, then the Courts could approve such a request.

Following the decision of the House of Lords in *Re F*, the courts have formulated clearer principles on which to base a non-consensual sterilisation.

Re GF [1992] 1 F.L.R. 293

The mother of a 29-year-old severely mentally handicapped woman sought the declaration of the court that a hysterectomy proposed to be performed on her daughter would be lawful. The woman suffered from severe menorrhea and was unable to cope with the condition. Although the operation was therapeutic in intention, it would have the incidental effect of sterilisation of the woman.

Held: No declaration was needed for the lawful performance of a hysterectomy which would have the incidental effect of the sterilisation of a patient who was unable to give her consent by reason of mental disability provided that the operation was necessary for therapeutic purposes and the operation was in the best interests of the patient and there was no alternative and practicable method of treatment. Sir Stephen Brown P said that two doctors would have to agree on three issues: first, the operation was necessary for therapeutic reasons; secondly, that the operation was in the best interests of the patient; and third, there was no practicable less intrusive treatment available. Where the three issues were agreed on, a declaration of lawfulness was not necessary.

Commentary

First, the Official Solicitor has now issued a Practice Note on Declaratory Proceedings in respect of Medical and Welfare Proceedings for Adults who Lack Capacity: see [2001] 2 F.L.R. 158. With regard to minors, a next friend seeking a specific issue

order under the Children Act 1989 may be an appropriate procedure for securing a sterilisation: *Re HG (specific issue order:
sterilisation)* [1993] 1 F.L.R. 587. In this case, the deputy judge
authorising the sterilisation of an epileptic teenager who also
suffered from an unspecified chromosomal abnormality said:

> "... a sufficiently overwhelming case has been established to justify
> interference with the fundamental right of a woman to bear a child.
> [Accordingly] it would be cruel to expose to an unacceptable risk of
> pregnancy and that that should be obviated by sterilisation in her
> interests".

By contrast, if a patient is cared for in a residential home that
offers a high standard of care which minimises the risk of
pregnancy or if the patient was not subjected to any great risk of
sexual exploitation and pregnancy, then sterilisation may be
refused: see *Re LC* [1997] 2 F.L.R. 258; *and Re S* [1998] 1 F.L.R. 944.

Key Principle: **It is now clear that mere satisfaction of the
Bolam test is no longer determinative of the patient's best
interests when considering non-consensual sterilisation. The
"medical paternalism run amok" in Re F has now been constrained by the courts limiting the *Bolam* test to the advisability of medical treatment.**

In Re S (Sterilisation; Patient's Best Interests) [2001] Fam 15

The mother of SL, a female aged 29 who had been born with
severe learning difficulties, was concerned about the possibility
of SL becoming pregnant when she moved into a local authority
home. Accordingly, she applied for a declaration that SL could
be lawfully sterilised or given a partial hysterectomy despite her
inability to consent. The judge held that both contraception and
surgery were lawful options so he left the decision to SL's
mother. The Official Solicitor appealed against the declaration,
contending that the judge (1) had wrongly rejected unanimous
medical opinion that the insertion of an intra uterine coil was a
more appropriate procedure on the principal of *primum non
nocere*, and (2) had misapplied the Bolam test by employing it as
a conclusive test rather than considering the patient's best
interest.

Held: The appeal was allowed because: (1) the judge had erred, given that the expert evidence had been unanimously in favour of intra uterine contraception as a less invasive procedure, notwithstanding that it would require repeated intervention, and: (2) once the *Bolam* test had been satisfied, it became irrelevant compared with the consideration of what was in the best interests of the patient. That was a judicial decision involving far broader considerations than the medical options and which could not be determined as a range of options. The correct decision was that the insertion of the intra uterine device was in the best interests of SL as it was the least invasive option, was not irreversible, and left room for surgical procedures if it were ineffective. Furthermore, it acknowledged the possibility that subsequent medical advances might provide alternative options.

Commentary

It was held in this case that the best interests test for adult incompetents was the same as the welfare test used in wardship. Moreover, with Thorpe L.J. confining the *Bolam* test to "the judgment of the adult patient's best interests when a dispute arises as to the advisability of medical treatment" the courts have now effectively closed the door on any more instances of medical paternalism running amok. That it is for the courts alone to determine the best interests of a patient—as there can be only one "best interest"—is a welcome clarification and limitation following on from Bennett J. in *Re Z (medical treatment: hysterectomy)* [2000] 1 F.L.R. 523 saying:

> "Experts are what they are—experts. They must be listened to with respect, but their opinions must be weighed and judged by the court."

9. ASSISTED REPRODUCTION

Regulating Assisted Reproduction

Key Principle: The establishment of a regulatory authority to oversee continuing developments in human fertilisation and embryology was a principal recommendation of the Warnock Committee that had been established four years after the birth of the world's first child conceived through in vitro fertilisation.

Report of the Committee of Inquiry into Human Fertilisation and Embryology

This Committee, chaired by Dame (now Baroness) Mary Warnock was established in 1982 with the terms of reference:

> "To consider recent and potential developments in medicine and science related to human fertilisation and embryology; to consider what policies and safeguards should be applied, including consideration of the social, ethical and legal implications of these developments; and to make recommendations."

Commentary

The Committee was established four years after four years after the birth in England in 1978 of Louise Brown, the world's first "test-tube baby", i.e. the first baby born via the IVF procedure developed by Patrick Steptoe and Robert Edwards.

Whilst the Warnock Committee acknowledged that IVF "opened up new horizons in the alleviation of infertility [to the extent that] It [became] possible to observe the very earliest stages of human development, and [brought about] the hope of remedying defects at this very early stage", they noted also that:

> "Society's views on the new techniques were divided between pride in the technological achievement, pleasure at the new-found means to relieve, at least for some, the unhappiness of infertility, and unease at the apparently uncontrolled advance of science, bringing with it new possibilities for manipulating the early stages of human development."

Thus, it was the *possibility of manipulating the early stages of human development* via IVF that brought about the perceived need for policies and safeguards along with consideration of the ethical and legal implications.

The Warnock Committee reported in July 1984, two years after it was set up. Many of the recommendations were subsequently enacted in the Human Fertilisation and Embryology Act 1990 (HFEA 1990). One of its recommendations, to establish a regulatory authority to oversee continuing developments in human fertilisation and embryology, came to fruition in the Human Fertilisation and Embryology Authority (HFEA) as provided for in s.5 of the 1990 Act.

In the following notes, the Human Fertilisation and Embryology Act 1990 will be referred to as "the Act" or "the 1990 Act", when distinguishing it from the proposed 2008 Act, and to distinguish it from the Human Fertilisation and Embryology Authority—as they refer to themselves as the HFEA: see, for example, "Infertility 2007/08 The HFEA guide", (accessible via the HFEA's website: http://www.hfea.gov.uk [Accessed February 28, 2008]).

Key Principle: **The Human Fertilisation and Embryology Authority, established under s.5 of the 1990 Act as the first statutory body of its type in the world, has the responsibility for licensing over 120 fertility clinics in the UK and the activities they carry out in connection with embryos and gametes.**

Human Fertilisation and Embryology Act 1990

The Human Fertilisation and Embryology Authority, its functions and procedure

5. The Human Fertilisation and Embryology Authority

(1) There shall be a body corporate called the Human Fertilisation and Embryology Authority.

(2) The Authority shall consist of—

    (a) a chairman and deputy chairman, and

    (b) such numbers of other members as the Secretary of State appoints.

Commentary

Composition of the HFEA

Walter Merricks, who is the UK's Financial Ombudsman, became the interim Chair of HFEA on the November 1, 2007. Unquestionably, he is far more than a mere figurehead in this role. Apart from his outstanding legal career, his biography notes that:

> "He and his wife have two children conceived by donor insemination, after having discovered that he was infertile. Together with other families they founded the Donor Conception Network in 1993, a self-help charity that supports parents of donor-conceived children and those contemplating treatment. The network has over 900 members."

There were 17 other members of the HFEA when Walter Merricks became the interim chair. The very contentious issue is whether a regulatory body containing non-medically qualified members should be authorised to permit or deny treatments that may be viewed as an intrusion on the doctor-patient relationship.

Functions of the HFEA

The home page of HFEA's web site (www.hfea.gov.uk/ [Accessed February 28, 2008]) proclaims that: "Our primary remit is to license and monitor UK clinics that offer IVF (in vitro fertilisation) and DI (donor insemination) treatments, and all UK-based research into human embryos. We also regulate the storage of eggs, sperm and embryos."

Licences

Human Fertilisation and Embryology Act 1990

Scope of licences

11. Licences for treatment storage and research.

  (1) The Authority may grant the following and no other licences—

      (a) licences ... authorising activities in the course of providing treatment services,

      (aa) licences ... authorising activities in the course of providing non-medical fertility services,

(b) licences ... authorising the storage of gametes and embryos, and

(c) licences ... authorising activities for the purposes of a project of research.

Licence conditions

12. General conditions

(1) The following shall be conditions of every licence granted under this Act—

(a) except to the extent that the *activities authorised* by the licence fall within paragraph (aa), that those activities shall be carried on only on the *premises to which the licence relates* and under the *supervision of the person responsible*,

(aa) that any activities to which section 3(1A)(b) or (1B) or 4(1A) applies shall be carried on only on the premises to which the licence relates or on relevant third party premises,

(d) that proper records shall be maintained in such form as the Authority may specify in directions,

(e) that no money or other benefit shall be given or received in respect of any supply of gametes or embryos unless authorised by directions,

(3) It shall be a condition of every licence to which this subsection applies that—

(a) such information as is necessary to facilitate the traceability of gametes and embryos, and

(b) any information relating to the quality or safety of gametes or embryos, shall be recorded and provided to the Authority upon request.

Commentary

The essence of s.12 is that licences are granted under this section in respect of *authorised activities* on *specified premises* that are carried out under the supervision of the *person responsible for the licensed activities*.

Procedures that cannot be licensed, except in pursuance of a licence,—prohibitions in connection with embryos and

gametes—are provided for in ss.3 and 4, respectively. In particular, note the provisions of s.3(3):

Activities governed by the Act

(3) A licence cannot authorise—

   (a) keeping or using an embryo after the appearance of
        the primitive streak,
   (b) placing an embryo in any animal,
   (c) keeping or using an embryo in any circumstances in
        which regulations prohibit its keeping or use, or
   (d) replacing a nucleus of a cell of an embryo with a
        nucleus taken from a cell of any person, embryo or
        subsequent development of an embryo.

With regard to s.3(3)(d), the "Report of how the HFEA made its
decision to licence the creation of embryos by cell nuclear
replacement", (therapeutic cloning) is available online at: http://
www.hfea.gov.uk/docs/HFEA_CNR_Decision_Report.pdf
[Accessed February 28, 2008].

Section 20 of the Act provides that an appeal against the
refusal to grant a licence for an activity must be made to the
HFEA and be heard by members of the Authority that do not
include those who made the ruling that is now being appealed.

Grant, revocation and suspension of licences

**20. Appeal to Authority against determinations of licence
committee.**

(1) Where a licence committee determines to refuse a licence
     or to refuse to vary a licence so as to designate another
     individual in place of the person responsible, the appli-
     cant may appeal to the Authority if notice has been given
     to the committee and to the Authority before the end of
     the period of twenty-eight days beginning with the date
     on which notice of the committee's determination was
     served on the applicant.

(2) Where a licence committee determines to vary or revoke a
     licence, any person on whom notice of the determination
     was served (other than a person who applied for the

variation or revocation) may appeal to the Authority if notice has been given to the committee and to the Authority before the end of the period of twenty-eight days beginning with the date on which notice of the committee's determination was served.

(3) An appeal under this section shall be by way of rehearing by the Authority and no member of the Authority who took any part in the proceedings resulting in the determination appealed against shall take any part in the proceedings on appeal.

Section 21 provides that any further appeal will be to the High Court or, in Scotland, the Court of Session on a point of law, only.

Code of Practice

Directions and guidance

25.—Code of practice.

(1) The Authority shall maintain a code of practice giving guidance about the proper conduct of activities carried on in pursuance of a licence under this Act and the proper discharge of the functions of the person responsible and other persons to whom the licence applies.

(2) The guidance given by the code shall include guidance for those providing treatment services about the account to be taken of the welfare of children who may be born as a result of treatment services (including a child's need for a father), and of other children who may be affected by such births.

(3) The code may also give guidance about the use of any technique involving the placing of sperm and eggs in a woman.

(6) A failure on the part of any person to observe any provision of the code shall not of itself render the person liable to any proceedings, but—

[a licence committee shall ... take account of any relevant provision of the code]

Commentary
Whilst s.25(1) provides, it is "guidance" that is provided to licensees, subs.6 makes it clear that failure to comply with provisions of the code may be taken into account for the purposes of revoking a licence. The "guidance" of s.25 contrasts with the mandatory "directions" provided for in ss.23 and 24, with breach of the latter, for example, by way of providing false or misleading information for the grant of a licence, providing for sanctions that includes a custodial sentence. Clearly, neither "guidance" nor "directions" are to be treated with contempt.

Information
Section 31 of the 1990 Act provides that the HFEA shall keep a register containing information of, inter alia, the provision of treatment services for any identifiable individual, and identifying information of a donor that it can impart to a donor-conceived person who has attained the age of 18 and who is requesting the information. No other comment is offered here on s.31 as this will undergo a whole scale revamp when the 1990 Act is amended by the proposed 2008 Act.

Summary
Overall, the roles of the HFEA include its duties to:

- licence and monitor fertility clinics that carry out in vitro fertilisation (IVF) and donor insemination;

- licence and monitor centres undertaking human embryo research;

- licence and monitor the storage of gametes and embryos;

- produce a Code of Practice which gives guidelines to clinics about the proper conduct of HFEA licensed activities;

- maintain a formal register of information about donors, fertility treatments and children born as a result of those treatments;

- monitor any subsequent developments in this area and where appropriate, advise the Secretary of State for Health on developments in these fields.

Infertility and Eligibility for Treatment

Key Principle: There is no consensus on what constitutes infertility and whether it should be regarded as an illness to be treated on the NHS.

Infertility 2007/08: The HFEA guide
This publication states that:

> "Getting pregnant can be harder than you think. If you are having intercourse regularly without using contraception you should conceive within two years, but in any one month your chances of conception are only around 20 to 30 per cent."

Commentary
Statistics from the same page (p.6) state that 95 per cent of couples will have conceived within two years. However, on p.8 it is noted that:

> "if you are over 35, it is a good idea to make an appointment with your GP after six months [of trying for a baby by having intercourse without contraception and without success], as fertility tests can take time to complete and your age may affect the treatments available to you".

If infertility (however it may be defined) is suspected, then the NHS aims to provide women between the ages of 23 and 39 at least one free cycle of IVF—but this assumes the eligibility criteria set out in guidelines published by NICE (see Ch.1 for notes on NICE) are met. For women under the age of 40, two embryos can be implanted whereas for women aged over 40 using their own eggs, up to three embryos can be implanted. A challenge to the policy of limiting implantation to three embryos to the over-40s was defeated in:

R. (on the application of Assisted Reproduction and Gynaecology Centre) v Human Fertilisation and Embryology Authority [2002] EWCA Civ 20
The authority's published code of practice stated that: "No more than three eggs or embryos should be placed in a woman in any one cycle, regardless of the procedure used." However, the clinic wished to treat the patient by using more than three embryos in one cycle. Whereas the clinic did not challenge the

appropriateness of the general rule contained in the code of practice, it argued that it was appropriate to make an exception to the rule in the patient's case, based on her particular treatment needs. The authority responded by rejecting the patient's case as an exception that justified a departure from the code of practice, however. The clinic appealed.

Held: On an examination of the facts of this case, the authority had produced an opinion which was plainly rational. Accordingly, the court had no power to intervene and strike down the authority's decision of limiting the implantation to three embryos.

Reform
Reform may be imminent, as an Expert Group produced a report *One Child at a Time: Reducing Multiple Births after IVF* which raised the issue of "single embryo transfer" because of fears that multiple births are putting the lives of mothers and their babies at risk. This policy may be applied to women under the age of 35 who have no history of miscarriages, for example. The possibility of reducing the number of embryos implanted followed research that indicated that in addition to multiple births being resource intensive and expensive, they put a mother's health at risk and increased the likelihood of disabilities in babies. Indeed, HFEA's website states that: "The risk of cerebral palsy is five times higher for twins and 18 times higher for triplets than for a single baby". See: www.hfea.gov.uk/en/1207.htm [Accessed February 28, 2008]

However, the adoption of a one-embryo policy—as in the Netherlands, Finland and Sweden—may deprive many women of the chance of having a baby. Indeed, in trials in the Netherlands where doctors implanted 150 women with one embryo and another 150 with two, the pregnancy rate among those with two embryos was 40 per cent while that for the rest of the group was barely half that, dropping to 21 per cent.

Ageism

Key Principle: **Significant and sustained criticism has been directed both at those who provide and those who receive IVF treatment when the woman undergoing treatment is 44 years of**

age, or older, as she will be of pensionable age when the child is still at school.

The HFEA website provides statistics on the likelihood of conception after IVF treatment. They range from just under 30 per cent for women under 30 years of age to less than 1 per cent for women over 44. The fact that IVF may be provided for women over the age of 40 has been no bar to a health authority refusing funding to a younger woman, however:

R. v Sheffield HA Ex p. Seale (1994) 25 B.M.L.R. 1

A 37-year-old woman applied for judicial review of the health authority's refusal to provide her with IVF treatment on the grounds of her age, claiming that the refusal was irrational, as it was not based on a sustainable clinical approach, and illegal under provisions of the NHS Act then prevailing, as the Secretary of State was under a duty to provide medical services to meet all reasonable requirements.

Held: The refusal was neither illegal as the authority's duty to provide a service did not mean that it had to be provided on demand for any patient who might benefit from it, nor was it irrational as fertility and the success of IVF treatment decreased with age. The authority was entitled to take age into account as a criterion when determining the allocation of scare resources.

Commentary

Much of the criticism of the age-related treatments for older women has focused on the "selfishness" of the woman and / or the fact that she lied about her age in order to obtain treatment. More recently, this criticism has been extended to encompass the almost inevitable association of advanced age with illness. In particular, it was reported that *"IVF mother who gave birth at 66 has cancer"* (Daily Telegraph, December 12, 2007). The news item referred to Maria del Carmen Bousada de Lara, a single woman, who became the world's oldest mother when she gave birth to twins just before her 67th birthday. It was reported that she was diagnosed as having cancer less than a year after the birth of her twin sons. The newspaper report noted that:

> "Miss Bousada de Lara became the world's oldest mother following IVF treatment at a private clinic in America for which she reportedly paid £30,000 after claiming to be just 55 years old".

Determination of who, in law, are the Parents of a Donor-Conceived Child.

Key Principle: **The 1990 Act has provisions for identifying who, in law, are the parents of a child born after using donor gametes or embryos.**

Human Fertilisation and Embryology Act 1990, Section 27(1)

Status

27.—**Meaning of "mother".**
  (1) The woman who is carrying or has carried a child as a result of the placing in her of an embryo or of sperm and eggs, and no other woman, is to be treated as the mother of the child.

Commentary
In essence, the section provides that in every instance the "carrying mother" or the "birth mother"—the one who gestates the child to term, irrespective of who donated the gametes or embryo—is, in law, the mother of the child. A potential mother may be denied treatment, however, because of her previous criminal record and doubts about her suitability as a parent, as in:

R. v Ethical Committee of St Mary's Hospital (Manchester) Ex p. Harriott [1988] 1 F.L.R. 512
H was unable to conceive a child and her application to the local authority to adopt was refused because of her criminal record for offences related to prostitution and the running of a brothel and because of her allegedly poor understanding of the role of a foster-parent and the local authority's social service department. A hospital consultant decided that IVF treatment should not be and the ethical committee that reviewed the case was of the opinion that this was a decision for the medical team to take. H then applied for judicial review of the committee's decision contending inter alia that the consultant was under a duty to act fairly when deciding whether to remove a woman from the IVF list on social grounds involving issues of contested fact.

Held: The applications were refused on the grounds that: (1) the committee had merely advised that it was for the consultant to make up her own mind as to whether treatment should be given or not. If the committee refused to give advice, the courts could not compel it to do so. (2) It could not be said on the facts that no reasonable consultant could have come to the decision to which the consultant had come.

Father

Human Fertilisation and Embryology Act 1990, Section 28(1)–(3)

28.—Meaning of "father".

(2) If—

    (a) at the time of the placing in her of the embryo or the sperm and eggs or of her insemination, the woman was a party to a marriage, and

    (b) the creation of the embryo carried by her was not brought about with the sperm of the other party to the marriage, then, subject to subsection (5) below, the other party to the marriage shall be treated as the father of the child unless it is shown that he did not consent to the placing in her of the embryo or the sperm and eggs or to her insemination (as the case may be).

(3) If no man is treated, by virtue of subsection (2) above, as the father of the child but—

    (a) the embryo or the sperm and eggs were placed in the woman, or she was artificially inseminated, in the course of treatment services provided for her and a man together by a person to whom a licence applies, and

    (b) the creation of the embryo carried by her was not brought about with the sperm of that man, then, subject to subsection (5) below, that man shall be treated as the father of the child.

(6) Where—

    (a)   the sperm of a man who had given such consent as is required by … this Act was used for a purpose for which such consent was required, or

    (b)   the sperm of a man, or any embryo the creation of which was brought about with his sperm, was used after his death,

he is not, subject to [other specified provisions], to be treated as the father of the child.

Commentary

Subsections (5A) to (5D) provide the rules for the determination of who is regarded as the father of the child following the death of a man who may or may not have been a party to a marriage with the woman and who may or may not have donated the sperm. Following the unique decision in Blood's case, however, the need for written consent is a specific provision of the subsections that would not be ignored.

R. v HFEA Ex p. Blood [1999] Fam 151

Diane Blood (DB) had requested that sperm be taken from her husband who had lapsed into a coma and was dying. After his death, she hoped to start a family that she claimed they had planned. Whilst the sperm was taken and stored pending legal argument, the HFEA refused to licence the treatment for her by artificial insemination on the basis that s.4(1) required that storage of the sperm had to be pursuant to a licence and, by Sch.3 of the 1990 Act, this required written consent. DB's husband had not given written consent. However, DB argued that by also refusing to grant her a licence to export the sperm abroad it had failed to take account of her rights under the Treaty of Rome 1957, Arts 59 and 60, to obtain medical treatment in other Member States where written consent was not required.

Held: The appeal was allowed. Strictly, the HFEA had been right to refuse treatment in the UK, but it had failed to take into account DB's rights under EU law. DB had a directly enforceable right to receive cross border medical treatment which had been infringed by the authority's decision and she was entitled to receive treatment in Belgium, in a clinic which adopted generally the same standards as the UK.

Commentary

The Court of Appeal made it clear that their decision would not constitute a precedent as they made it clear that a criminal act had been committed in what was a previously untested area of the law. Diane Blood received treatment in Belgium and, over a period of a few years, gave birth to two boys. Significantly, her campaign to change their birth certificates from reading "father unknown" to include the name of her deceased husband resulted in a change in the law with the enactment of the Human Fertilisation and Embryology (Deceased Fathers) Act 2003. This amended the 1990 Act by inserting new provisions in s.28(5A)—(5I).

A further problem that focused on s.28 in determining who "the father of the child" fell to be determined in:

Leeds Teaching Hospital NHS Trust v A [2005] Q.B. 506

Mr & Mrs A and Mr & Mrs B were two couples treated via ICSI (intracytolplasmic sperm injection) by L. Mr and Mrs A were both white but the twins born were of mixed race because Mrs A had been mistakenly impregnated with sperm from Mr B. Whilst it was agreed that Mr & Mrs A would raise the twins, it was necessary to determine who the legal father was.

Held: The consent Mr A gave to the placing in his wife of an embryo did not embrace consent to the embryo that was placed inside her as it was fundamentally different from the one that would have been created with his sperm. Accordingly, s.28 did not apply and Mr A was not the legal father of the twins, Mr B was. Mr B was not a sperm donor (which would have meant he relinquished his right to be treated as a father of the child) under s.28(6)(a). Moreover, whereas Mr & Mrs A's rights under Art.8 of the European Convention on Human Rights would be breached by denying the presumption that Mr A was the father, this interference was in accordance with the law and could be rectified in domestic law by way of adoption. There was no violation of Mr B's rights under the Convention nor were the twins rights violated.

Commentary

Whereas Mr B was the legal father in this case, it was decided by the House of Lords in another case, Re D [2005] 2 A.C. 621, that where an unmarried couple began "treatment together" but then parted before an embryo, created with donor sperm, was planted into the woman who, by then had a new partner, her original partner, B, was not the legal father. Whereas B had given his consent in writing at the time they were being treated together and he had stated that he intended to become the legal father of any resulting child, the House of Lords upheld the decision of the Court of Appeal that for B to be regarded as the father under s.28(3), the embryo had to be placed in the woman at the time the treatment services were being provided for her and her partner together.

Need for a father

Human Fertilisation and Embryology Act 1990, Section 13(5)

13. Conditions of licences for treatment
  (5) A woman shall not be provided with treatment services, other than basic partner treatment services, unless account has been taken of the welfare of any child who may be born as a result of the treatment (including the need of that child for a father), and of any other child who may be affected by the birth.

Commentary
The proposed amendments of the 1990 Act omit the reference for the need for a father, so as to bring the amended Act into conformity with the Adoption and Children Act 2002 and the Human Rights Act 1998. The focus on the welfare of the child will remain, however.

Determining the Fate of an Embryo When Couples Separate

Key Principle: Case law has confirmed that if, after being "treated together", one partner of a couple that has undergone IVF treatment decides to withdraw consent to the storage of the embryos created, the embryos must be allowed to perish.

Evans v Amicus Healthcare [2005] Fam 1; and Evans v UK (6339/05) 1 F.C.R. 585

E and J, an unmarried couple, had given their written consents to each other's treatment "together" to include the "use" and storage of their embryos. Later, they separated and J withdrew his consent. E, who was infertile, appealed against a decision that after J had withdrawn his consent, she was not entitled to use frozen embryos created by IVF treatment. Her appeal was dismissed by the Court of Appeal as, under the 1990 Act, "together" was an adverb which qualified the treatment to a man and a woman whilst the couple were united about the treatment, and this applied irrespective of the nature of their relationship. J was entitled under the 1990 Act to withdraw his consent and E's future treatment would not be "treatment together" with him. E then appealed to the European Court of Human Rights.

Held: Appeal dismissed. The competing interests of the individual and the community as a whole had to be considered. In this respect the state enjoyed a "margin of appreciation", which varied in accordance with the nature and importance of the issues at stake. In view of the lack of international consensus on the issue of regulation of IVF treatment and the moral sensitivities involved, the margin of appreciation enjoyed by the state had to be a wide one. That wide margin applied both to the initial decision to legislate and to the detailed rules set down to achieve a balance between the competing public and private interests. Moreover, in balancing the competing rights of the individuals, the Art.8 rights of a male donor were not necessarily less worthy of protection than those of the female. Accordingly, the UK had not exceeded its margin of appreciation nor upset the fair balance by preferring J's Art.8 rights to those of E's.

Commentary

The great difficulty here was in balancing the Art.8 rights of E and J—rights that even Thorpe L.J. thought were incommensurate. Both parties wished to assert their incompatible "rights" but, in this case, E's wish to be a mother was overridden by J's wish not to be a "father".

Embryo Selection

Key Principle: Embryos created during IVF treatment may be analysed before implantation not only to reject those that might lead to the birth of a child with genetic disability but also to determine if those selected can lead to the birth of a child whose tissue may be used in life-saving treatment for an existing ill sibling.

R. (On the Application of Quintavalle) v HFEA [2005] 2 A.C. 561

A couple (H) wished to undergo IVF treatment in order to bear a child who would be free of the potentially life-threatening genetic blood disorder which affected their existing son, Z, and who would share the same tissue type as Z, so that stem cells from the newborn child could be used to treat him. The proposed IVF treatment involved taking cells from embryos and testing those cells for the existence of the genetic disorder in a procedure known as pre-implantation genetic diagnosis ("PGD"); and for the cells to be simultaneously tested to identify those embryos whose tissue type matched that of the existing child ("HLA typing"). The HFEA had decided in principle to allow HLA typing where PGD was already necessary to avoid passing on a serious genetic disorder. Applications for such licences would be decided on a case by case basis. The authority subsequently granted a licence, limited to the H's, that permitted PGD and HLA typing. Q, who succeeded at first instance in challenging the grant of the licence, but failed on an appeal to the Court of Appeal, then appealed to the House of Lords.

Held: Appeal dismissed. The process of HLA typing would be an activity "in the course of" providing that IVF treatment within s.11(1) of the 1990 Act provided it was an activity falling within the meaning of a practice to determine whether embryos were "suitable" for the purpose of being placed in the woman and appeared to the HFEA "necessary or desirable" within para.1 of Sch.2. In interpreting "suitability", the HFEA had not been precluded from interpreting it as including the selection of an embryo with a characteristic that a woman desired. Accordingly, the authority had power to authorise both PGD and HLA typing as activities to determine the suitability of an embryo for implantation.

Commentary

Mrs H was implanted with selected embryos but she miscarried. As for operating on a healthy baby that has no clinical need for an operation, the operation must be performed in the child's best interests. To some, this is impossible in a "saviour sibling" case, as the baby has been born for reasons that include providing tissue for its older sibling. That is, the baby has become a "means to an end" rather than "an end in itself", thus contravening Kantian ethics (see Ch.3). Such objections have not subsequently prevented the HFEA granting licences to other couples for similar purposes.

Note that a proposed amendment to the Human Fertilisation and Embryology Bill 2007 would, if accepted, prohibit tissue typing for the purposes of seeking a match for existing children. Kantian ethics would prevail at the possible expense of a loss of life that might have been saved.

Embryo screening that would be carried out for sex selection purposes is not permitted other than for medical reasons, however. Sex selection was not permitted for the Masterton family who sought IVF treatment plus PGD to ensure they had another daughter after N, their only daughter in five children, had died in a bonfire accident. Although Mrs M had been sterilised after N's birth, no clinic in the UK applied for a licence to help the family.

There is no change in policy in the proposed 2008 Act: no sex selection for non-medical reasons.

A significant point about embryo selection that cannot be overlooked, is the liability that may attach to the negligent selection of the embryo or the negligent extraction or fertilisation of the mother's eggs (perhaps by ICSI) leading to the creation of the embryo and the birth of a disabled child. The child, if born alive and surviving for at least 48 hours, could sue in his own name under the Congenital Disabilities (Civil Liability) Act 1976. Given that this Act contains, in effect, a statutory enactment of the *Bolam* standard, however, the likelihood of receiving compensatory damages is small.

Excusal from assisting in the provision of fertility treatment via Conscientious Objection

Section 38 HFEA 1990 provides that:

(1) No person who has a conscientious objection to partici-
     pating in any activity governed by this Act shall be under
     a duty, however arising, to do so.

(2) In any legal proceedings the burden of conscientious
     objection shall rest on the person claiming to rely on it.

Surrogacy

Key Principle: **An infertile couple may be assisted in their
quest to have a child by a surrogate mother providing the
surrogacy is not underpinned by a commercial agreement.**

Surrogacy Arrangements Act 1985, Section 1A
No surrogacy arrangement is enforceable by or against any of the
persons making it.

Commentary
In the Warnock Report, surrogacy was expressed as being: "the
practice whereby one woman carries a child for another with the
intention that the child should be handed over after birth".
Under statute, s.1 Surrogacy Arrangements Act 1985 provides,
inter alia, the meaning of surrogate mother.

**1.—Meaning of "surrogate mother", "surrogacy arrangement"
and other terms.**
(1) The following provisions shall have effect for the inter-
     pretation of this Act.

(2) "Surrogate mother" means a woman who carries a child
     in pursuance of an arrangement—

     (a) made before she began to carry the child, and
     (b) made with a view to any child carried in pursuance
          of it being handed over to, and parental responsi-
          bility being met (so far as practicable) by, another
          person or other persons.

(3) An arrangement is a surrogacy arrangement if, were a
     woman to whom the arrangement relates to carry a child
     in pursuance of it, she would be a surrogate mother.

Also under this statute, s.2 provides, inter alia, that no person
shall initiate or take part in making a surrogacy arrangement on

a commercial basis or knowingly cause another person to do the same; and s.3 makes it clear that advertising for surrogacy services is an offence.

Where a child is born under a surrogacy arrangement, the mother is the gestational mother and it is immaterial that the eggs of the commissioning mother may have been used; and the father is the genetic father unless, of course, he is a sperm donor. In essence, the same principles as in the 1990 Act apply. Re Q (A minor)(Parental Order) [1996] 1 F.L.R. 369 made it clear that in this judicially sanctioned surrogacy arrangement, where the commissioning mother's eggs and donated sperm were used to create the embryo, the commissioning man (the husband of the commissioning woman) was not undergoing "treatment together" with the unmarried surrogate mother. Accordingly, as their was no legal father under s.28(2) or (3) of the 1990 Act, there was no man whose consent was required for the making of a parental order.

Statutory regulation of surrogacy has not followed the 1997 Brazier Review.

2007/08: Proposals for Reform of the Human Fertilisation and Embryology Act 1990

Human Fertilisation and Embryology Bill 2007
The Human Fertilisation and Embryology Bill 2008 introduced into the House of Lords in November 2007 was in three Parts with the first Part amending the 1990 Act, the second Part (when in force) providing for who is to be treated as the parents of a child who has been born as a result of assisted reproduction techniques and with Part three providing for miscellaneous and general provisions.

Provisions of the Surrogacy Arrangements Act 1985 also would be amended.

If the Bill receives Royal Assent, it is projected that it will come into force in 2009.

The Department of Health website provides a link that shows the Human Fertilisation and Embryology Act 1990 (c.37) as it would appear following the amendments made by the original draft of the Human Fertilisation and Embryology Bill, as introduced on the November 8, 2007. The URL is:

http://www.dh.gov.uk/en/Publicationsandstatistics/

Publications/PublicationsLegislation/DH_080205   [Accessed February 28, 2008].

Purpose and Provisions of the Bill

The purpose of Pt 1 was to address the scientific developments that had been made since enactment of the 1990 Act; to reflect societal changes towards assisted conception; and to make provisions enabling the Human Fertilisation and Embryology Authority to perform its regulatory role according to the principles of better regulation.

Part 2 makes new provisions for the determination of legal parenthood. It introduces this concept of "agreed female parenthood", in certain circumstances, for the mother's female partner and makes equivalent provision for that of opposite sex couples, where the concept of "agreed fatherhood" applies to the male partner.

The Bill addressed the controversial provision of the 1990 Act of an unmarried couple being "treated together" in a licensed clinic using donated sperm by making a new provision that both the prospective mother and her partner (whether male or female) who is intended to be the second parent of the child must consent to such in writing.

Particular Provisions

Section 1 of the 1990 act would be amended so as to ensure that the Act applies to all live human embryos regardless of their manner of creation and a "live human embryo" will no longer be assumed to be created by fertilisation, only. A regulation-making power will be inserted so as to enable future definitions of "embryo", "eggs", "sperm" and "gametes" so as to enable the law to keep pace with scientific change.

Section 3 of the Act will be amended so as to ensure that embryos created by artificial gametes or genetically modified gametes cannot be placed in a woman and neither can genetically modified embryos nor embryos created by cloning. The prohibition of reproductive cloning will supersede the Human Reproductive Cloning Act 2001.

A new s.4A will be inserted into the 1990 Act to regulate "inter-species embryos". The mixing of animal and human gametes will be permitted only under licence and the product may be kept for a very limited time, only.

A "cooling-off" period of up to one year is provided for where one person in a couple decides to withdraw consent to an embryo remaining in storage. If agreement between them cannot be reached in that time, the embryos will be allowed to perish.

A particularly interesting provision to be inserted into Sch. 3 of the 1990 Act is based on the recommendation of Professor Sheila McLean that (say) in the case of a child who may be left infertile after undergoing therapy for cancer, or an adult rendered mentally incapacitated by way of a coma, gametes can be taken without consent and stored provided that a clinician certifies that specified conditions have been met; but those gametes cannot be used unless and until the person from whom they were taken becomes competent and consents to such use.

Section 13 of the 1990 Act would be amended to include the provision that:

Persons or embryos that are known to have a gene, chromosome or mitochondrion abnormality involving a significant risk that a person with the abnormality will have or develop—

(a)   a serious physical or mental disability;

(b)   a serious illness; or

(c)   any other serious medical condition,

must not be preferred to those that are not known to have such an abnormality.

A similar provision rejecting the use of embryos that would result in a child having a serious gender-related medical condition when embryos free of the risk are available also would be inserted into the 1990 Act

The former provision is clearly intended to ensure there will be no repetition of the American case where deaf lesbians wanted to select embryos that would result in deaf children: an appalling abuse of Kantian ethics and a potential abuse of Mill's harm to others principle.

Finally, for the purposes of this summary, s.31 of the 1990 Act will be amended to record a host of provisions relating to identifying information of the donor and the donor-conceived person

Summary

The following summarises some of the key proposals contained in the Bill. The Bill aims to:

- ensure that all human embryos outside the body—whatever the process used in their creation—are subject to regulation;

- regulate "inter-species" embryos created from a combination of human and animal genetic material for research;

- ban sex selection of offspring for non-medical reasons;

- retain a duty to take account of the welfare of the child in providing fertility treatment, but remove the reference to "the need for a father";

- recognise same-sex couples as legal parents of children conceived through the use of donated sperm, eggs or embryos; and

- increase the scope of legitimate embryo research activities, subject to controls.

Given the controversial nature of some of the provisions, the government decided in March 2008 to allow Labour MP's to have a free vote on:

- the creation of inter-species embryos;

- removing the references to "the need for a father"; and

- the creation of saviour siblings.

The parliamentary vote is expected in May 2008.

10. PREGNANCY AND ABORTION

Pregnancy

(1) Non-invasive monitoring of foetal development

Key Principle: Whilst monitoring foetal development by way of ultrasound scans has become a non-invasive norm, frequent reports casting doubt over the safety of the scans has permeated the generally accepted safe nature of the procedure.

Reports on the perceived safety of ultrasound scans have been inconsistent over the past 15 years. Reports from outside the UK, casting doubt over the safety of ultrasound scans, were published in newspapers circulating in England and Wales in 1993, viz;

Australia
Here, "Results of a study of women who had five or more ultrasound examinations during pregnancy show that they were more than twice as likely to have babies with restricted growth as those who had just one ultrasound." (*The Times*, October 8, 1993).

Norway
In September 1993, " ... a Norwegian study found a link between ultrasound and left-handedness, suggesting a possible effect on the developing central nervous system". (*The Times*, October 8, 1993).

America
Here there was a comparison of two groups. "In the first group there was no routine use of ultrasound and scans were only performed if there was a serious medical reason. The second group were routinely scanned at around 20 and 32 weeks. There were nearly four times as many stillbirths in the second group as in the others, so what is the value of routine screening[?]." (*Western Mail*, December 29, 1993).

Canada

A much smaller scale study carried out in Canada appeared to yield a result that was a cause for concern. When 72 children with speech defects were compared with another group of children without speech defects it was discovered that "the majority of the problem youngsters had been exposed to ultrasound scans, but those with normal speech had not". (*Western Mail*, December 29, 1993).

Commentary on the "non-UK" results

Whilst the use of ultrasound scanning now appears to be part of routine ante-natal care, frequently there is no "medical" reason for a scan: it has been reported that scans are often used for "social" reasons—to introduce prospective parents to their new baby—as well as to check for abnormalities. The wisdom of this was questioned towards the end of the 1970s by Michel Odent, a hospital consultant in France. He outlawed the use of routine scans because at that time there was not enough evidence to prove that they were safe. The reasoning was that, ultrasound waves are not neutral: they have powerful biological effects. Accordingly, he insisted that they should be used only when there is an obvious medical need for more information about the growing baby.

A perceived problem with the results, however, is the lack of consistency in the reported problems and the apparent absence of any replication of the results. By contrast, it is difficult to be assured that there is no problem with ultrasound scans when such a range of issues has been reported.

1993: Results of scans administered in the UK

"An analysis of four trials of 16,000 pregnancies published in the *British Medical Journal* [in July 1993] concluded that ultrasound had no effect on parents' chances of having a healthy baby". ((1993) *The Times*, October 8).

Clearly, if a disabled child alleged that ultrasound scans caused the disabilities he was born with, he would be met with a number of major obstacles, viz;

i.   if a responsible body of medical practitioners would recommend the use of ultrasound scans then a *Bolam* standard would be challenged;

ii. a causal link between the use of the ultrasound and the disability would have to be established; and, presumably,

iii. the child's mother would have to establish that had she been informed of the risk, multiple ultrasound scans might have on her ability to have a healthy child then she would have refused to have them.

1998: Positive and questionable aspects of scans administered in the UK

In November 1998, BBC news reported that: "a six-year study [by doctors at Oxford's John Radcliffe Hospital] of prenatal ultrasound, published in *The Lancet* .. found that it can detect 68% of congenital abnormalities which could lead to miscarriages or other problems". The news item continued by noting that:

"The researchers studied more than 30,000 babies, of whom .. 2% were deemed abnormal on delivery.

"Another 174 foetuses had signs suggesting abnormality, but went on to be normal at birth. These are known as 'false positives'. [It was also said that:] 'The Oxford study' shows that ultrasonography is increasingly sensitive for the detection of many serious anomalies and therefore capable of providing good information to allow parents to make important decisions about their unborn child.

"Unfortunately, it also shows that ultrasonography may also provide information that is confusing or even misleading."

2004: Again, no clear "picture"

Results were published in *The Times* of nearly 3,000 children whose mothers had been randomly assigned to receive *either* five ultrasound scans from 18 to 38 weeks gestational age *or* a single scan at 18 weeks. The children were monitored from birth to 8 years of age. Whereas it was reassuring that no difference was found after the age of one year between groups in terms of physical size, speech, language, behaviour or neurological development, the potential for concern was in discovering that at birth, the length of newborns in the "5 ultrasound scans" group was "significantly less" than in the "single ultrasound" group. This appears very similar to the Australian results published in 1993: indeed, restricted growth is the single condition common to a couple of published results.

February 2007: New causes for concern?
At present (February 2007) the statistics may indicate some cause for concern but it is by no means clear that any statistical risk has been established—indeed the results of the further tests published in 2004 (noted above) seemed to suggest that there is no discernible risk. However, a report published in the British Medical Journal (BMJ) in February 2007 has again cast doubt on the safety of ultrasound scans. Commenting on the report, CBC news[1] said:

> "While non-medical ultrasound scans offer parents an irresistible sneak peek, *the practice may not be entirely benign*, . .
>
> Dramatic improvements in technology, from the fuzzy polaroids of the past to the current 3-D photographs, have shifted ultrasound from its original medical intent, . .
>
> But the report notes that the U.S. Food and Drugs Administration, the American Institute of Ultrasound in Medicine and the French Academy of Medicine have all expressed reservations about ultrasound for non-medical purposes. The FDA suggests that casual exposure to ultrasound should be avoided, *particularly during pregnancy*.
>
> Health Canada also cautions parents, saying ultrasounds should only be performed for diagnostic purposes. The federal agency also suggests *fetal ultrasounds should only be performed when the expected medical benefits exceed any foreseeable risks*."

The concerns relate to what is now being called "4-D ultrasonography" or "boutique ultrasonography"—the "4th dimension" being the movement of the developing foetus—and the increasingly rapid expansion of the provision of commercial scans for "social" purposes.

Commentary
A number of results have suggested that foetal development has been adversely affected when the mothers of the children had been subjected to multiple scans, but that no long-term adverse effects had been experienced by the mothers or by the growing children. It seems too simplistic, however, to suggest that foetal "problems" manifested at birth simply disappear with age. Unless a specific adverse condition is positively linked to the use of ultrasound scans, however, it seems as if the practice will

1 http://www.cbc.ca/technology/story/2007/02/06/ultrasound-scans.html?ref=rss

remain an acceptable, convenient diagnostic tool with the added
bonus of promoting "parental bonding".

In 2008, the Royal College of Obstetricians and Gynaecologists
is due to publish its guidelines on scanning for *vasa praevia*,
which kills one baby in every 2,500,—i.e. 300 each year. Pregnant
women at risk of vasa praevia will now be screened during the
routine scan at 20 weeks pregnancy.

(2) Invasive Diagnostic Testing Procedures

(i) Amniocentesis

Key Principle: **By contrast with ultrasound scans, amniocentesis is an invasive procedure involving the insertion of a
needle through the mother's abdomen and the uterine wall
into the sac surrounding the foetus. The object of the procedure is to remove a small volume of amniotic fluid and test it
for substances which indicate abnormalities such as spina
bifida and Down's syndrome. If such an abnormality is indicated it would permit an abortion under (s.1(1)(d)) Abortion
Act 1967.**

Reasons for offering amniocentesis include:

- The pregnant woman has had a previous pregnancy affected by a chromosomal or genetic disorder;

- The results of a blood test to measure the levels of pregnancy hormones in her blood together with her age indicate
she is at risk of having a child with Down's syndrome; and

- An ultrasound scan has detected features or abnormalities
that indicate an increased risk of the developing foetus
having a chromosome abnormality.

Commentary

Ultrasound is employed to guide a needle through the mother's
abdomen and the uterine wall into the sac surrounding the
foetus. The procedure normally takes no longer than about 10
minutes and about 20ml of the amniotic fluid is removed for
analysis. Whereas a preliminary result may be obtained within
48 hours, the final result may take as long as three weeks to
obtain. It is estimated that amniocentesis is more than 99 per cent
accurate in identifying chromosome abnormalities. The test may
be used from 15 weeks of pregnancy onwards.

Amniocentesis may precipitate legal action

Key Principle: Legal action following amniocentesis may arise from any one of at least three issues: first the pregnant woman would have an action in battery against the health authority / NHS Trust if her consent had not been obtained. Secondly, amniocentesis carries about a 1 per cent risk of causing a miscarriage. Accordingly, the woman would have to establish that had she been informed of the risk of miscarriage she would not have consented to the procedure. Thirdly, if the procedure is carried out negligently and the woman is not informed that there is a probability of her giving birth to a disabled child, then, if she can prove that she would seek an abortion had she been given the correct information, then she would have an action in negligence.

Commentary

First, the effect of the Abortion Act 1967 as amended by s.37 Human Fertilisation and Embryology Act 1990 is to reverse the judgment the third point as decided in *Rance v Mid Downs Health Authority* (1991). (See above and below).

Secondly, in February 2007, it was announced by two separate groups of scientists in America and Hong Kong that blood tests for detecting Downs syndrome may be possible by 2010. The tests would be safer but more expensive than amniocentesis.

(ii) Chorionic Villus Testing (CVS)

This test may be carried out from 11 weeks gestation. Here, ultrasound is used to guide a needle through the mother's abdomen into the developing placenta of the foetus. A small sample of tissue is extracted via suction and a preliminary result is available within 48 hours with the final result being available within two weeks. CVS testing carries a slightly higher risk of miscarriage when compared to amniocentesis.

Commentary

The legal issues that may arise in respect of CVS are the same as for amniocentesis. As to which test may be offered to the pregnant woman is likely to be dependent on procedures adopted in the hospital where she intends to give birth (this may be independent of any decision to favour a home birth: see the next chapter).

Abortion

Law and Abortion

Permissive Abortion: The Abortion Act 1967 (as amended)

Key Principle: The principal statutory provisions on abortion are contained within the Abortion Act 1967 (as amended). The Act is *permissive only*: i.e. abortion is allowed only on certain clearly defined grounds. Failure to observe the provisions of this Act may result in an action for criminal abortion.

Section 1, as amended by the Human Fertilisation and Embryology Act 1990 now reads;

(1)   ... a person shall not be guilty of an offence under the law relating to abortion when a pregnancy is terminated by a registered medical practitioner if two registered medical practitioners are of the opinion, formed in good faith—

    (a)   that the pregnancy *has not exceeded its twenty-fourth week* and that the continuance of the pregnancy would involve risk, greater than if the pregnancy were terminated, of injury to the physical or mental health of the pregnant woman *or* any existing children of her family; or

    (b)   that the termination is necessary to prevent grave permanent injury to the physical or mental health of the pregnant woman; or

    (c)   that the continuance of the pregnancy would involve risk to the life of the pregnant woman, greater than if the pregnancy were terminated; or

    (d)   that there is a substantial risk that if the child were born it would suffer from such physical or mental abnormalities as to be seriously handicapped.

Commentary

Legally permissive—but moral?

The Abortion Act 1967 introduced permissive abortion into England and Wales. In a non-emergency case, "permissive" means that no-one will be guilty of an offence under the law relating to abortion if a woman's pregnancy is terminated by a registered medical practitioner ("doctor") after two registered medical practitioners are of the opinion, formed in good faith, that the woman's physical or mental health will be affected in such a way specified by s.1(1) or any other condition specified in s.1(1) is satisfied. In emergency situations, the requirement for *two* doctors to form an opinion in good faith is dispensed with: if one doctor deems a termination to be immediately necessary, then the woman may lawfully be aborted: s.1(4) No abortion carried out in accordance with the provisions of the Abortion Act 1967 (as amended) will constitute a criminal offence of "procuring a miscarriage" under the Offences Against the Person Act 1861 (see below).

It should be noted that the amendment of the 1967 Act by the Human Fertilisation and Embryology Act 1990 introduced a time limit in s.1(1)(a) of 24 weeks. This was the first time limit enacted in the Abortion Act and, to date, it remains the only current limit. The "previous limit" of 28 weeks was not part of the Abortion Act: it was a provision of the s.1 Infant Life (Preservation) Act 1929; and this time limit, which remains "good law" in the 1929 Act, is distinct from, and not part of, the Abortion Act 1967 (see below).

That there is no time limit specified in s.1(1)(b)–(d) means that abortion under these grounds may be performed up to term. Note that only para.(d) refers to the developing "child". Whereas this "child" could be subjected to a late-term abortion, if it is born with "such physical or mental abnormalities as to be seriously handicapped", then, whilst it may be "allowed to die", it cannot be killed as this would constitute murder (see the next chapter).

Recent proposals for the reform of English law on abortion are noted at the end of this chapter.

The Morality of Abortion

Key Principle: **There is no consensus on the morality of abortion and none will be achieved by theorising about when life "begins".**

Commentary
MaClean & Maher (*Medicine, Morals & the Law*) have analysed and dismissed the arguments attaching moral significance to life

beginning at quickening (i.e. the time when the mother first feels the foetus move); viability (i.e. the stage when the foetus is a "child capable of being born alive"); and birth. Moreover, to claim that life begins at conception will satisfy only the pro-life point of view in so far as conception is the start of a *continuous process* of development from the single-cell stage containing an equal number of chromosomes from both parents, through the multi-cellular stage, ... then the embryo stage, to a foetus and, finally, a new-born baby. The counter-argument is that the single-cell, or even multi-cellular pre-embryo stage, is totally unlike anything which could be recognised as a human being: just as an acorn is a *potential* tree, but nothing more, so a zygote (the single or multi-cell stage of the pre-embryo) is no more than a *potential* human being—hence, no argument can be based on the alleged *autonomy* of the foetus.

Moreover, the claim of the "right to life" of the developing foetus contrasts with the rights of the autonomous mother to "determine what shall be done with her own body" and a sterile debate ensues. In short, no argument on the morality of abortion achieves a consensus.

Judicial Development of Permissive Abortion law

Key Principle: **The judicial development of permissive abortion law, based on the Abortion Act 1967 (as amended), may be conveniently classified into categories that include: (1) the status of the parents; (2) whether the foetus has any rights; (3) the rights, if any, of third party participants in an abortion, viz; (i) doctors; (ii) nurses; and (iii) medical receptionists.**

1(a) The Competent Pregnant Woman

Emeh v Kensington and Chelsea and Westminster A.H.A. [1985] Q.B. 1012

P, a mother of three healthy children, underwent an abortion and sterilisation operation in May, 1976. In January 1977, when she discovered she was 18–20 weeks pregnant, she decided not to have another abortion. She later sued K in negligence and for breach of contract.

Held: She was successful on both counts, and her refusal to undergo a second abortion was not so unreasonable as to eclipse the surgeon's negligence: *it was **not** a novus actus interveniens*. She was awarded damages amounting to more than £20,000 which included the cost of a second sterilisation operation. As Slade L.J. said:

> "Save in the most exceptional circumstances, I cannot think it right that the court should ever declare it unreasonable for a woman to decline to have an abortion in a case where there is no evidence that there were any medical or psychiatric grounds for terminating the particular pregnancy".

Commentary

Whatever the "most exceptional circumstances" meant in *Emeh*, it must be remembered that a competent pregnant woman can refuse treatment, including a Caesarean section, even if that refusal brings about her death and that of her unborn baby: *Re MB* (1997); *St George's NHS Trust v S* (1998): see Ch.4.

N.B. Where the pregnant female is a *Gillick*-competent minor, her right to confidentiality means that she does not have to inform her parents of her wish to seek an abortion. The approach adopted in *Gillick* to seeking advice and treatment on contraceptive matters applied equally in relation to abortion: *R. (on the application of Axon) v SS for Health* [2006] Q.B. 539.

1(b) Abortion and the Incompetent Female

Initially, the legal basis for the abortion of an adult incompetent female posed problems for the court, as evidenced in *T v T*:

T v T [1988] Fam 52

A declaration was sought to abort and sterilise a severely handicapped 19-year-old woman with a mental age of 3 who was about 11 weeks pregnant. However, not only was she was unable to comprehend her condition and consent to the abortion but there was no power for anyone to consent on her behalf under the Mental health Act 1983 nor did the court have such power under *parens patriae* jurisdiction.

Held: Whilst it was a tortious act to perform surgical treatment without a defence or other justification, the declaration would be given as it was in T's best interests and the "demands" of good medical practice.

Commentary

The year after this decision, the House of Lords rejected "demands of good medical practice" as a legal basis for the sterilisation of an adult incompetent female. The central issue remained what was in the best interests of the subject, and sterilisation would be lawful on the basis of necessity if it was in the patient's best interests to perform it. The best interests were to be based on a "Bolam standard"—but see now Ch.8 and the limitations placed on *Bolam* in In *Re S (Sterilisation; Patient's Best Interests)* [2001] Fam 15.

With regards to abortion, irrespective of whether the female is of adult years, i.e. she has reached the age of majority, or she is a minor, the Abortion Act 1967 as amended provides the necessary safeguards and, thus, any abortion which complies with one of the provisions in s.1(1) will be lawful. Consequently, it has been decided that a declaration of the lawfulness of the procedure will not be a prerequisite for such an abortion.

In re SG (Adult Mental Patient: Abortion) [1991] 2 F.L.R. 329

Held: There was no requirement to seek a Court declaration for performing an abortion on a pregnant mentally handicapped woman: the Abortion Act 1967 provided fully adequate safeguards for the doctors involved.

If no expert evidence is adduced favouring a termination as being in the best interests of the incompetent female, then such a declaration is likely to be refused: *Re SS (Medical Treatment: Late Termination)* [2002] 1 F.L.R. 445.

Commentary

Decision-making concerning adults lacking capacity is now governed by the Mental Capacity Act 2005.

1(c) The Putative Father

Paton v British Pregnancy Advisory Service [1979] Q.B. 276

Held: A father has no rights in respect of an unborn child and the Abortion Act 1967 gave him no right even to be consulted prior to an abortion. In this case it was said that the father had "no legal right enforceable at law or in equity to stop his wife having this abortion or to stop the doctors from carrying out the abortion". Although the abortion was performed, the father took his case to the European Commission on Human Rights ((1980) 3 E.H.R.R. 408), arguing that this decision infringed the European Convention on Human Rights. Whereas he argued that his right to family life and the unborn child's right to life had been infringed, the Commission dismissed his claim. It was said that where an abortion was carried out on medical grounds, his (the father's) right to family life must necessarily be subordinated to the need to protect the rights and health of the mother.

Commentary

It would seem that the pursuit of a claim by a father for standing (*locus standi*) in challenging a decision to abort his wife would be confined to challenging the decisions of two doctors purportedly made in good faith that a proposed abortion would be lawful within the scope of the 1967 Act. Thus, in May 1997, James Kelly succeeded in having his wish to prevent his estranged wife from having an abortion, being referred to the House of Lords. However, he instructed his lawyers not to proceed with the case when, it was said, that he realised not only the consequences of the financial hardship he had endured in pursuing the case but that it was "no longer about me and her, it was about changing the law". ((1997) *The Times*, May 28).

2. Foetal "rights"?

In essence, English law does not accord a foetus legal personality. Consequently, a foetus has no standing in a claim of "a right to life": *Paton v BPAS* (1980) 3 E.H.R.R. 408; *B v Islington Health Authority* [1991] 1 Q.B. 638; *Re MB (Caesarean Section)* [1997] 2 F.L.R. 426; and *Kelly v Kelly* [1997] 2 F.L.R. 828. See also the judgments of Balcombe and Staughton L.J.J. in *Re F (In Utero)* [1988] Fam 122.

In *Vo v France* (2005) 10 E.H.R.R. 12, a French woman had had to have an abortion following the negligent piercing of the amniotic sac during a routine medical examination. She complained that the failure of the French courts to classify the taking of her unborn child's life as intentional homicide amounted to a violation of Art.2 ECHR. Accordingly, took her case to the European Court of Human Rights.

Held: By 14 votes to 3 it was decided that there had been no violation. In particular, in para.84 of the judgment it was said that:

"At European level, ... there is no consensus on the nature and status of the embryo and/or foetus, ... At best it may be regarded as common ground between States that the embryo/foetus belongs to the human race. The potentiality of that being and its capacity to become a person ... require protection in the name of human dignity, without making it a 'person' with the 'right to life' for the purposes of Article 2 [ECHR]."

Third Parties' Rights

(i) Doctors

A doctor claiming conscientious objection under s.4(1) Abortion Act 1967 must prove it. Section 4(1) provides that: "... no person shall be under any duty ... *to participate* in any treatment authorised by this Act to which he has a conscientious objection". A conscientious objection does *not* absolve a doctor from treating a woman when the continuation of her pregnancy threatens her life, however.

Codes of ethics are inconsistent in relation to abortion with the Hippocratic Oath's declaration of: "I will not give a woman a pessary to produce abortion" contrasting with the Declaration of Oslo proclaiming that: "Diversity of response to [abortion] results from the diversity of attitudes towards the life of the unborn child. This is a matter of individual conviction and conscience"(!)

On the other hand, it is of paramount importance that a doctor who is willing to abort a woman ensures that he acts in good faith in expressing an opinion that a proposed abortion comes within a permissive category if he is to remain within the law, as failing to do so provides for criminal liability under the Offences Against the Person Act 1861 (below): *R. v Smith* [1973] 1 W.L.R. 1510.

Commentary

In June 2007, the BMA voted by 67 per cent to 33 per cent in favour of removing the need for two doctors' signatures to allow abortion in the first trimester. The Government says it has no plans to change the law.

(ii) Nursing Staff

Section 4 of the Abortion Act 1967 provides that no person is under a legal duty to assist in an abortion to which (s)he has a conscientious objection, *except* where immediate treatment is necessary *to save the life of the woman or to prevent grave permanent damage to her health.* The question which then arose was: if a midwife or a nurse was prepared to help a registered medical practitioner would (s)he be guilty of any offence since s.1 Abortion Act 1967 only provided that no offence would be committed when a pregnancy is terminated by that registered practitioner in prescribed circumstances. The answer was given in:

Royal College of Nursing v DHSS [1981] A.C. 800
Here, Lord Diplock said:

> "The doctor need not do everything with his own hands; the requirements of the sub-section are satisfied when the treatment for termination of a pregnancy is one prescribed by the registered medical practitioner carried out in accordance with his directions and of which a registered medical practitioner remains in charge throughout."

Commentary
An article in the *Journal of Family Planning and Reproductive Health Care*, March 2007, expressed the view that specially-trained nurses could perform abortions without a doctor being present. The authors of the article also claimed that the law which prevents nurses from carrying out surgical abortions has been represented. Basically, they contend that the 1981 RCN case (above), which permitted nurses to carry out medical abortions using drugs, could be extended to permitting nurses to carry out surgical abortions that involve the insertion of a catheter into the womb.

(iii) Medical Receptionists
The first case to provide guidance on s.4(1) Abortion Act 1967 was *Janaway v Salford A.H.A.* As noted, s.4(1) provides that: "... no person shall be under any duty ... *to participate* in any treatment authorised by this Act to which he has a conscientious objection".

Janaway v Salford A.H.A. [1988] A.C. 537
In June 1984 Mrs Janaway, the applicant, became employed by the respondent health authority as a medical receptionist at a health centre. Her duties included the typing of correspondence for doctors at the centre. In September, she discovered that her employers expected her to type letters referring patients to

specialists with a view to the termination of pregnancy. Being a practising Roman Catholic and regarding all abortions as immoral, she refused, and sought to rely on s.4(1). Her employers, taking the view, on legal advice, that the section only applied to those with direct, clinical responsibility for the patients, dismissed her. Mrs Janaway applied for judicial review, seeking an order of certiorari to quash her employers' decision and a declaration that she was not under any duty to type the abortion referral letters.

Held: A secretary who typed a letter could not be said to be counselling or procuring an abortion: she would have been intending merely to carry out the obligations of her employment. She could not invoke the protection of s.4(1).

Criminal Abortion

Key Principle: **An abortion which is performed outside the scope of the Abortion Act 1967 may result in an indictment, leading to life imprisonment, under the Offences Against the Person Act 1861.**

The law relating to *criminal abortion* is to be found in ss.58 & 59 Offences Against the Person Act 1861. In particular, s.58 provides for criminal offences, punishable by a maximum of *life imprisonment*, in particular circumstances.

58. Administering drugs or using instruments to procure abortion.

Every woman, being with child, who, with intent to procure her own miscarriage, shall unlawfully administer to herself any poison or other noxious thing, or shall unlawfully use any instrument or other means whatsoever with the like intent, and whosoever, with intent to procure the miscarriage of any woman, whether she be or be not with child, shall unlawfully administer to her or cause to be taken by her any poison or other noxious thing, or shall unlawfully use any instrument or other means whatsoever with the like intent, shall be guilty of felony, and being convicted thereof shall be liable to be kept in penal servitude for life.

Commentary

Self-induced abortion by the woman herself is criminal, under s.58, only if the woman is, in fact, pregnant. Any Act by a third party is criminal *regardless of whether or not the woman can be proved to be pregnant*.

The unmitigating harshness of the 1861 provisions were tempered by a common law defence and a defence enacted in the Infant Life (Preservation) Act 1929, viz;

At Common Law

In *R. v Collins* [1898] 2 Brit Med J 59; 122 at 129, Grantham J. said that:

> "It could well be understood that there were cases where it was necessary, in order to save the life of a woman, that there should be forcible miscarriage, and a properly qualified doctor had to say when that time had arrived. That was not unlawful."

Under Statute

Section 1 Infant Life (Preservation) Act 1929 contained the qualified defence that:

> "...no person shall be found guilty of an offence ... unless it is proved that the act which caused the death of the child was not done in good faith for the purpose only of *preserving the life* of the mother."

The first case that raised this defence of therapeutic abortion was:

R. v Bourne [1939] 1 K.B. 687

A 14-year-old girl became pregnant after being raped. Dr Bourne agreed to perform an abortion on her. He had previously carried out other abortions and had written: "I have done that before and shall not have the slightest hesitation in doing it again. I have said that the next time I have the opportunity, I will write to the Attorney-General and invite him to take action." Following the operation, Dr Bourne was indicted under the Offences Against the Person Act 1861.

Held: Macnaghten J., Where an abortion was performed for the purpose of saving the life of a woman, *or for preserving her health*—physical or mental—then it would not have been performed unlawfully. There was no clear distinction between danger to life and danger to health "... since life depends on health, and it may be that health is so gravely impaired that death results." Furthermore, "... the word 'unlawfully' [in s.58 of the OAP Act 1861] is not ... a meaningless word ... it imports the meaning expressed by the proviso in s.1(1) [of the 1929 Act], and that s.58 of the Offences Against the Person Act 1861, must be read as if the words making it an offence to use an instrument with intent to procure a miscarriage were qualified by a similar proviso." So Macnaghten J. was able to conclude that:

> "...if the doctor is of the opinion, on reasonable grounds and with adequate knowledge, that the probable consequence of continuance of the pregnancy will be to make the woman a physical or mental wreck, the jury are quite entitled to take the view that the doctor who, under those circumstances and in that honest belief, operates, is operating for the purpose of preserving the life of the mother." Dr Bourne was acquitted.

Commentary
In essence, prior to the enactment of the Abortion Act 1967, the "*Bourne* defence" was the only available defence for a person charged with the unlawful procurement of a miscarriage.

The Meaning of "Capable of being born alive"

Key Principle: **The Infant Life (Preservation) Act 1929 introduced the offence of *child destruction*, or causing death of a child presumed *capable of being born alive*, before it has an existence independent of its mother: i.e. at a time after the expiry of the limitation on an abortion—which was put at 28 weeks. This time limit was found only in the Infant Life (Preservation) Act 1929: no time limit was specified in the Abortion Act 1967 when originally enacted.**

Modern case law illustrating the meaning of "capable of being born alive" includes:

C v S [1987] 1 All E.R. 1230
While this case confirmed that a father has no legal right to be consulted prior to the legal termination of a pregnancy, the principal issue to be decided was whether or not an abortion carried out on an 18 to 21 week-old foetus constituted an offence under the Infant Life (Preservation) Act 1929.

Held: The foetus was not capable of being born alive because it would not be able to breathe "either naturally or with the aid of a ventilator" per Lord Donaldson M.R.. No offence was committed under the 1929 Act.

Rance v Mid-Downs Health Authority [1991] 1 Q.B. 587

Held: A foetus which had reached that stage in its development where it was capable, if born, of living and breathing through its own lungs without any connection to its mother was a child "capable of being born alive" within the meaning of s.1 of the Infant Life (Preservation) Act 1929 and accordingly an abortion of a foetus at that stage in its development was unlawful *even if carried out within the period of 28 weeks referred to in* s.2 of the 1929 Act. Accordingly, it was not possible to found a course of action against a hospital if its medical staff negligently failed to discover an abnormality in a foetus which was "capable of being born alive", thereby depriving the parents of the possibility of having the pregnancy terminated.

Commentary

The significant feature about a child being "capable of being born alive" is that breathing must take place other than by or through connection with its mother. There is no requirement that the child should be able to sustain its lung function without mechanical ventilation. If it were otherwise, it would mean that all the situations in which severely handicapped newborn babies might require ventilation would be cases of "children who were not capable of being born alive, and failure to attend or render medical assistance would not be culpable", per Morgan & Lee, *Blackstone's Guide to the Human Fertilisation and Embryology Act 1990*.

N.B.: The decision in *Rance* would now not be followed, following the amendment to the 1967 Act by the Human Fertilisation and Embryology Act 1990 if there was "a substantial risk that if the child were born it would suffer from such physical or mental abnormalities as to be seriously handicapped": s.1(1)(d) 1967 Act.

Abortion procedures that have raised doubts as to their legality

Key principle: **Classifying an abortion procedure as "permissive" or "criminal" can be fraught with difficulties and only recently have a couple of procedures been clarified.**

Selective Reduction of Multiple Pregnancy: "Selective Feticide"

"Selective reduction" is the term used to describe the procedure "whereby one or more embryos in a multiple pregnancy are selectively killed to allow others to develop". Margaret Brazier (Medicine, Patients and the Law,3/e. London: Penguin, 2003, p.331) states that:

> "The dead foetuses are not expelled from the uterus, but may become 'foetus papyraceous', flattened and mummified, and emerge on delivery of their healthy brothers and sisters".

With regard to the legality of the procedure, it would appear that two questions have to be answered, viz: (i) does the procedure fall within the offence under s.58 OAPA 1861 of acting "with intent to procure a miscarriage"?; and, if it does, (ii) would compliance with the terms of the Abortion Act 1967, as amended, render it lawful?

Commentary

Prior to the amendment of the abortion Act 1967 by the Human Fertilisation and Embryology Act 1990, a persuasive article on this issue was John Keown's "*Selective Reduction of Multiple Pregnancy*" (1987) N.L.J. 1165. Keown argued that a miscarriage does not necessitate the expulsion of the foetus from the uterus or to the emptying of the uterus; that "miscarriage" pertains not to the destination of the foetal remains but to the failure of gestation. He argued that s.58 prohibits the termination of pregnancy even if the foetus is not thereafter expelled. Furthermore, "[s.58] is infringed whether the woman miscarries all of the foetuses or only of one". Keown's argument was supported by David Price who concluded that: "it is the causing of foetal death which is the essence of the crime of abortion and not simply the expulsion of the foetus from the mother".

However, since s.37(5) of the 1990 Act amended s.5(2) of the

1967 Act to refer to "a woman's miscarriage (or, in the case of a woman carrying more than one foetus, her miscarriage of any foetus) is unlawfully done unless authorised by section 1 of this Act ...", it was soon recognised that if a selective reduction was performed on one of the grounds for which a termination for the whole pregnancy was lawful, then the procedure would be *not unlawful*. Accordingly, selective reduction of a multiple pregnancy is now recognised and accepted as lawful by most of the major academics writing on this area of law.

RU486: The "abortion pill"

To the original s.1(3) Abortion Act 1967, which provided that "any treatment for the termination of pregnancy must be carried out in a hospital vested in the Minister of Health or the Secretary of State under the National Health Service Acts, or in a place for the time being approved for the purposes of this section ...", has been added a new s.(3A) which provides that:

> "The power ... to approve a place includes the power, in relation to treatment consisting primarily in the use of such medicines as may be specified in the approval and carried out in such a manner as may be specified, to approve a class of places."

Commentary

The purpose of the amendment was to anticipate the marketing of the French "abortion pill", *RU486* (mifepristone), the administration of which requiresis no surgery or anaesthetic, and to acknowledge that there is no need for its administration to be confined to a woman within a hospital or approved clinic. This method of abortion can be used for pregnancies up to nine weeks gestation. Surprisingly, perhaps, one of the major issues was defining "termination of pregnancy". Since there has to be a pregnancy before a termination can take place, administration of the pill prior to implantation would render this provision redundant as, then, there could be no "termination of pregnancy" because there would be no pregnancy and, thus, no abortion. There seems to be little doubt that a nurse could administer the pill—in common with many other drugs—while a doctor remained in charge of the patient's treatment (See the *RCN* (1981) Case, above), but whether there would be any likelihood of a woman being permitted to self-administer without being indicted under the Offences Against the Person Act 1861 remains a matter for conjecture.

Note: The "morning after" pill is a contraceptive measure not an abortifacient: *R. (on the application of Smeaton) v Secretary of State for Health and Others* [2002] 2 F.L.R. 146 (See Ch.8). By contrast, the results of research published in July 2007 indicated that daily (5 mg) doses of mifepristone [the drug in the abortion pill] is an effective oral contraceptive pill which has a better pattern of menstrual bleeding than an existing progesterone-only pill.

Proposals for Reforming Abortion Law
Focusing on English law:

- In March 2007, the *Journal of Family Planning and Reproductive Health Care*, published an article expressing the view that specially-trained nurses could perform abortions without a doctor being present;

- In June 2007, the BMA voted by 67 per cent to 33 per cent in favour of removing the need for two doctors' signatures to allow abortion in the first trimester; and

- Abortion limit of 24 weeks in s.1(1)(a) of the 1967 Act to be reduced to 20 weeks (a possible reform to be introduced by the Human Fertilisation and Embryology Bill 2008).

11. CHILDBIRTH; CIVIL LIABILITY TO A CHILD BORN WITH CONGENITAL DISABILITIES; AND LIFE-OR-DEATH DECISION-MAKING IN RESPECT OF SEVERELY HANDICAPPED NEWBORN BABIES

(I) Medico-Legal Aspects of Childbirth

The "Home vs Hospital" debate

(a) Home Births
Key Principle: In *"Making it Better for Mother and Baby"*, a report published by the Department of Health in February 2007, proposals for reconfiguring maternity care included more women being encouraged to have their babies born at home under the supervision of a midwife.

Nursing and Midwifery Order 2001 (SI 2002/253)
Currently, Art.45 of SI 2002/253 provides that it is a criminal offence for a person other than a registered midwife or a registered medical practitioner to attend a woman in childbirth except "in a case of sudden or urgent necessity".

Commentary
The strictness of a predecessor of SI 2002/253 (s.17 of the Nurses, Midwives and Health Visitors Act 1979), was demonstrated when, in August 1982, a man from Wolverhampton was convicted and fined £100 for attending his wife in the delivery of his own child! Furthermore, should a pregnant woman seek the assistance of an unqualified attendant, but neither a doctor nor a midwife, she risks being accused of counselling and procuring a criminal offence.

The stark reality is that whereas a seemingly simple decision to have a baby at home requires the presence of a qualified attendant it does not take into account the potential need for a Caesarean section because of sudden foetal distress or the onset of eclampsia.

Yet those who take a strong stand against home births may be seen to be anachronistic, however, following the report published in February 2007, *Making it Better for Mother and Baby*, by Dr Sheila Shribman, the Government's chief adviser on childcare and maternity services. The report advocates fewer consultant-led centres of excellence with the majority of routine maternity cases being in midwife-led birth-centres or be home births under the supervision of midwives. However, there is no evidence to support that larger centres are safer for mother and baby. The nearest centre of excellence may be an hour's drive away for some mothers-to-be and there is a shortage of midwives. Moreover, in March 2007, NICE (National Institute for Health and Clinical Excellence—see Ch.2) warned that babies born at home have a higher risk of dying if serious complications occur. Accordingly, any action on the report will have to be very carefully considered before implementation.

(b) Childbirth in Hospital

Key Principle: **In essence, the legal issues surrounding childbirth in hospital relate to precisely what it is that a woman consents to by deciding to have her child born in a hospital; and whether the standard of care owed to her has been breached, causing her and/or the child harm.**

The validity of consenting to epidurals

To combat the pain of going through labour, many women are given epidurals, i.e. an injection of anaesthetic into the base of the spine in order to numb the lower half of the body. It has been recorded that:

> "Thirty per cent of first-time mothers in Britain are routinely given epidurals." *Sunday Express* January 23, 1994.

Apart from the fact that some women find this "unnatural", research in Kansas City, Missouri, USA, by James Thorp, has found that

> "...those who had been given an epidural were four times more likely to have a caesarean birth. Labour also lasted longer and was more difficult."

Commentary

First, it is well established that "Every human being of adult years and sound mind has the right to determine what shall be done with his own body", (per Cardozo J., in *Schloendorff* (1914)). However, if a woman wishes to avoid a caesarean section, then, according to Dr Thorp: "It is imperative that women are told that an epidural increases the chances of a caesarean". If they are not, then it is arguable that they've not given real consent because they've not been informed in "broad terms of the nature of the procedure intended": *Chatterton v Gerson* (1981). Equally, if a woman had avoided an epidural but is then advised at the time of labour that she should undergo a caesarean section, even though she had previously made her objections known, there is a strong case for contending that any consent she gives to the procedure is not real: that is, she might be incapable of full and free consent because of the pain and ordeal of the delivery. Note that an Area Health Authority has been found negligent in attempting to obtain a woman's consent to subsequent sterilisation when she was on her way into theatre to give birth to her second child: *Wells v Surrey AHA* (1978): see Ch.8.

Caesarean Sections

Key Principle: **It is no defence for a health authority to claim necessity for performing a Caesarean section in order to save the life of a competent woman refusing to consent or to save the life of her unborn baby who is capable of being born alive.**

The 1992 case of *Re S*, in which a non-consenting competent woman was ordered to have a Caesarean section against her wishes has been disapproved and will no longer be followed "even though the consequence may be the death or serious handicap of the child she bears or her own death", per Butler Sloss L.J. in *Re MB* (1997): see Ch.8. The mother's right "is not reduced or diminished merely because her decision to exercise it may appear morally repugnant", per *St George's NHS Trust v S* (No. 2) [1998] 3 W.L.R. 936.

Commentary
It must be remembered that until birth, English law does not accord legal personality to a foetus: *Burton v Islington Health Authority* (1992); *St George's Healthcare NHS Trust v S* (1998); and that no attempt to save the life of the unborn child "capable of being born alive" can displace the autonomy of competent woman *refusing* consent.

Equally contentious is the issue of whether a fit and healthy woman should be allowed to *elect* a Caesarean section as opposed to vaginal birth when the former is thought to be clinically unjustifiable. The principal tension is between the cost of a Caesarean—five times more than a natural birth—and the woman's "right to choose". This "right of choice" should be viewed in the light of there being "... no evidence to suggest that a caesarean birth is any safer than a normal delivery" (*"Curb on caesarean births to save costs"*, *The Times*, March 6, 1998). Indeed, in February 2007, it was reported in the *Journal of Obstetrics and Gynaecology* that a Caesarean section in one pregnancy increases the risk of a woman having a still birth (i.e. an infant being delivered dead after 24 weeks gestation) in following pregnancies. The possibility of associating 4 per cent of still births with women who had previously had a Caesarean birth was based on the records of 82,000 live and still births in Oxfordshire and West Berkshire between 1968 and 1989.

Water Births

Key Principle: **The perceived benefits of water births appear to outweigh the potential disadvantages, though the latter should not be ignored.**

The concept of water births was pioneered by Igor Tjarkovsky in Russia in the 1960s; and recommended for pain relief during labour, rather than in birth, by the French doctor, Michel Odent in the 1970s.

It was reported in the *British Journal of Midwifery*, November/December 1993, Vol.1, No.6, p.264 that

> "... pioneer Igor Tjarkovsky performed his first water delivery after seeing the benefit of warm water in the treatment of his premature daughter ... Tjarkovsky believed that delivery into water was less dramatic for the baby than being subjected to a cold world where the force of gravity 'strikes like a blow from a club'".

Indeed, the benefits of a water birth to the baby were described in the following terms:

> "Having spent 9 months in fluid, protected from the harshness of light, sound, and touch, what could be more natural than to extend these features past the moment of birth? The characteristics of the pool

water are very similar to those in the womb, so a delivery into this environment is surely less traumatic than the sudden, combined experience of a drop in temperature, gravity, bright lights and noise. . . .

The baby does not attempt to breathe under water, taking the first breath only when brought into contact with air (Balaskas and Gordon, 1990). Despite recent concern, there have been no reports of babies drowning in this country. ((1993) 1BJM 265)."

Commentary

It is reported that there are also a number of benefits to the mother in the use of a birthing pool, viz;

"Th[e] [buoyancy afforded by the water in the birthing pool] together with the non-supine position, reduces the strain on the heart and spine; women with back problems find this particularly helpful. (1993) 1BJM 265"

In addition, the use of pain-killing drugs, such as pethidine, has been reduced. Consequently, there has been a cost saving on analgesics. Furthermore, "Of the 100 births reported by Odent (1983), 29 women tore. [However] No episiotomies were performed" (*ibid*).

(II) Congenital Disabilities: Possible Causes and Potential Actions and Liabilities

Key Principle: That medical research "into the growth of the foetus in the womb has established the crucial importance of good ante-natal care" there is no doubt (per *Brazier, Medicine, Patients and the Law*, 3/e. London: Penguin, 2003, p.372).

Commentary

What appeared to be at least strong circumstantial evidence of the need for good ante-natal care resulted from the severe disabilities suffered by children whose mothers, during their pregnancy, had taken the drug Thalidomide to help them sleep. Distillers, the manufacturers of Thalidomide, had claimed that it was non-toxic and safe for pregnant women and nursing mothers. It was never proved that this was incorrect, i.e. legal causation was never established, as out-of-court settlements were reached.

The Congenital Disabilities (Civil Liability) Act 1976

Key Principle: **The enactment of the Congenital Disabilities (Civil Liability) Act 1976 applies to all births from its coming into force in July 1976. The Act was intended to protect children from pre-conception injury as well as injury *in utero*. Moreover, it governs the rights of the child to sue a person for the wrongful act(s) that resulted in the child's injuries.**

Section 1 of the 1976 Act: Civil liability to child born disabled

1. (1) If a child *born* disabled as a *result* of such an *occurrence* before its birth as is mentioned in subsection (2) below, and a *person* (other than the child's own mother) is under this section *answerable to the child* in respect of the occurrence, the child's disabilities are to be regarded as damage resulting from the wrongful act of that person and actionable accordingly at the suit of the child.

   (2) An occurrence to which this section applies is one which—

      (a) affected either parent of the child in his or her ability to have a normal, healthy child; *or*
      (b) affected the mother during her pregnancy, or affected her or the child in the course of its birth, so that the child is born with disabilities which would not otherwise have been present.

... (See also subss. 3 (below) and 4–7).

The Human Fertilisation and Embryology Act 1990 has extended s.1 to cover infertility treatments by inserting s.1A into the 1976 Act which provides that:

   (1) In any case where—

      (A) a child carried by a woman as the result of the placing in her of an embryo or of sperm and eggs or her artificial insemination is born disabled,
      (B) the disability results from an act or omission in the course of the selection, or the keeping or use outside the body, of an embryo carried by her or of the gametes used to bring about the creation of the embryo, and

(C) a person is under this section answerable to the child
     in respect of the act or omission,

the child's disabilities are to be regarded as damage
resulting from the wrongful act of that person and
actionable accordingly at the suit of the child.

... (See also subss. 2–4).

Commentary

Whereas, at common law, the parents of children who were
mentally or physically disabled by (say) a drug regime prescribed by a GP for the use of the woman when she was pregnant, could sue the GP in negligence, there was no authority to
suggest either that doctors (GPs or hospital doctors) or drug
companies could be sued by children for injuries they suffered
before their birth. This *lacunae* was filled by the enactment and
coming into force of the Congenital Disabilities (Civil Liability)
Act 1976. (Hereafter: CD(CL)A 1976).

Employing Provisions of the 1976 Act

Key Principle: **Invocation of provisions of the Act requires:
first, that the child must be born alive and must live for at least
48 hours: ss.4(2)(a) and 4(4); secondly, the child, via his next
friend, must establish that his disabilities resulted from an
occurrence which is provided for in s.1(2)(a) and (b) (above).**

Commentary

An occurrence is a tortious, usually negligent, act. Accordingly,
for the tortfeasor to be answerable to the child it must be proved
that: (i) the tortfeasor was negligent; and (ii) that the tortfeasor
breached the duty of care he owed to the affected parent. The
rights of the child to sue arise from this relationship, i.e. the
child's rights are derivative only: s.1(3). Clearly, (iii) causation is
the major hurdle which has to be overcome if the plaintiff/clai-
mant is to discharge the burden of proof.

Prescribed Drugs and Consequential Damage to the Foetus

Key Principle: If a drug prescribed to the child's mother during her pregnancy is alleged to have caused the child's disability, then it may be possible to sue the doctor who prescribed the drug(s) and/or the manufacturer(s) of the drug(s).

Suing Doctors: the difficulty of overcoming a statutory "*Bolam* standard".
Section 1(5) of the 1976 Act provides that:

> "The defendant is *not answerable to the child*, for anything he did or omitted to do *when responsible in a professional capacity* for treating or advising *the parent*, if he took reasonable care having due regard to *the then received professional opinion* applicable to the particular class of case; but this does not mean that he is answerable *only* because he departed from received opinion."

Commentary

For the child to succeed in his claim, he must prove, inter alia, that (1) the doctor knew that his (the child's) mother was pregnant at the time he prescribed the drug(s) for her or at least he ought to have known; and that (2) the doctor should have been aware of the risk posed by the drug. Whereas the doctor has no defence in claiming that the drug regime he prescribed was beneficial for the mother if he then failed to take into account the possibility of harm to her developing foetus, the doctor does have a defence if he acted in accordance with the practice of a responsible body of medical practitioners. Accordingly, the infant claimant, via his next friend, has the onus of discharging the burden of proof, i.e. he has to overcome, inter alia, the *Bolam* standard and establish causation: a difficult task as evidenced, perhaps, by the lack of any significant case law after more than 30 years of the statute being in force.

Suing Drug Companies

Consumer Protection Act 1987 (CPA 1987)

Section 2(1) of the CPA 1987 places the onus on the plaintiff to prove that: (a) the drug was defective; and (b) it caused the relevant injury to the foetus. If causation is established via application of standard tort principles of causation, then liability is strict. Section 3(1) provides that there is a defect in a product if the safety of the product is not such as persons generally are entitled to expect. However, S.4(1)(e) provides that it is a defence for a drug company to show:

> "That the state of scientific and technical knowledge at the relevant time was not such that a producer of products of the same description as the product in question might be expected to have discovered the defect if it had existed in his products while they were under his control."

Commentary
It is evident that this is another statute that places a substantial burden of proof on the infant claimant: one that is not easy to discharge when challenging (say) multi-national drug companies, as evidenced in the (pre-CPA 1987) *Thalidomide* cases.

Limitation of the grounds on which the disabled child is permitted to seek damages

Key Principle: **It must be remembered that as the CD(CL)A 1976 applies to all births from July 1976, any claim for damages must be supported by the provisions of this Act.**

Given that s.1(2) of the 1976 Act specifies that the "occurrence" ("negligent act") is one that "affected the mother in her pregnancy, or affected her or the child in the course of its birth, so that the child is *born* with disabilities which would not otherwise have been present", then it is evident that a claim will be limited to wrongful disabilities and a claim for "wrongful life"—a contention that the child would have been better off not being born at all—will not be entertained: *McKay v Essex A.H.A.* (1982).

Commentary
The limitation in *McKay* (a case involving a girl born before the 1976 Act was enacted) is an example of public policy and the literal approach to statutory interpretation combining to elevate the sanctity of life above the quality of life. By contrast, a severely handicapped new born baby may be allowed to die where the quality of life is minimal and if death is in his "best interests" (below).

Pre-Conception and Post-Conception Occurrences

Key Principle: Section 1(3) of the Congenital Disabilities (Civil Liability) Act 1976 provides the disabled child with the opportunity to pursue damages for pre-conception occurrences and s.2 enshrines a matter of public policy so enabling the pursuit of damages against the child's mother for post-conception occurrences.

Section 1(3)

... a person (here referred to as "the defendant") is answerable to the child if he was liable in tort to the parent or would, if sued in due time have been so; and it is no answer that there could not have been such liability because the parent suffered no actionable injury, if there was breach of a legal duty which, accompanied by injury, would have given rise to the liability.

Commentary

The rights of the child derived from s.1(3) are clearly expressed and they would apply if, say, a man's reproductive capacity is damaged at work by the negligence of his employers and, as a consequence, he has a much reduced likelihood of fathering a normal child. The employer then becomes answerable to the child even if the father appeared to suffer no actionable injury. The general rule is, however, that if either of the parents knew of the risk of begetting an abnormal child, then the employer would not be answerable to the child: s.1(4). However, if the father is the defendant and he knew of the risk but the mother did not, this subsection is inapplicable.

The one post-conception event specifically provided for in s.2 of the CD(CL)A 1976 is where the mother is made liable for her child being born with disabilities which, apart from her breach of duty, would not otherwise be present. s.2 provides that:

> "A woman driving a motor vehicle when she knows (or ought reasonably to know) herself to be pregnant is to be regarded as being under the same duty to take care for the safety of her unborn child as the law imposes on her with respect to the safety of other people; and if in consequence of her breach of that duty her child is born with disabilities which otherwise would not have been present, those disabilities are to be regarded as damage resulting from her wrongful act and actionable accordingly at the suit of the child."

Commentary
The duty referred to in s.2 provides an exception to the general rule in s.1 of the mother having no liability in respect of her disabled child. The specific reference to "motor vehicle" thereby excludes liability for disabilities if the mother had had an accident when riding a bicycle or a horse, for example. The public policy element emerges from the mother having to have motor insurance for driving on the roads and the insurers having to meet the cost of the damages.

(III) Choosing between life and death for a severely handicapped newborn child

Key Principle: **The decision-making in respect of attempting to save the life of a severely handicapped new born baby must be made in the light of the child's right to life, the duties of care owed to him and the quality of life he would lead if the sanctity of life was deemed to outweigh his quality of life.**

Re B [1981] 1 W.L.R. 1421
B was a Down's syndrome baby who also had an intestinal obstruction. The baby's parents refused authorisation for the relatively simple surgery required to save her life. In response, the doctors contacted the local authority, B was made a ward of court, and a judge was asked to authorise the operation. He supported the parents and refused. The case then went to the Court of Appeal.

Held: The operation was authorised, the decision being made "in the best interests of the child". Templeman L.J. said that the Court has to decide:

> "... whether the life of this child is demonstrably going to be so awful that in effect the child must be condemned to die, or whether the life of this child is still so imponderable that it would be wrong for her to be condemned to die".

Commentary
In *Re B*, Templeman L.J. thought the choice was between:

> "whether to allow an operation to take place which may result in the child living for 20 or 30 years as a mongoloid or whether ... to terminate the life of a mongoloid child because she also has an intestinal

complaint. Faced with that choice I have no doubt that it is the duty of this court to decide that the child must live".

Of course:

"There may be cases ... of severe proved damage where the future is so uncertain and where the life of the child is so bound to be full of pain and suffering that the court might be driven to a different conclusion". (per Templeman LJ).

The significance of a decision based on such "a different conclusion" is that the outcome would reflect a judgment made on a "quality-of-life" standard, not a "sanctity-of-life" standard—a decision that has significance also for those of "adult years and sound mind" (See the "right to die" cases in Ch.14).

The ratio from *Re B*, together with those from *Re C* (1989), *Re J* (1990) and *An NHS Trust v MB* (2006) (all discussed below) provides the basis for decision-making in this area of English law.

Key Principle: **For those who adhere to the principle of the sanctity of life being inviolable, decision-making favouring the handicapped newborn being allowed to die is impermissible.**

Re F (1986) {An Australian Case}

Here, Vincent J. expressed the opinion that:

"No parent, no doctor, no court, has any power to determine that the life of any child, however disabled that child may be, will be *deliberately taken from it* ... [*the law*] does *not* permit decisions to be made concerning the quality of life, nor does it enable any assessment to be made as to the value of any human being".

Commentary

First, and stopping short of "deliberately taking the life of a severely handicapped newborn", English law, in s.1 of the Children & Young Persons Act 1933, provides that (inter alia) any wilful ill-treatment or neglect by or on behalf of a person who has attained the age of 16 years could result in a criminal offence carrying a sentence of up to 10 years on indictment; and unreasonable refusal to permit a surgical operation may amount to wilful neglect: *Oakey v Jackson* [1914] 1 K.B. 216.

Secondly, with respect to Vincent J., his dictum doesn't even have the force of a persuasive precedent in English law. Here, decisions are made in the best interests of the child. It has been repeatedly stated that neither parental wishes nor provisions of the European Convention on Human Rights can prevail over the best interests of the child if those interests are best served by avoiding resuscitation and initiating treatment enabling the child's life to be ended peacefully and with dignity: *A National Health Service Trust v D* [2000] 2 F.L.R. 677. This results from:

> "The court's prime and paramount consideration [being concerned with] the best interests of the child. This of course involves ... consideration of the views of the parents concerned ... [but] those views cannot themselves override the court's view of the ward's best interests". (per Cazalet J.).

Cazalet J. decided that Art.2 ECHR ("Everyone's right to life shall be protected by law") was not infringed because the decision was based on D's best interests, and that Art.3 ECHR ("No one shall be subjected to ... inhuman or degrading treatment .. ") encompassed the right to die with dignity.

Key Principle: **Whilst English law will never sanction the deliberate taking of a severely handicapped newborn's life, it is prepared to sanction treatment that will allow the child's life to come to an end peacefully and with dignity.**

Re C (a minor)(wardship: medical treatment) [1989] 2 All E.R. 782

Baby C was born with hydrocephalus. She suffered from "gross and abnormally severe" damage to the cortex of the brain. The damage was irreparable and the prognosis for the child's life was "hopeless": death was inevitable. There was "no prospect of a happy life for this child". She was blind, probably deaf and suffered from generalised spastic cerebral palsy of all four limbs. She was made a ward of court because the local social services department had formed the view that her parents would be unable to properly care for her. An operation to relieve pressure on the brain was authorised by the court and duly took place. The questions then arose as to what further treatment should be provided and whether she should be treated as a non-handi-capped child or in a manner appropriate to her condition.

Held: (CA) The hospital authority was to be allowed "to *treat the baby to allow her life to come to an end peacefully and with dignity*"; and that "the opinion of the local nurses and carers should be taken into account [because] if they believed she was in pain or would suffer less by a particular course of action, it would be correct to consider that course of action, always bearing in mind the balance between short-term gain and needless prolongation of suffering".

Commentary
First, As Derek Morgan noted:

> "This is the first time an English court has acknowledged and condoned the paediatric practice of managing some neonates towards their death, rather than striving with heroic interventions to 'save' or 'treat' at all cost".

Secondly, without affecting the key principle, above, there is the unique case of Re A (Children) (Conjoined Twins: Surgical Separation) [2001] Fam 147. Here, the Court of Appeal upheld the first instance decision of Johnson J. in permitting the separation of conjoined twins knowing that in doing so one of the twins, "Mary", would die: her heart and lungs had no capacity to sustain her life independently of her sister, Jodie, and the severance of the shared aorta through which blood was pumped from Jodie's heart through Mary's body had the inevitable impact of bringing about Mary's death.

However, Court of Appeal said the reasons for the lawfulness of the operation to separate the twins were based on necessity not, as Johnson J. had decided, that Mary's life would be worth nothing to her. The sanctity of life doctrine, enshrined as a fundamental principle of law, commanded such respect that it had to be accepted that each life had inherent value in itself, however grave the impairment of some of the bodily functions of the particular individual.

Key Principle: **The Court of Appeal has sanctioned "life-or-death" decision-making in respect of a severely handicapped** child who was *neither on the point of death nor on the point of dying* at the time the decision was made.

Re J (a minor) (wardship: medical treatment) [1990] 3 All E.R. 930

J, a ward of court, had been born nearly 13 weeks prematurely. At birth, J was not breathing; he was immediately placed on a ventilator, drip fed and given antibiotics to counteract infection. He was taken off ventilation after a month though he required additional oxygen at irregular intervals. He was epileptic, and the consensus of the medical evidence was that he was likely to develop serious spastic quadriplegia (i.e. paralysis of both arms and legs) and that he would be both blind and deaf. He was unlikely ever to be able to speak or to develop even limited intellectual abilities but he would experience pain. The prognosis was that any further collapse which required ventilation would be fatal. However, he was *neither on the point of death nor on the point of dying*. The question arose whether if he suffered further collapse the medical staff at the hospital where J was being cared for should reventilate him in the event of his breathing stopping.

Held: (CA) *The appropriate course was that J should not be ventilated were he to cease breathing again.* In determining the best interests of the child, Lord Donaldson said that:

"What doctors and the court have to decide is whether ... a particular decision as to medical treatment should be taken which as a *side effect* will render death more or less likely. ... What can never be justified is the use of drugs or surgical procedures with the *primary* purpose of doing so".

Surprisingly, however, Lord Donaldson approved a passage originally expressed in an American case, where Asch J. had put forward the "subjective" test, i.e. "the court must decide what the patient would choose, *if he were able to make a sound judgement*".

Also, in *Re J*, Taylor L.J. said that:

"Two decisions of this court have dealt with cases at the extremes of the spectrum of affliction [viz.,] Re C ... [and] the earlier case of Re B ...

"Those two cases ... decide[d] [that] where the child is terminally ill the court will not require treatment to prolong life; but where, at the other extreme, the child is severely handicapped although not intolerably so and treatment for a discrete condition can enable life to continue for an appreciable period, albeit subject to that severe handicap, the treatment should be given.

"It is to be noted that [in *Re B*] Templeman LJ did not say, even *obiter*, that where the child's life would be bound to be full of pain and suffering there would come a point at which the court should rule against prolonging life by treatment. He went no further than to say there may be cases where the court might take that view.…

"I consider that the correct approach is for the court to judge the quality of life the child would have to endure if given the treatment and decide whether in all the circumstances such a life would be so afflicted as to be *intolerable to that child*."

Commentary

It was wholly inappropriate of Lord Donaldson M.R. and Taylor L.J. to adopt the utterly baseless position of associating "intolerability" with a consideration of what the child in question, *if capable of exercising sound judgement*, would deem to be an intolerable life. To seek the impossible cannot be meaningful at any time: to seek a rational decision from a severely handicapped neonate is beyond the bounds of credibility. Moreover, McKenzie J. in the Canadian case of *Re Superintendent of Family and Child Service and Dawson (Re Stephen Dawson)* (1983) had made it clear that the child at the beginning of life would have no yardstick by which to judge this "intolerability" when he said that the child:

".. would not [be able to] compare his life with that of a person enjoying normal advantages. He would know nothing of a normal person's life having never experienced it".

Key Principle: **The courts are the sole arbiters of what is in the best interests of a severely handicapped newborn and decisions can be made which are contrary to all medical opinions heard in court.**

An NHS Trust v MB [2006] 2 F.L.R. 319

The claimant NHS trust (N) sought a declaration that it would be lawful and in M's best interests for N to withdraw all forms of ventilation from him, and M's parents applied for a declaration that it should be lawful and in M's best interests for a tracheostomy to be performed to enable long term ventilation to be carried out. M had been in hospital since the age of seven weeks. He suffered from Type 1 spinal muscular atrophy (SMA) i.e. *the*

*most severe type for those who are not born dead. The condition was
progressive and degenerative. Even with the continuation of treatment
death was inevitable.* M could survive for a small number of years
or could die suddenly and soon. M had not been able to breathe
unaided since before his first birthday and required positive
pressure ventilation via an invasive endotracheal tube. It was
said that M's cognitive function was impossible to assess; and
that it was very difficult to assess how much discomfort or distress M experienced, but it was inevitable that some interven-
tions were uncomfortable for him. N considered that the quality
of life for M was so low and the burdens of living so great that it
was unethical to continue artificially to keep him alive. At least
10 doctors and consultants were of the opinion that: M "has an
intolerably poor quality of life, and this will only get worse ...
The treatments currently provided for M are futile and sadly will
not change the outcome of his illness". (para.26 of the judgment)

Held: It   was probable and had to assumed that M continued to
see and to hear and to feel touch; to have an awareness of his
surroundings, in particular of the people who were closest to
him, namely his family; and to have the normal thoughts and
thought processes of a small child of 18 months, with the proviso
that because he had never left hospital he had not experienced
the same range of stimuli and experiences as a more normal 18
month old. Accordingly, *it was **not** in M's best interests to discontinue ventilation with the inevitable result that he would die.* M
had age appropriate cognition, a relationship of value with his
family, and other pleasures from sight, touch and sound. Those
benefits were precious and real and *the routine discomfort, distress
and pain that M suffered did **not** outweigh those benefits.* However, it
would not be in M's best interests to undergo procedures that
went beyond maintaining ventilation, if they involved the positive infliction of pain and would mean, if they became necessary,
that M had moved naturally towards death, despite the ventilation. Those procedures were cardio pulmonary resuscitation,
electro-cardiogram monitoring, administration of intravenous
antibiotics and blood sampling. It was in M's best interests and
lawful to withhold or not to administer any of those forms of
treatment. The declaration reflecting that decision would be
permissive in effect and therefore would **not** prevent a doctor
giving such treatment.

Commentary

It is remarkable that Holman J. overrode unanimous medical opinion, particularly when the list of "burdens" far outweighed the list of "benefits" that were presented to him. Of course, M's perceived cognitive abilities contrasted with the absence of those in *Re C*, above, though for both M and C, death very early in life was inevitable. M's death was announced in December 2006.

Generally, the medical profession would be supported in their application for a declaration—sometimes by the parents of the handicapped child—but they could also be granted the declaration in the face of parental opposition.

In another Re C case (the first was discussed, above), *Re C (a baby)* [1996] 2 F.L.R. 43, the President of the Family Division, Sir Stephen Brown, permitted a declaration on behalf of the medical profession and the child's parents to discontinue the ventilation of a baby girl experiencing "almost a living death" {The baby had become blind and deaf and was suffering repeated convulsions after contracting meningitis}. The medical profession were able to terminate the treatment as soon as they thought appropriate.

Even if the parents disagreed with the medical profession—as was the case in the third Re C case, *Re C (a minor)(medical treatment)* (1997) 40 B.M.L.R. 31—a declaration permitting the medical profession to refrain from reventilating a child who had suffered a respiratory relapse and who was in a "no chance situation" would be appropriate because:

> "[To be subjected to parental determination] would be tantamount to requiring the doctors to undertake a course of treatment which they are unwilling to do. The court could not consider making an order which would require them so to do". (per Sir Stephen Brown P).

Whereas Holman J. did not grant the NHS Trust the declaration they sought, other judges have faced equally severe criticism for agreeing with medical professionals and not the parents of the severely handicapped children—particularly in the cases of Charlotte Wyatt & Luke Winston-Jones.

"Best interests" and the cases of Charlotte Wyatt & Luke Winston-Jones

Both sets of parents of the severely handicapped neonates opposed applications for declarations that it would not be unlawful to withhold ventilation, should it be required. The judges agreed with the medical prognosis in each case, however, and against parental wishes. Luke Winston-Jones, who had Edwards syndrome (average life span of a child with this condition is less than two months) died shortly after the hearing in his case, whereas Charlotte Wyatt (who has serious heart and lung problems and who, prior to the declaration being sought, had to resuscitated at least three times after she had stopped breathing) remains alive and the initial order in her case has been relaxed. She was due to go into foster care when she was released from hospital, however, as she "may no longer have a stable home to go to" following the separation of her parents and the reported drug overdose her father took "after his wife walked out with their other three children": "Baby Charlotte faces foster care as parents separate", *The Sunday Times*, February 12, 2006, p.3.

Of course, where the judiciary agrees with the parent(s) of the handicapped child, the anomalous position of *Re T* can arise:

Re T (a minor) (Wardship: medical treatment) 1 All E.R. 906
As in the third Re C case (above), there was a disagreement between the medical profession and the child's mother—only this time it was the mother that didn't want the child to be treated when the medical profession thought that there was a good chance of a successful transplant and that the operation would be in the child's best interests. Indeed, even in the absence of a transplant, the child might live for two and-a-half years. However, the mother's wishes prevailed given "... the prospect of forcing the devoted mother of this young baby to the consequences of this major invasive surgery ...".

The point about the last case is that it has introduced an uncertain delimitation between what is "acceptable" as selective non-treatment in the best interests of a neonate and what constitutes involuntary, passive euthanasia for an older person.

Key Principle: **Notwithstanding "dubious judicial decision-making" if a decision to allow a severely handicapped newborn to die is contemplated, it must be made by the courts. A doctor, who acts on the wishes of parents, but without the approval of the courts, may be indicted on a homicide charge.**

R. v Arthur (1981) 12 BMLR 1

A baby boy was born with uncomplicated Down's syndrome in the hospital where Dr Arthur was consultant paediatrician. The parents of the baby boy did not wish him to survive. Accordingly, Dr Arthur noted: "Parents do not wish it to survive. Nursing care only". Dr Arthur then prescribed a sedative drug, DF118, which also suppresses appetite. The baby died within 69 hours of birth. The prosecution alleged that the prescription of the drug would not only suppress appetite but starve the baby to death; that apart from being a Down's syndrome baby, the baby was otherwise healthy, and that his death resulted from lack of sustenance and the effect of the drug causing him to succumb to broncho-pneumonia. However, following the defence adducing evidence that the baby suffered from severe brain and lung damage; that Dr Arthur had followed established practice in the management of such an infant; and, that in the first three days of life, normal babies take in little or no sustenance and usually lose weight (which the dead baby had not done), the judge directed that the charge be altered to attempted murder. On the law for the jury, the judge stressed that there is "... no special law in this country that places doctors in a separate category and gives them special protection over the rest of us ... [i.e.] if the doctor gives [the severely handicapped child] drugs in excessive amount so that drugs will cause death then the doctor commits murder". However, in his summing-up, the trial judge, Farquharson J., concluded that the jury would have to think long and hard before deciding that eminent doctors "have evolved standards which amount to committing crime".

Held: Dr Arthur was acquitted.

Commentary

First, it seems impossible to reconcile the jury's decision-making in the criminal case of R. v Arthur (1981) with that of the Court of Appeal in the civil case of *Re B* (1981). The parents' wishes prevailed in the former—a case of uncomplicated Down's syndrome—but were rejected in the latter—a case of intestinal obstruction in addition to Down's syndrome.

Secondly, it is clear that *R. v Arthur* cannot be followed as: "What can never be justified is the use of drugs or surgical procedures with the *primary* purpose of [bringing about the child's death]" per *Re J* (1990) (above). This, of course, is subject to necessity, as in the case of *Re A (children) (Conjoined Twins: Surgical Separation)* [2001] Fam 147, above.

The Brazier Report: Guidelines for Future Practice

The *Brazier Report, Critical Care Decisions in Fetal and Neonatal Medicine*, was published in November 2006. It recommended that premature babies born after only 22 weeks in the womb or earlier should not be routinely resuscitated.

The Report noted that it is "extremely rare" for babies born before 22 weeks to survive and only around 1 per cent of babies born between 22 and 23 weeks survive to leave hospital.

Guidelines put forward recommend that intensive care should not be given to babies born before 22 weeks and babies born between 22 and 23 weeks should not, in normal practice, be given intensive care unless parents make a request and doctors agree. Professor Margaret Brazier, who chaired the committee that produced the guidelines, said:

> "Natural instincts are to try to save all babies, even if the baby's chances of survival are low. However, we don't think it is always right to put a baby through the stress and pain of invasive treatment if the baby is unlikely to get any better and death is inevitable."

There's always an exception...

The recommendations in the *Brazier Report* should be contrasted with the report in *The Times*, February 21, 2007, entitled *"Tiniest baby is heading for home"*, where it was reported that:

> "*Amillia Taylor* should not have been born until next month. Incredibly, she is already four months old and should soon be at home with her parents after a phenomenal fight for survival.
>
> She was born in October after only 21 weeks and six days in her mother's womb, and is *the first baby to survive delivery at less than 22 weeks*.
>
> Her parents, who went through in-vitro fertilisation treatment to conceive, chose the name Amillia for their 10oz (300g) infant because they read that it meant 'resilient'. Now aged 17 weeks, she has lived up to her name and beaten the medical odds. She weighs 4½lbs (2kg) and doctors are ready to let her go home."

12. RESEARCH

Research and Competent Adult Participants

Key Principle: Ethical guidance and the law relating to medical research on human subjects (participants) each aims to eliminate, and avoid a repetition of, the abusive practices carried out prior to and during Second World War and to protect the consenting participants.

Ethical Guidance
The principal ethical guidance emerged, and has evolved, from the 10 principles that constituted the Nuremberg Code, which was formulated in the Nuremberg War Crimes Tribunal.

NUREMBERG CODE
The points include:

1.   The voluntary consent of the human subject is absolutely essential. This means that the person involved should have legal capacity to give consent; should be so situated as to be able to exercise free power of choice, without the intervention of any element of force, fraud, deceit, duress, over-reaching, or other ulterior form of constraint or coercion; and should have sufficient knowledge and comprehension of the elements of the subject matter involved as to enable him to make an understanding and enlightened decision....

2.   The experiment should be such as to yield fruitful results for the good of society, unprocurable by other methods or means of study, and not random and unnecessary in nature.

3.   The experiment should be so designed and based on the results of animal experimentation and a knowledge of the natural history of the disease or other problem under study that the anticipated results will justify the performance of the experiment.

4. The experiment should be so conducted as to avoid all unnecessary physical and mental suffering and injury...

6. The degree of risk to be taken should never exceed that determined by the humanitarian importance of the problem to be solved by the experiment.

7. Proper preparations should be made and adequate facilities provided to protect the experimental subject against even remote possibilities of injury, disability, or death

9. During the course of the experiment the human subject should be at liberty to bring the experiment to an end if he has reached the physical or mental state where continuation of the experiment seems to him to be impossible.

Commentary

Whereas the Nuremberg Code was formulated by a War Crimes Tribunal, the first international code developed by the World Medical Association (an international representative body of doctors)—the Declaration of Helsinki—is regarded as the first major contribution of the medical profession at self-regulation over matters of medical research on human subjects. Of course, this element of self-regulation has no connection with the degree of self-regulation the medical profession experienced under the Medical Act 1983 prior to the 2002 and later amendments: see Ch.2.

DECLARATION OF HELSINKI
Elements of the Declaration include:

A INTRODUCTION
4. Medical progress is based on research which ultimately must rest in part on experimentation involving human subjects.

5. In medical research on human subjects, considerations related to the well-being of the human subject should take precedence over the interests of science and society.

6. The primary purpose of medical research involving human subjects is to improve prophylactic, diagnostic and therapeutic procedures and the understanding of the aetiology and pathogenesis of disease. Even the best proven prophylactic, diagnostic, and therapeutic methods

must continuously be challenged through research for their effectiveness, efficiency, accessibility and quality.

8. Medical research is subject to ethical standards that promote respect for all human beings and protect their health and rights. Some research populations are vulnerable and need special protection. The particular needs of the economically and medically disadvantaged must be recognized. Special attention is also required for those who cannot give or refuse consent for themselves, ...

B BASIC PRINCIPLES FOR ALL MEDICAL RESEARCH

10. It is the duty of the physician in medical research to protect the life, health, privacy, and dignity of the human subject.

13. The design and performance of each experimental procedure involving human subjects should be clearly formulated in an experimental protocol. This protocol should be submitted for consideration, comment, guidance, and where appropriate, approval to a specially appointed ethical review committee, which must be independent of the investigator, the sponsor or any other kind of undue influence. This independent committee should be in conformity with the laws and regulations of the country in which the research experiment is performed. ...

15. Medical research involving human subjects should be conducted only by scientifically qualified persons and under the supervision of a clinically competent medical person. The responsibility for the human subject must always rest with a medically qualified person and never rest on the subject of the research, even though the subject has given consent.

18. Medical research involving human subjects should only be conducted if the importance of the objective outweighs the inherent risks and burdens to the subject. This is especially important when the human subjects are healthy volunteers.

20. The subjects must be volunteers and informed participants in the research project.

24. In any research on human beings, each potential subject must be adequately informed of the aims, methods,

sources of funding, any possible conflicts of interest, institutional affiliations of the researcher, the anticipated benefits and potential risks of the study and the discomfort it may entail. ... After ensuring that the subject has understood the information, the physician should then obtain the subject's freely-given informed consent, preferably in writing. If the consent cannot be obtained in writing, the non-written consent must be formally documented and witnessed.

C ADDITIONAL PRINCIPLES FOR MEDICAL RESEARCH COMBINED WITH MEDICAL CARE

28. The physician may combine medical research with medical care, only to the extent that the research is justified by its potential prophylactic, diagnostic or therapeutic value. When medical research is combined with medical care, additional standards apply to protect the patients who are research subjects.

31. The physician should fully inform the patient which aspects of the care are related to the research. The refusal of a patient to participate in a study must never interfere with the patient-physician relationship.

32. In the treatment of a patient, where proven prophylactic, diagnostic and therapeutic methods do not exist or have been ineffective, the physician, with informed consent from the patient, must be free to use unproven or new prophylactic, diagnostic and therapeutic measures, if in the physician's judgement it offers hope of saving life, re-establishing health or alleviating suffering. Where possible, these measures should be made the object of research, designed to evaluate their safety and efficacy.

Commentary

The Declaration of Helsinki was adopted by the 18th World Medical Association General Assembly in 1964 and has been amended five times (up to 2000) and required addenda on the clarification of a couple of paragraphs in 2002 and 2004. As in the Nuremberg Code, the focus on "informed consent" in the Declaration of Helsinki is designed to ensure that the abuses masquerading as "medical research", such as those carried out under the Nazi regime and the 40 years of the infamous Tuskegee Syphilis Study (see below) in America, are not replicated.

The rights of the individual, as expressed in the Declaration of Helsinki, are not absolute, however. Note that para.5 expresses the view that: "considerations related to the well-being of the human subject *should* take precedence over the interests of science and society". However, whereas "should", not "must", clearly gives scope for exceptional circumstances, it does indicate that consequentialism / utilitarianism isn't the prevailing ethical theory underpinning medical research on human subjects. By contrast, see s.33(3) of the Mental Capacity Act 2005, below.

It should also be noted that the latest version of the Declaration of Helsinki does not stress any distinction between supposedly "therapeutic" and "non-therapeutic" research—but note para.28, above.

More importantly, perhaps, in medical research, is the focus on the ethical requirement of *primum non nocere* (first, do no harm) unless, of course, the risk of harm can be justified by the potential benefits of the research; and the ethical and legal requirement to act in the patient's best interests—particularly so in relation to incompetent patients. Indeed, with regard to experimental treatment, as sanctioned by para.32, see the case of *Simms v Simms*, below.

Tuskegee Study of Untreated Syphilis in the Negro Male

"Arguably the most infamous biomedical research study in U.S. history" (per Katz, *et al.*, (2006)) was that which was carried out to observe and note the succession of phases syphilis exhibited when left untreated. Initially, the research was intended to discover whether the patients would benefit by not being treated with the then known remedies which were toxic and of questionable effectiveness.

The study was carried out in Tuskegee, Alabama, which was identified as the area having the highest prevalence of syphilis in the six southern States examined. 399 African-American men with latent syphilis and a control group (those without the disease) of 201 were enrolled on the study.

Throughout the 40 years of the study—1932 until 1972—the subjects were told they were being treated for "bad blood". Some were given placebo "treatments", but no-one received any anti-syphilitic treatment. Indeed, no one in the study group was treated with, or even informed of, penicillin, which had become recognised as an effective drug from the time of its availability in 1943.

The subjects were provided with warm meals on the days they

were examined and, having an agreed to an autopsy following their deaths, given free burials. By the time the study ended, 28 men had died of syphilis, 100 others died from syphilis-related complications, at least 40 wives had been infected and 19 children had been born with congenital syphilis.

"The longest non-therapeutic experiment on human beings in medical history" (Sharma (2005)) ended in 1972, when the press were informed by a Public Health Services venereal-disease investigator who had first expressed his concerns six years earlier.

The study was notorious for: having no experimental data from animal studies; for not providing any proper medical protection or management; and for not obtaining any of the subjects' informed consent.

In 1974, an out-of-court settlement was agreed with each survivor receiving $37,500 in damages and heirs of the deceased received $15,000; and in 1997, President Bill Clinton said: ". . . on behalf of the American people, what the United States government did was shameful and I am sorry".

Key Principle: **The emphasis on the need for the full, free and uncoerced "informed consent" of a competent participant in medical research is a feature of codes of ethics and English law.**

Code of Ethics
Paragraph 23 Declaration of Helsinki
23. When obtaining informed consent for the research project the physician should be particularly cautious if the subject is in a dependent relationship with the physician or may consent under duress. In that case the informed consent should be obtained by a well-informed physician who is not engaged in the investigation and who is completely independent of this relationship.

Law
At law, para.3(1) of Pt 1, Sch. 1 to the Medicines for Human Use Regulations 2004 (SI 2004 /1031) provides that:

"A person gives informed consent to take part in a clinical trial only if his decision:

(a) is given freely after that person is informed of the nature, significance, implications and risks of the trial; and

(b) either

(i) is evidenced in writing, or otherwise marked, by that person, so as to indicate his consent, or

(ii) if the person is unable to sign or to mark a document so as to indicate his consent, is given orally in the presence of at least one witness and recorded in writing."

Commentary

Whilst it remains debateable whether English law has a doctrine of "informed consent" as developed in the American cases of *Salgo* and *Canterbury v Spence* (see Ch.4), the amount of information to be disclosed to a competent research subject prior to the beginning of the research project in England is unlikely to vary from another North American case, the Canadian case of *Halushka v University of Saskatchewan*:

Halushka v University of Saskatchewan (1965) 52 W.W.R. 608

Here, Hall J.A. expressed the view that:

> "There can be no exception to the ordinary requirements of disclosure in the case of research as there may well be in ordinary medical practice. The researcher does not have to balance the probable effect of lack of treatment against the risk involved in treatment itself. The example of risks being properly hidden from a patient when it is important that he should not worry can have no application in the field of research. The subject of medical experimentation is entitled to a full and frank disclosure of all the facts, probabilities and opinions which a reasonable man might be expected to consider before giving his consent."

Key Principle: **It may be doubted that full, free and uncoerced "informed consent" can be given in respect of payment for "voluntary" participation in the early stages of clinical trials for a new drug.**

TGN1412

In essence, before a new drug is marketed, the research programme on human beings that follows successful trials on animals, is divided into three phases each phase involving an increasing number of people. Phase 1 involves only a small number of healthy volunteers and the aim is to establish the safety of the drug and to determine what the most effective dosage of the drug might be.

TGN1412 was a biological agent, a "monoclonal antibody" targeted as treating diseases such as rheumatoid arthritis. In laboratory tests, TeGenero, the German developer of the drug, said it had performed as they had hoped.

Because Phase 1 trials confer no benefits on those who take part in them, payment was offered at about £150 per day or just over £2,000 for a commitment of a couple of weeks. Half-a-dozen healthy volunteers and a control group of two injected with a placebo, participated in the trial at Northwick Park Hospital, London, in March 2006.

All six who were injected with TGN1412 became very ill very quickly and all suffered some degree of multiple organ failure and required admission to intensive care. One volunteer was so badly affected that he had to have some fingers and toes amputated. This followed the heart, liver and kidney failure and pneumonia and septicaemia he had already suffered.

The trials that were due to start in Germany were abandoned.

Commentary
The report published by the MHRA (Medicines and Healthcare Products Regulatory agency) concluded that the harm suffered by the volunteers was due to an "unpredicted biological action" in human beings. The conclusion was reached after finding no evidence of crime or a technical error.

However, the report of the Expert Scientific Group on Phase One Clinical Trials that followed made 22 recommendations and accused the MHRA of being too lax in its decision to approve the TGN1412 trial.

Perhaps the most controversial element of being offered inducements for taking part in Phase 1 trials, however, is that it is offering a financial "reward" to healthy participants for accepting unknown risks—albeit that proper testing on animals should alert the developers to any possible risks / side effects.

Yet, whereas the ethics of offering financial inducements to those who are not financially independent and are willing to accept risks may be questionable, the risks remain the same if they are accepted by those acting altruistically—though, perhaps, the market for such do-gooders is appreciatively smaller.

The law relating to the clinical trials of medicines is discussed later in the chapter. Here, it will suffice to note that: regulation 32 of SI 2004/1031 (The "Clinical Trials Regulations") requires an investigator to report "any serious adverse event which occurs in a subject at a trial site at which he is responsible for the conduct of a clinical trial immediately to the sponsor"; and that reg.15 requires provision to be made for the insurance or indemnity of the investigator (researcher) or sponsor.

Key Principle: **Whereas providing a patient with a placebo (a pharmacologically inert substance) may be said to be "harmful" when an existing therapy exists, the WMA has attached a note of clarification to para.29 of the Declaration of Helsinki explaining the circumstances under which a placebo-controlled trial may be ethically acceptable.**

29. The benefits, risks, burdens and effectiveness of a new method should be tested against those of the best current prophylactic, diagnostic, and therapeutic methods. This does not exclude the use of placebo, or no treatment, in studies where no proven prophylactic, diagnostic or therapeutic method exists.

Note of clarification on paragraph 29 of the WMA Declaration of Helsinki

The WMA hereby reaffirms its position that extreme care must be taken in making use of a placebo-controlled trial and that in general this methodology should only be used in the absence of existing proven therapy. However, a placebo-controlled trial may be ethically acceptable, even if proven therapy is available, under the following circumstances:

— Where for compelling and scientifically sound methodological reasons its use is necessary to determine the efficacy or safety of a prophylactic, diagnostic or therapeutic method; or

— Where a prophylactic, diagnostic or therapeutic method is being investigated for a minor condition and the patients who receive placebo will not be subject to any additional risk of serious or irreversible harm.

All other provisions of the Declaration of Helsinki must be
adhered to, especially the need for appropriate ethical and scientific review.

Commentary
A number of ethical and legal issues arise from providing
patients with placebos. First, from the doctor's perspective, it
may be questioned whether the doctor can act in his patient's
best interests (as required by the Hippocratic Oath) if he provides him with a placebo when there is a known, effective drug
that can be administered. Secondly, it must be queried whether a
patient can be said to have consented to a placebo unless, of
course, he was specifically informed either that that was what he
was going to receive or that he would be in a group that might be
given the placebo. In either case, if the patient is informed that he
will, or might, receive such "treatment", it may negate any
psychological impact the placebo could be intended to provide.
Thirdly, the legitimacy of providing a placebo when a known,
effective drug is available, is questionable as, at best, it delays—if
not prevents—any therapeutic benefit accruing to the patient.
(Refer to the Tuskegee study, above).
    Of course, as provided for in para.29 of the Helsinki Declara-
tion, the provision of a placebo may be acceptable in the absence
of any proven treatment.

Research and Incompetent Adult Patients

Key Principle: **Research (and experimental treatment) on
incompetent adults is permitted under paras 24 and 25 of the
Declaration of Helsinki, it has been sanctioned at common law
and is now provided for under provisions of the Mental
Capacity Act 2005, as amended.**

Declaration of Helsinki, paragraphs 24 and 25
24. For a research subject who is legally incompetent, physically
or mentally incapable of giving consent or is a legally incompetent minor, the investigator must obtain informed consent
from the legally authorized representative in accordance with
applicable law. These groups should not be included in research
unless the research is necessary to promote the health of the
population represented and this research cannot instead be
performed on legally competent persons.

25. When a subject deemed legally incompetent, such as a minor child, is able to give assent to decisions about participation in research, the investigator must obtain that assent in addition to the consent of the legally authorized representative.

(See also para.32, above, and its sanctioning of experimental treatment)

At common law

Simms v Simms [2003] Fam 83

In two separate cases the patients, an 18-year-old male (JS) and a 16-year-old female (JA), were suffering from probable variant Creutzfeldt-Jakob disease ("vCJD"). Whereas no recognised effective treatment or cure had yet been found, overseas medical research had identified a treatment which seemed successful in mice. The parents of the incompetent teenage patients sought declaratory relief that it was lawful for them, as being in their best interests, to have the treatment which, of course, had not been tested on humans.

Held: The declarations were granted in each case. There was a responsible body of relevant medical opinion which supported the innovative treatment proposed; and that the concept of "benefit" to a patient suffering from vCJD encompassed an improvement from the present state of illness, a continuation of the existing state of illness without deterioration and the pro-longation of life. Thus, it was decided that there were possible benefits to the patients from such pioneering treatment where there was no alternative treatment available. Accordingly, it was in the best interests of each patient that the proposed treatment be carried out.

Commentary

First, at para.48 of her judgment, Dame Elizabeth Butler Sloss P said:

"To the question: 'Is there a responsible body of medical opinion which would support the ... treatment within the United Kingdom?', the answer in one sense is unclear. This is untried treatment and there is so far no validation of the experimental work done in Japan. The *Bolam* test ought not to be allowed to inhibit medical progress. And it is clear that if one waited for the *Bolam* test to be complied with to its fullest extent, no innovative work such as the use of penicillin or performing heart transplant surgery would ever be attempted: see

Lord Diplock in *Sidaway v Board of Governors of the Bethlem Royal Hospital and the Maudsley Hospital* [1985] A.C. 871, 893. I do, however, have evidence from responsible medical opinion which does not reject the research."

Secondly, the distinction between "research" and "experimental treatment" (if one exists) is debatable. Generally, research is subject to a pre-determined protocol, including a control group, and ethical approval; and research on the effect of drugs human participants generally follows extensive testing on animals. By contrast, experimental treatment may be the "last resort": the only possible course deemed available in the absence of any proven therapeutic procedure. Even so, experimentation must be carried out in the best interests of the patient. As noted in *Simms v Simms*, the performance of experimental treatment is likely to be subject to the granting of a declaration of lawfulness from the courts. Of course, the reference to "experimentation" in para.4 of the Declaration of Helsinki and "medical research" in para.5 clouds any perceived distinction between experimentation and medical research. Moreover, it is just as debatable as to when research on (say) organ transplants evolves into what is akin to "routine" *treatment*.

Thirdly, not only is there is no statutory definition of what constitutes research, there is no primary legislation exclusively devoted to regulating the conduct of research on human subjects. (The limited provisions of the Mental Capacity Act 2005 are discussed below). By contrast, the Animals (Scientific Procedures) Act 1986 regulates research on non-human vertebrates.

By contrast with *Simms v Simms*, in *An NHS Trust v J*, the patient's family opposed the administration of innovative treatment.

An NHS Trust v J [2006] EWHC 3152 (Fam)

An application was made by the NHS trust to withdraw all life sustaining treatment to a 53-year-old woman who had been in a persistent vegetative state for more than three years. The proceedings had the support of J's family—J's husband, two daughters and J's mother—who were devoted to her. However, just before the hearing, an article was published suggesting that patients in the PVS might be revived to a level of wakefulness that would enable them to communicate in a meaningful manner upon the administration of Zolpidem, a drug normally used for the treatment of insomnia. On the basis of expert testimony that if the drug was administered and there was no response within three days there would be no response at all, the Official Solicitor opposed the declaration. Following administration of Zolpidem on three consecutive days, noting there was no increased mental awareness and hearing then that there were no clinical reasons why artificial nutrition and hydration should not be removed, Sir Mark Potter P granted the declaration sought by the trust.

Commentary

Now that the Mental Capacity Act 2005 is in force, invocation of certain of its provisions could ensure that a different outcome would be perfectly possible. See ss.1–5 and 24 for some principles and advance decisions to refuse treatment, respectively. The more pertinent provisions for the purposes of this chapter follow.

Elements of the Provisions of the Mental Capacity Act 2005 relating to the participation of adults lacking capacity to consent to research:

Mental Capacity Act 2005, sections 30–34

30. Research

(1) Intrusive research carried out on, or in relation to, a person who lacks capacity to consent to it is unlawful unless it is carried out—

    (a) as part of a research project which is for the time being approved by the appropriate body for the purposes of this Act in accordance with section 31, and

    (b) in accordance with sections 32 and 33.

(2) Research is intrusive if it is of a kind that would be unlawful if it was carried out—

    (a) on or in relation to a person who had capacity to consent to it, but

    (b) without his consent.

(4) "Appropriate body", in relation to a research project, means the person, committee or other body specified in regulations made by the appropriate authority as the

appropriate body in relation to a project of the kind in question.

...

31. Requirements for approval

(1) The appropriate body may not approve a research project for the purposes of this Act unless satisfied that the following requirements will be met in relation to research carried out as part of the project on, or in relation to, a person who lacks capacity to consent to taking part in the project ("P").

(2) The research must be connected with—

  (a) an impairing condition affecting P, or
  (b) its treatment.

(3) "Impairing condition" means a condition which is (or may be) attributable to, or which causes or contributes to (or may cause or contribute to), the impairment of, or disturbance in the functioning of, the mind or brain.

(4) There must be reasonable grounds for believing that research of comparable effectiveness cannot be carried out if the project has to be confined to, or relate only to, persons who have capacity to consent to taking part in it.

(5) The research must—

  (a) have the potential to benefit P without imposing on P a burden that is disproportionate to the potential benefit to P, or
  (b) be intended to provide knowledge of the causes or treatment of, or of the care of persons affected by, the same or a similar condition.

(7) There must be reasonable arrangements in place for ensuring that the requirements of sections 32 and 33 will be met.

32. Consulting carers etc.

(1) This section applies if a person ("R")—

  (a) is conducting an approved research project, and

(b) wishes to carry out research, as part of the project, on or in relation to a person ("P") who lacks capacity to consent to taking part in the project.

(2) R must take reasonable steps to identify a person who—

(a) otherwise than in a professional capacity or for remuneration, is engaged in caring for P or is interested in P's welfare, and

(b) is prepared to be consulted by R under this section.

(3) If R is unable to identify such a person he must, in accordance with guidance issued by the appropriate authority, nominate a person who—

(a) is prepared to be consulted by R under this section, but

(b) has no connection with the project.

(4) R must provide the person identified under subsection (2), or nominated under subsection (3), with information about the project and ask him—

(a) for advice as to whether P should take part in the project, and

(b) what, in his opinion, P's wishes and feelings about taking part in the project would be likely to be if P had capacity in relation to the matter.

(5) If, at any time, the person consulted advises R that in his opinion P's wishes and feelings would be likely to lead him to decline to take part in the project (or to wish to withdraw from it) if he had capacity in relation to the matter, R must ensure—

(a) if P is not already taking part in the project, that he does not take part in it;

(b) if P is taking part in the project, that he is withdrawn from it.

. . .

33. Additional safeguards

(1) This section applies in relation to a person who is taking part in an approved research project even though he lacks capacity to consent to taking part.

(2) Nothing may be done to, or in relation to, him in the course of the research—

    (a) to which he appears to object (whether by showing signs of resistance or otherwise) except where what is being done is intended to protect him from harm or to reduce or prevent pain or discomfort, or

    (b) which would be contrary to—

        (i) an advance decision of his which has effect, or
        (ii) any other form of statement made by him and not subsequently withdrawn,

of which R is aware.

(3) The interests of the person must be assumed to outweigh those of science and society.

(4) If he indicates (in any way) that he wishes to be withdrawn from the project he must be withdrawn without delay.

34. Loss of capacity during research project

(1) This section applies where a person ("P")—

    (a) has consented to take part in a research project begun before the commencement of section 30, but

    (b) before the conclusion of the project, loses capacity to consent to continue to take part in it.

(2) The appropriate authority may by regulations provide that, despite P's loss of capacity, research of a prescribed kind may be carried out on, or in relation to, P if—

    (a) the project satisfies prescribed requirements,

    (b) any information or material relating to P which is used in the research is of a prescribed description and was obtained before P's loss of capacity, and

    (c) the person conducting the project takes in relation to P such steps as may be prescribed for the purpose of protecting him.

. . .

Commentary
The requirement for ethical approval and the potential for the research to benefit the patient should be noted. Together with the

"additional safeguards", the provisions of ss.30–34 aim to protect the patient from harm and promote treatment that would be beneficial to him. Note that the provisions apply to adults, only: s.2(5) provides that the Act does not apply to minors under the age of 16.

Research involving children

Key Principle: **Whereas research involving children may be deemed ethically acceptable under paras 24 and 25 of the Declaration of Helsinki and it may be sanctioned by the BMA, the legal regulation of non-invasive research on minors under the age of 16, that involves their participation in clinical trials of medicines, is provided for under the Medicines for Human Use (Clinical Trials) Regulations 2004, SI 2004/1031.**

Declaration of Helsinki
See again paras 24 and 25 of the Declaration of Helsinki, above.

The Medicines for Human Use (Clinical Trials) Regulations 2004, SI 2004/1031 Interpretation

Regulation 2–(1) In these regulations—
"minor" means any person under the age of 16 years;

Schedule 1 Part 4

CONDITIONS AND PRINCIPLES WHICH APPLY IN RELATION TO A MINOR

Conditions
9.   The clinical trial relates directly to a clinical condition from which the minor suffers or is of such a nature that it can only be carried out on minors.

10. Some direct benefit for the group of patients involved in the clinical trial is to be obtained from that trial.

11. The clinical trial is necessary to validate data obtained—

(a) In other clinical trials involving persons able to give informed consent, or

(b) By other research methods

Principles

13. Informed consent given by a person with parental responsibility or a legal representative to a minor taking part in a clinical trial shall represent the minor's presumed will.

14. The clinical trial has been designed to minimise pain, discomfort, fear and any other foreseeable risk in relation to the disease and the minor's stage of development.

16. The interests of the patient always prevail over those of science and society

Commentary

A minor is provided with information "according to his capacity of understanding" (Sch.1 Pt 4 reg.6) and any explicit wish (s)he expresses in refusing to participate in, or be withdrawn from the clinical trial at any time must be "considered by the investigator" (reg.7). *Re W* [1992] 4 All E.R. 627 provides authority that no minor has the ultimate authority to refuse treatment. However, any such involvement is, of course, subject to the satisfaction of regs.10 and 16 in this Part.

With regard to voluntary involvement of minors in research, the safest course of action is to try and obtain consent both from the minor and either a person having parental responsibility for the minor or the minor's legal representative. *Gillick* competence alone (see Ch.4) is unlikely to suffice unless in clear and exceptional circumstances it is in the minor's best interests that his / her parents are not informed.

Research Governance

Key Principle: **The regulation of clinical research in the NHS has developed and evolved over the past 40 years and particularly so since the start of the new millennium.**

History

The Department of Health first recommended the establishment of local research ethics committees in 1975. The committees would aim to ensure that researchers achieved acceptable minimum standards in the protocols underpinning their studies and that they managed risk acceptably. It was another 16 years, however, before more formal guidance was given to the then local health authorities who were each required to establish at least one local research ethics committee (LREC). Given that such committees were unsuitable for appraising the proposals for research carried out at simultaneously at one site, the Governance Arrangements for Research Ethics Committees (GAfRECs) led to the establishment in 1997 of multi-centre research ethics committees (MRECs) and the continuation of LRECs. MRECs would complete the ethical review and then disseminate the protocol to LRECs for consideration of local issues. In 2000 came another development with the establishment of COREC—the Central Office for NHS Research Ethics Committees—having the functions of, inter alia, issuing guidance to RECs and appointing MRECs whilst Strategic Health Authorities became the appointing authorities for LRECs. Further change took place in 2005 with the National Patient Safety Agency (NPSA) (see Ch.1) assuming the responsibility for COREC. The evolution has continued and a new body, the National Ethics Research Service (NRES), which is a part of the National Patient Safety Agency (NPSA), took over from COREC and NHS RECs on June 1, 2007. Under NRES, research ethics advisers at both national and local level will, hopefully, be able to speed-up decisions via a more effective triage system that has been implemented to permit quicker decision-making in respect of research which doesn't have any contentious ethical content. Moreover, ethical approval is, henceforth, likely to be given by specialist advisors rather than a local committee.

Note, also, that in all cases NHS researchers require Research and Development Management approval and the research must not start until this approval is obtained. This will not be granted unless NHS indemnity arrangements are in place.

The coming into force of the Medicines for Human Use (Clinical Trials) Regulations 2004, SI 2004/1031 established the UK Ethics Committee Authority (UKECA) as part of the NPSA. Regulation 5 provides that the UKECA recognises and monitors the subordinate bodies that are permitted to review the protocols for clinical trials in investigational medicinal products (CTIMP).

Commentary
Acronyms! Acronyms apart, there is clearly a significant focus on
the requirements of adherence to the formalities deemed necessary for the protection of patients' safety. This is not simply a
matter of bureaucracy: the protection is part of Good Clinical
Practice which is an international ethical and scientific quality
standard for the design and conduct, etc. of clinical trials
involving the participation of human subjects.

Medicines for Human Use (Clinical Trials) Regulations 2004

Key Principle: **The 2004 Regulations, SI 2004/1031 (as now
amended), were enacted to give the force of law to Directive
2001/20/EC and to ensure compliance with the principles of
Good Clinical Practice.**

Interpretation
2.–(1) In these Regulations—
    "the Directive" means Directive 2001/20/EC of the European
    Parliament and of the Council on the approximation of laws,
    regulations and administrative provisions of the Member
    States relating to the implementation of good clinical practice
    in the conduct of clinical trials on medicinal products for
    human use;

Commentary
It is important to note that four other Directives are referred to in
the interpretation provisions and that, of those, Directive 2005/
28/EC is, for the purposes of this section, the most important as
it is the good clinical practice Directive.
    Some noteworthy provisions of Directive 2001/20/EC are:

- The statutory establishment of ethics committees;

- The additional safeguards for protection of vulnerable
  groups (minors and incapacitated adults); and

- The requirement that all clinical trials be conducted in
  accordance with good clinical practice.

Regulation 28 and Sch.1 contain the principles of good clinical
practice

Good clinical practice and protection of clinical trial subjects

28.–(1) No person shall—

(a) Conduct a clinical trial; or

(b) perform the functions of the sponsor of a clinical trial .. otherwise than in accordance with the conditions and principles of good clinical practice.

SCHEDULE 1

Regulation 2(1)

CONDITIONS AND PRINCIPLES OF GOOD CLINICAL PRACTICE AND FOR THE PROTECTION OF CLINICAL TRIAL SUBJECTS

PART 1

APPLICATION AND INTERPRETATION

1.–(3) If any subject of a clinical trial is a minor, the conditions and principles specified in Part 4 apply in relation to that subject.

(5) If any person—

(a) is an adult unable by virtue of physical or mental incapacity to give informed consent, and

(b) has, prior to the onset of incapacity, refused to give informed consent to taking part in the clinical trial,

that person cannot be included as a subject in the clinical trial.

3.–(1) For the purposes of this Schedule, a person gives informed consent to take part, or that a subject is to take part, in a clinical trial only if his decision—

(a) is given freely after that person is informed of the nature, significance, implications and risks of the trial; and

(b) either—

    (i) is evidenced in writing ... so as to indicate his consent, or

   (ii) if the person is unable to sign or mark a document so as to indicate his consent, is given orally in the presence of at least one witness and recorded in writing.

PART 2

CONDITIONS AND PRINCIPLES WHICH APPLY TO ALL CLINICAL TRIALS

Principles based on Articles 2 to 5 of the GCP Directive

1.   The rights, safety and well-being of the trial subjects shall prevail over the interests of science and society

6.   Clinical trials shall be conducted in accordance with the principles of the Declaration of Helsinki

9.   All clinical information shall be recorded, handled and stored in such a way that it can be accurately reported, interpreted and verified, while the confidentiality of records of the trial subjects remains protected.

Conditions based on Article 3 of the Directive

12.   A trial shall be initiated only if an ethics committee and the licensing authority comes to the conclusion that the anticipated therapeutic and public health benefits justify the risks and may be continued only if compliance with this requirement is permanently monitored.

13.   The rights of each subject to physical and mental integrity, to privacy and the protection of the data concerning him in accordance with the Data Protection Act 1998 are safeguarded.

14.   Provision has been made for insurance or indemnity to cover the liability of the investigator and sponsor which may arise in relation to the clinical trial.

Commentary

The concept of good clinical practice (GCP) was developed by a steering group comprised of members of the regulatory authorities from the EU, Japan and the USA.

The steering group was named the Tripartite International Conference on Harmonisation (ICH) and GCP "came into effect" as guidance in 1997. It is crucial to note, now, that the concept of GCP is no longer mere guidance but is firmly established on a statutory basis.

Other Parts of the Schedule contain principles and conditions which relate to a minor (Pt 4) and an incapacitated adult (Pt 5).

13. ORGAN TRANSPLANTS

Regulating Transplants via the Human Tissue Act 2004

Key Principle: Enactment of a single Act, the Human Tissue Act 2004, to regulate all aspects of transplantation of human organs and tissue, replaced and repealed a number of older statutes, particularly the Human Tissue Act 1961, The Anatomy Act 1984 and the Human Organ Transplants Act 1989.

Human Tissue Act 2004

Schedule 7 REPEALS AND REVOCATIONS

Part 1 REPEALS [abridged version]

Short title and chapter	Extent of repeal
Human Tissue Act 1961 (c. 54)	The whole Act.
Anatomy Act 1984 (c. 14)	The whole Act.
Corneal Tissue Act 1986 (c. 18)	The whole Act.
Human Organ Transplants Act 1989 (c. 31)	The whole Act.

Commentary

Reasons for enacting the new (2004) Act

Prior to the enactment of the 2004 Act, organ transplants had been regulated by the Human Tissue Act 1961 (transplants from cadavers) and the Human Organ Transplants Act 1989 (concerning transplants from living donors). Each Act was contentious enough in its own right to warrant a reform of the law. For example, the provisions of s.1 of the HTA 1961 stated:

Section 1(1)

"If any person, either in writing at any time or orally in the presence of two or more witnesses during his last illness, has expressed a request that his body or any specified part of his body be used after his death for therapeutic purposes or for purposes of medical education or research, the person lawfully in possession of his body after his death *may*, unless he has reason to believe that the request was subsequently withdrawn, authorise the removal from the body of any part or, as the case may be, the specified part, for use in accordance with the request."

Being in lawful possession of a body attached a right and a duty to the possessors to dispose of the body. However, this is qualified at common law by noting that there is no property in a dead body that enables the possessors to do anything they so wish with the body other than for arranging its disposal according to social mores and the law. The problem in this sub-section was compounded by not specifying who was in lawful possession of a body when a person died in hospital, for example.

Moreover, as no age limit was specified below which a potential donor could not make a valid request, it appeared possible that a *Gillick competent* minor could consent to "his body or any specified part of his body be[ing] used after his death for therapeutic purposes or for purposes of medical education or research", a point that contrasts with Lord Donaldson's view in *Re W* (1992) of a minor's ability to give consent to organ donation (below).

The most notable uncertainty, however, was whether a deceased donor's express wishes would be respected as any donation could be decided upon at the discretion of "the person lawfully in possession of [the deceased's body]" provided that that person had no reason to believe that the deceased's request was subsequently withdrawn.

As for s.1(2), it provided that:

"Without prejudice to the foregoing subsection, the person lawfully in possession of the body of a deceased person may authorise the removal of any part from the body for use for the said purposes if, having made such reasonable enquiry as may be practicable, he has no reason to believe—

(a) that the deceased had expressed an objection to his body being so dealt with after his death, and had not withdrawn it; or
(b) that the surviving spouse or any surviving relative of the deceased objects to the body being so dealt with."

Amongst the uncertainties introduced by this sub-section were the interpretation of "such enquiry as may be reasonably practicable"—particularly as the Act came into force at a time when there were very few landline telephones, no mobile phones, no internet on which to send emails and only a nascent motorway system on which to drive far fewer cars than presently congest our roads—and uncertainties over how far the relationship of "any surviving relative" extended.

Restrictions introduced under the Human Organ Transplants Act 1989

With regard to transplants involving living donees, the Human Organ Transplants Act 1989 was enacted quickly and in response to the perceived revulsion of engaging in the commercial trading of organs at a London hospital in 1989. Accordingly, s.1 of the Act made it a criminal offence to trade in organs and s.2 prohibited a donation from an unrelated donee unless it was established that it was an altruistic donation.

It may be argued that the focus on the genetic relationship, provided for in s.2, was unnecessary and unwarranted given that "every human being of adult years and sound mind [which clearly encompasses an individual wishing to make an altruistic donation] has a right to determine what shall be done with his own body" (per Cardozo J. in *Schloendorff* (1914)); and the familial pressure that may be exerted on a relative to make a donation could infringe the requirement for a full, free and uncoerced consent. The questionable need for the unrelated donee to be interviewed by a person approved by a statutory body (ULTRA—Unrelated Live Transplant Regulatory Authority) before the donee's consent is accepted, partly to obtain an assurance that the donation was not a commercial transaction, is a principle that is retained in the 2004 Act, with an assessor interviewing the prospective, altruistic donor before reporting to a Human Tissue authority committee of at least three members.

Section 7(2) of the 1989 Act defined "organ" as "any part of a human body consisting of a structured arrangement of tissues which, if wholly removed, cannot be replicated by the body". (See, now: HTA 2004, s.34 and SI 2006/1659, Part 3, below).

Organ Retention Scandals

More recently, and sadly, the perceived need for a change in the law became evident following the "organ retention scandals" at Bristol Royal Infirmary and the Royal Liverpool Children's Hospital at Alder Hey. For years, organs and tissue had been removed from children's bodies on which post-mortems had been performed at the Bristol Royal Infirmary and used ".. for a variety of purposes, including audit, medical education and research, or had simply been stored". Following the publication of the Kennedy Report on the Bristol inquiry, *Removal and Retention of Human Material*, it was reported that an even larger collection of children's hearts had been retained at Alder Hey. This led to another, separate, inquiry under the chairmanship of Michael Redfren QC.

The Redfern Report published details of what had become established practices of removing and retaining children's organs without consent or even any knowledge of the parents. This was compounded by withholding this information when the bodies of babies—minus many organs—were returned to the parents for burial.

Notwithstanding the value attached to the taking and retaining organs after post-mortem examination for specific and warranted research purposes, it was evident that the law was in urgent need of reform. Indeed, the Bristol Interim Report had noted that:

> "... we have no doubt that the complexity and obscurity of the current law will be manifest to all. Equally we have no doubt that there will be general agreement that this state of affairs is regrettable and in need of attention".

That reform of the law was prompted more by the "organ retention scandals" than by the perceived need to increase the number of organs harvested and save lives prompted Mason & Laurie to remark that "the 2004 Act was born under the wrong star".

At least, the reforms brought in by the HTA 2004 gave prominence to the need for appropriate consent and such provisions were enacted in ss.1 to 3 of the Act.

Provisions of the Human Tissue Act 2004

Key Principle: **Part 1 of the HTA 2004, entitled "Removal Storage and Use of Human Organs and Other Tissue for Scheduled Purposes", provides, in s.1(1), the activities which shall be lawful if done with appropriate consent.**

Part 1 Removal Storage and Use of Human Organs and Other Tissue for Scheduled Purposes

1. Authorisation of activities for scheduled purposes

(1) The following activities shall be lawful if done with appropriate consent—

(a) The storage of the body of a deceased person for use for a purpose specified in Schedule 1, other than anatomical examination;

(b) the use of the body of a deceased person for a purpose so specified, other than anatomical examination;

(c) the removal from the body of a deceased person, for the purpose specified in Schedule 1, of any relevant material of which the body consists or which it contains;

(d) the storage for use for a purpose specified in Part 1 of Schedule 1 of any relevant material which has come from a human body;

(e) the storage for use for a purpose specified in Part 2 of Schedule 1 of any relevant material which has come from the body of a deceased person;

(f) the use for a purpose specified in Part 1 of Schedule 1 of any relevant material which has come from a human body;

(g) the use for a purpose specified in Part 2 of Schedule 1 of any relevant material which has come from the body of a deceased person.

Human Tissue Act 2004

Schedule 1

Section 1 Scheduled Purposes

Part 1 Purposes Requiring Consent: General
7. Transplantation

Commentary

"Transplantation" is the only word in para.7. However, this ultra-brief reference to a scheduled purpose should not detract from the fact that the 2004 Act is *the* Act that regulates transplantation from all donors, living or cadaveric. "Transplantable material", for the purpose of s.34 of the 2004 Act (Information about transplant operations) is defined in part 3, reg.9 of SI 2006/1659 as meaning:

(a) the whole or part of any of the following organs if it is to be used for the same purpose as the entire organ in the human body—

(i) kidney,
(ii) heart,
(iii) lung or a lung lobe,
(iv) pancreas,
(v) liver,
(vi) bowel,
(vii) larynx;

(b) face, or

(c) limb.

Under reg.10, SI 2006/1659, "Transplantable material" for the purposes of s.33 (below) extends beyond "organs" to include bone marrow and peripheral blood stem cells.

Section 33 HTA 2004: Restriction on transplants involving a live donor

(1) Subject to subsections (3) and (5), a person commits an offence if—

(a) he removes any transplantable material from the body of a living person intending that the material be used for the purpose of transplantation, and

(b) when he removes the material, he knows, or might reasonably be expected to know, that the person from whose body he removes the material is alive.

(2) Subject to subsections (3) and (5), a person commits an offence if—

(a) he uses for the purpose of transplantation any transplantable material which has come from the body of a living person, and

    (b) when he does so, he knows, or might reasonably be
        expected to know, that the transplantable material
        has come from the body of a living person.

(3) The Secretary of State may by regulations provide that
    subsection (1) or (2) shall not apply in a case where—

    (a) the Authority is satisfied—

        (i) that no reward has been or is to be given in
            contravention of section 32, and
       (ii) that such other conditions as are specified in
            the regulations are satisfied, and

    (b) such other requirements as are specified in the reg-
        ulations are complied with.

The "transplantable materials" specified in SI 2006/1659 are the,
"relevant material" for the purpose of s.53 of the 2004 Act:

Section 53 HTA 2004: "Relevant material"

(1) In this Act, "relevant material" means material, other than
    gametes, which consists of or includes human cells.

(2) In this Act, references to relevant material from a human
    body do not include—

    (a) embryos outside the human body, or
    (b) hair and nail from the body of a living person.

Providing, then, that a person has given "appropriate consent",
"any relevant material which has come from a human body"
may be authorised for use in transplantation.

The Requirements for, "Appropriate Consent"

Key Principle: **Consent is not only the fundamental principle
that underpins the lawful storage and use of bodies, body
parts, organs and tissue and the removal of material from the
bodies of deceased persons, but what constitutes "appropriate
consent" is defined by reference by who may give it.**

HTA 2004

Sections 2 and 3

2. "Appropriate consent": children

(2) Subject to subsection (3), where the child concerned is alive, "appropriate consent" means his consent.

(3) Where—

   (a) the child concerned is alive,

   (b) neither a decision of his to consent to the activity, nor a decision of his not to consent to it, is in force, and

   (c) either he is not competent to deal with the issue of consent in relation to the activity, or though he is competent to deal with that issue, he fails to do so, "appropriate consent" means the consent of a person who has parental responsibility for him.

(7) Where the child concerned has died and the activity is not one to which subsection (5) applies, "appropriate consent" means—

   (a) if a decision of his to consent to the activity, or a decision of his not to consent to it, was in force immediately before he died, his consent;

   (b) if paragraph (a) does not apply—

      (i) the consent of a person who has parental responsibility for him immediately before he died, the consent of a person who stood in a qualifying relationship to him at that time.

Commentary

There is now clear, statutory authority for a *"Gillick competent"* minor to consent to organ donation. Moreover, this is not qualified by the need for supplemental parental consent. This contrasts with the position at common law, where it had been said that:

> "It is inconceivable that [a doctor] should proceed in reliance solely upon the consent of an under-age patient, however *"Gillick competent"*, in the absence of supporting parental consent and equally inconceivable that he should proceed in the absence of the patient's consent. In any event he will need to seek the opinions of other doctors and may be well advised to apply to the court for guidance ..." (per Lord Donaldson in *Re W* (1992)).

3. "Appropriate consent": adults

(2) where the person concerned is alive, "appropriate consent" means his consent.

(3) where the person concerned has died and the activity is one to which subsection (4) applies, "appropriate consent" means his consent in writing.

(5) Consent in writing for the purposes of subsection (3) is only valid if—

     (a) it is signed by the person concerned in the presence of at least one witness who attests the signature,

     (b) it is signed at the direction of the purpose concerned, in his presence and in the presence of at least one witness who attests the signature, or

     (c) it is contained in a will of the person concerned made in accordance with the requirements of—

         (i) section 9 of the Wills Act 1837 (c.26).

Commentary

Living donors

Notwithstanding the risk of the donee dying during the removal of (say) a kidney, or the likelihood of his developing end stage renal failure, the Att-Gen's Reference (No.6 of 1980) permits the donee to consent to the infliction of bodily injury in the course of what, essentially, amounts to a non-therapeutic operation, on the basis that it is in the public interest to do so.

Obtaining, or attempting to obtain consent from a living relative, who felt pressurised into donating, has resulted in litigation in America. In particular, in *McFall v Shimp* (1978) 10 Pa D & C (3d) 90, whilst Flaherty J. thought it was morally indefensible for a man to refuse a bone marrow donation that would save his cousin's life, he refused to compel him to do so because: "For our law to compel the defendant to submit to an intrusion of his body would change every concept and principle upon which our society is founded".

Key Principle: **Under s.6 HTA 2004 and SI 2006/1659, a mentally incapacitated patient may be deemed to consent to donate material from his body providing it is in his best interests to do so.**

Incapacitated patients

6. Activities involving material from adults who lack capacity to consent

Where—

(a) an activity of a kind mentioned in section 1(1)(d) or (f) involves material from the body of a person who—

    (i)   is an adult, and
    (ii) lacks capacity to consent to the activity, and

(b) neither a decision of his to consent to the activity, nor a decision of his not to consent to it, is in force,

there shall for the purposes of this Part be deemed to be consent of his to the activity if it is done in circumstances of a kind specified by regulations made by the Secretary of State.

Further details are provided for in SI 2006/1659, Pt 2, reg.3.

Commentary

The legislative provisions, alone, do nothing to counter the claims of those who believe that the removal of relevant material from the bodies of mentally incapacitated persons is carried out as much for the convenience of others as it is for the best interests of the mentally incapacitated person. One American case and one English case, respectively, illustrate judicial decisions that focus, first, on the fiction of trying to "read the mind" of the mentally incapacitated man; and, secondly, acting, supposedly, in the best interests of the woman:

Strunk v Strunk (1969) 35 A.L.R. (3d) 683

This case involved the brothers Tom and Jerry. Tom Strunk, the older brother, was 28 years of age, married, in employment, a part-time student and in need of a kidney transplant. His younger brother, Jerry, was 27 and incompetent, having a mental age of six years; he had a speech defect which made it difficult for him to communicate with others, and he was committed to a state institution for the feeble minded. However, Jerry was in good physical health and he was found to be a suitable potential donor. The brothers' mother petitioned the court for authority to proceed with the operation.

Held: (By a majority decision). The transplant would be authorised as it was beneficial not only to Tom but also to Jerry because "Jerry was greatly dependent on Tommy, emotionally and psychologically, and that his well-being would be jeopardised more severely by the loss of his brother than by the removal of a kidney."

Commentary

The decision was made on the basis of "substituted judgment", i.e. the court claimed to declare the decision that Jerry would have made if he were competent to do so: a complete fiction, of course.

The notable contribution from English law has been:

Re Y (Mental Patient: Bone Marrow Transplant) [1997] Fam 110
25-year-old Y, mentally and physically handicapped from birth, lived in a community home where she been regularly visited by members of her family. Her mother's health was precarious and her older sister, P, who suffered from a serious illness, required a bone marrow transplant from a healthy compatible donor. By reason of her disabilities, Y was unaware of P's illness and unable to consent to the operations required for a donation. P applied for declarations that they were lawful nonetheless.

Held: the declarations were granted. The operations were in Y's best interests as they would tend to prolong the life of both P and the mother, and Y would receive emotional, psychological and social benefit, by way of continued regular visits, with minimal detriment to herself.

Commentary

The law and ethics of cases such as *Strunk v Strunk* and *Re Y* (above) and those relating to life created via IVF treatment in order to have the characteristics that not only ensure the children born as a result are free of the genetic condition that has blighted the life of an older sibling but that also they will be tissue compatible with the older sibling, so enabling a transplant of material from the "saviour sibling" (see Ch.9) are amongst the most controversial that fall to be decided in any legal system. However, the presence of statutory provisions pertaining to "deemed consent" in the 2004 Act contrasts with a proposed amendment to the Human Fertilisation and Embryology Bill 2008, that would ban tissue-typing for "saviour sibling" purposes. If the latter were to be accepted, then, while material could continue to be taken from one human being unable to consent to the procedure that would help save the life of another (2004 Act), no one having the capacity to consent would be permitted to do so in respect of a procedure that would be intended to create a life to save another: Human Fertilisation and Embryology Act 1990 as amended by a 2008 Act. See Ch.9.

Key Principle: **Unlike the repealed HTA 1961, the HTA 2004 prohibits certain activities and provides for penalties if the prohibitions are breached.**

Offences under the Act
Section 5 Prohibition of activities without consent etc.

(1)   A person commits an offence if, without appropriate consent, he does an activity to which subsection (1), (2) or (3) of section 1 applies, unless he reasonably believes—

   (a)   that he does the activity with appropriate consent, or
   (b)   that what he does is not an activity to which the subsection applies.

(2)   A person commits an offence if—

   (a)   he falsely represents to a person whom he knows or believes is going to, or may, do an activity to which subsection (1), (2) or (3) of section 1 applies—

      (i)   that there is appropriate consent to the doing of the activity, or
      (ii)   that the activity is not one to which the subsection applies, and

   (b)   he knows that the representation is false or does not believe it to be true.

(7)   A person guilty of an offence under this section shall be liable—

   (a)   on summary conviction to a fine not exceeding the statutory maximum;
   (b)   on conviction on indictment—

      (i)   to imprisonment for a term not exceeding 3 years, or

      (ii) to a fine, or
     (iii) to both.

See also s.25, which provides for the breach of a licence requirement and s.32:

Section 32 Prohibition of commercial dealings in human material for transplantation

  (1) A person commits an offence if he—

    (a) gives or receives a reward for the supply of, or for an offer to supply, any controlled material;
    (b) seeks to find a person willing to supply any controlled material for reward;
    (c) offers to supply any controlled material for reward;
    (d) initiates or negotiates any arrangement involving the giving of a reward for the supply of, or for an offer to supply, any controlled material;

  (2) Without prejudice to subsection (1)(b) and (c), a person commits an offence if he causes to be published or distributed, or knowingly publishes or distributes, an advertisement—

    (a) inviting persons to supply, or offering to supply, any controlled material for reward, or
    (b) indicating that the advertiser is willing to initiate or negotiate any such arrangement as is mentioned in subsection (1)(d).

  (4) A person guilty of an offence under subsection (1) shall be liable—

    (a) on summary conviction—

       (i) to imprisonment for a term not exceeding 12 months, or
      (ii) to a fine not exceeding the statutory maximum, or
     (iii) to both;

    (b) on conviction on indictment—

       (i) to imprisonment for a term not exceeding 3 years, or
      (ii) to a fine, or
     (iii) to both.

(5) A person guilty of an offence under subsection (2) shall be liable on summary conviction—

   (a) to imprisonment for a term not exceeding 51 weeks, or
   (b) to a fine not exceeding level 5 on the standard scale, or
   (c) to both.

Commentary

The clear aims of the provisions of ss.32 and 33 are to prohibit, so far as the Act can provide for, all transplants other than those that are wholly altruistic and for which "appropriate consent" has been given. There is no wholly convincing argument why such a blanket ban on the trade in organs should exist, however. Accordingly, the terms of imprisonment provided for in ss.5 and 32 may be perceived as being harsh.

Cadaveric donations

Key Principle: **By contrast with the HTA 1961, ss.1(1) and 3(3) of the 2004 Act make it clear that a decision made by a person giving appropriate consent to donate relevant material after his death remains his, and is not subjected to the discretion of the person in lawful possession of the body.**

Sections 1(1) and 3(3): see above.

Commentary

The clear authority for the use of relevant material from the cadaver (dead body) that was made in writing by the donor when he gave appropriate consent during his lifetime was intended to boost the number of cadaveric donations from those who had "opted in" and had registered their wishes on the NHS Organ Donor Register. In January 2008, the media gave much prominence to the call made by Prime Minister Gordon Brown call for a debate on proposals to change from the current system of "opting in", to a system that would presume a person's consent unless there had been an express withdrawal, or "opting out" of the system. Mr Brown said: "A system of this kind ['opting out'] seems to have the potential to close the aching gap between the potential benefits of transplant surgery in the UK and the limits imposed by our current system of consent". The perceived need for change was an attempt to rectify the shortfall between (for example) nearly 7,000 people being registered for and awaiting a kidney transplant, whereas just over 1,000 kidneys per year were becoming available.

The "call for a debate" was hardly a new initiative, however, although somewhat less attention had been paid to the publication of the annual report of the Chief Medical Officer (CMO), Sir Liam Donaldson, six months earlier, in July 2007, when Sir Liam said:

> "I believe that we would be able to get up to much higher levels of donation and we would save a lot of people's lives who are currently dying unnecessarily at a rate of one a day.
> "To meet the current demand for organs the number of people on the NHS Organ Donor Register would need to approximately treble. I believe we can only do this through changing the legislation to an opt-out system with proper regulation and safeguards."

The proposals should be treated with caution, however, as any change of policy designed to harvest more organs in the absence of explicit approval would probably not be welcome on the basis of "presumed consent", a phrase having unwelcome connotations with the recent past. Much more emphasis on education and making people aware of the plight of those who suffer and, perhaps, die for want of organs that could so easily be retrieved, may be a preferable method for achieving donation at the levels experienced by some other European States.

Key Principle: **Rather than make a decision to donate relevant material following his death, a person may decide to authorise a nominated representative to make the decision for him. However, in the absence both of the appropriate consent of the deceased donor and his failure to nominate a representative, the HTA 2004 provides a hierarchy of family relationships from which consent may be obtained.**

Section 4: Nominated Representatives

(1) An adult may appoint one or more persons to represent him after his death in relation to consent for the purposes of section 1.

(2) An appointment under this section may be made orally or in writing.

The validity of the request will also be dependent on complying with the formalities in sub-sections (4) and (5), relating to oral and written appointments, respectively.

In the absence of the deceased's appropriate consent and his failure to nominate a representative, s.27 provides:

Section 27 Provision with respect to consent

(4) The qualifying relationships for the purpose of sections 2(7)(b)(ii) and 3(6)(c) should be ranked in the following order—

    (a) spouse, civil partner or partner; [see s.54(8) for the definition of "partner"]

    (b) parent or child;

    (c) brother or sister;

    (d) grandparent or grandchild;

    (e) child of a person falling within paragraph (c);

    (f) stepfather or stepmother;

    (g) half-brother or half-sister;

    (h) friend of longstanding.

(5) Relationships in the same paragraph of subsection (4) should be accorded equal ranking.

(6) Consent should be obtained from the person whose relationship to the person concerned is accorded the highest ranking in accordance with subsections (4) and (5).

(7) If the relationship of each of two or more persons to the person concerned is accorded equal highest ranking in accordance with subsections (4) and (5), it is sufficient to obtain the consent of any of them.

(8) In applying the principles set out above, a person's relationship shall be left out of account if—

    (a) he does not wish to deal with the issue of consent,

    (b) he is not able to deal with that issue, or

    (c) having regard to the activity in relation to which consent is sought, it is not reasonably practicable to communicate with him within the time available if consent in relation to the activity is to be acted on.

Commentary

Notwithstanding the very clear policy of giving every opportunity for the provision of consent to the use of relevant material from a cadaver for the purposes of transplantation, the shortfall in the number of organs required for potential transplant recipients means that the "opting in" / "opting out" debate is likely to remain current for the near future, at least.

However, a further source of organs may arise from the provisions of s.43 which authorises the minimum steps necessary for the preservation of part of a body whilst consent is sought for the removal of the part for transplantation.

Section 43 Preservation for transplantation

(1) Where part of a body lying in a hospital, nursing home or other institution is or may be suitable for use for transplantation, it shall be lawful for the person having the control and management of the institution—

(a) to take steps for the purpose of preserving the part for use for transplantation, and

(b) to retain the body for that purpose.

(2) Authority under subsection (1)(a) shall only extend—

(a) to the taking of the minimum steps necessary for the purpose mentioned in that provision, and

(b) to the use of the least invasive procedure.

(3) Authority under subsection (1) ceases to apply once it has been established that consent making removal of the part for transplantation lawful has not been, and will not be, given.

The authority responsible for optimising the safety and supply of organs is the NHS Blood and Transplant (NHSBT), a Special Health Authority established in October 2005 under SI 2005/2529.

Dropped Proposal for Reform

The dropped proposal for reform relates to the merger of the Human Tissue Authority, established under s.13 of the 2004 Act, with the Human Fertilisation and Embryology Authority to form the Regulatory Authority for Tissue and Embryos (RATE). This was scheduled for 2008—but the proposal was certainly not short of critics—as evidenced, it would seem, by the proposal being dropped.

14. THE MANAGEMENT OF DYING: EXERCISING AUTONOMY (THE "RIGHT TO DIE"), ASSISTED SUICIDE AND EUTHANASIA

Ethical guidance on preserving and respecting human life

Key Principle: Codes of ethics provide guidance of variable quality to doctors in respect of end-of-life decision-making.

The World Medical Association's International Code of Medical Ethics (1949, as amended in 1968 and 1983) includes the premise that: "**A PHYSICIAN SHALL** always bear in mind the obligation of preserving life." [Emphasis as in the Code].

Commentary (I)
This unqualified obligation elevates the sanctity of life to a position of supreme importance without any consideration of quality of life. Moreover, the focus is on beneficence and non-maleficence: it excludes any reference to a patient's right to self-determination.

By contrast, the guidance from the GMC is far more detailed and it includes a clear instruction that doctors are legally bound to obey the decisions of a competent person who refuses what may be potentially life-saving treatment.

Withholding and Withdrawing Life-Prolonging Treatments: Good Practice in Decision-Making
(GMC, August 2002)

Respect for human life and best interests [Extracts]
9. Doctors have an ethical obligation to show respect for human life; protect the health of their patients; and to make their patients' best interests their first concern. This means offering those treatments where the possible benefits outweigh any burdens or risks associated with the

treatment, and avoiding those treatments where there is no net benefit to the patient.

11. Prolonging life will usually be in the best interests of a patient, provided that the treatment is not considered to be excessively burdensome or disproportionate in relation to the expected benefits. Not continuing or not starting a potentially life-prolonging treatment is in the best interests of a patient when it would provide no net benefit to the patient....

End of natural life

12. Life has a natural end and doctors and others caring for a patient need to recognize that the point may come in the progression of a patient's condition where death is drawing near. In these circumstances doctors should not strive to prolong the dying process with no regard to the patient's wishes, where known, or an up to date assessment of the benefits and burdens of treatment or non-treatment.

Adult patients who can decide for themselves

13. Adult competent patients have the right to decide how much weight to attach to the benefits, burdens, risks, and overall acceptability of any treatment. They have the right to refuse treatment even where refusal may result in harm to themselves or in their own death, and doctors are legally bound to respect their decision....

Adult patients who cannot decide for themselves

14. Any valid advance refusal of treatment—one made when the patient was competent and on the basis of adequate information about the implications of his/her choice—is legally binding and must be respected where it is clearly applicable to the patient's present circumstances...

Commentary (II)

The guidelines in this GMC publication were challenged in *R. (On the Application of Burke) v GMC* (2005) (below). The Court of Appeal approved them, however.

Doctors, Dying Patients and the Law

Key Principle: **Whilst it may be lawful for a doctor to withhold or withdraw treatment in appropriate circumstances, the active administration of a lethal substance may lead to an indictment on a count of murder or attempted murder.**

R. v Cox (1992) 12 B.M.L.R. 38

Dr Nigel Cox was indicted on a charge of attempted murder. His patient, 70-year-old Lillian Boyes, was in the terminal stages of rheumatoid arthritis and was beyond the control of painkillers. Eventually, he injected with potassium chloride in a quantity that had no therapeutic purpose.

Held: Ognall J. (directing the jury) said:

> "Even the prosecution acknowledge that [Dr Cox acted the way he did] because he was prompted by deep distress at Lillian Boyes' condition; by a belief that she was totally beyond recall and by an intense compassion for her fearful suffering. Nonetheless, ... if he injected her with potassium chloride *for the primary purpose of killing her, or hastening her death,* he is guilty of the offence charged."

The jury convicted Dr Cox on a count of attempted murder.

Commentary

Although Dr Cox was convicted at Winchester Crown Court, he was given only a suspended prison sentence and a reprimand by the GMC. Unquestionably, the perceived leniency was attributable to the tremendous support given to Dr Cox both by Mrs Boyes family and the general public. Dr Cox returned to practice as a GP.

By contrast with Dr Cox's case, in May 1999, Dr David Moor was cleared of the murder of 85-year-old George Liddell. Dr Moor had admitted giving Mr Liddell a lethal dose of diamorphine but he maintained he had done so only to relieve pain, not to kill him. Where the primary purpose of treatment was to kill pain, then a doctor was entitled to administer it even if an incidental effect was a hastening of the patient's death: the doctrine of double effect (see below).

The right to refuse treatment

Key Principle: **A decision by a competent person to refuse treatment must be obeyed if, in the event of an emergency, a treatment decision has to be made for that person, who is now mentally incapacitated, and the original decision, which has not been rescinded, applies to the current circumstances.**

Airedale NHS Trust v Bland [1993] A.C. 789
(See below for the case notes)

Commentary
It was decided in *Re T* (1992) and reaffirmed in *Bland* that a competent patient who *anticipates the possibility* of becoming incompetent in the future and in doing so specifies the circumstances in which he would not wish to receive particular medical treatment should be at liberty to refuse that medical treatment even where the decision leads to his death. In *Bland*, Lord Keith said:

> "Such a person is completely at liberty to decline to undergo treatment, even if the result of his doing so will be that he will die. This extends to the situation where the person, in anticipation of his, through one cause or another, entering into a condition such as PVS, gives clear instructions that in such event he is not to be given medical care, including artificial feeding, designed to keep him alive."

However, as Lord Goff pointed out:

> "Special care may be necessary to ensure that the prior refusal of consent is still properly to be regarded as applicable in the circumstances which have subsequently occurred."

Key Principle: **A prior refusal to consent that might "be regarded as applicable in the circumstances" includes carrying an unsigned card containing a statement of refusal to accept blood or blood products.**

Malette v Shulman (1990) 67 D.L.R. (4th) 321
Mrs M, a Jehovah's Witness, was unconscious and bleeding profusely as a result of a road traffic accident. She carried a card requesting that "no blood or blood products be administered to

me under any circumstances". Nevertheless, soon after arrival at the hospital the doctor in the emergency department decided that her condition was serious and she needed a transfusion.

Held: Despite the doctor's good motives and his thinking that he was acting in her best interests, the intervention constituted a battery and M was awarded damages of $20,000.

Commentary
Although the card was unsigned, it had to be accepted that the card belonged to Mrs Malette, in the absence of evidence to the contrary, and the "prior refusal" could not be overridden by claiming the administration of the blood transfusion was "necessary".

Key principle: **A competent patient on a ventilator has a right to insist that treatment be withdrawn; and a failure to respect the wishes may lead to an action in respect of the unlawful administration of treatment.**

Re B (Consent to Treatment: Capacity) [2002] 2 All E.R. 449
Ms B, a tetraplegic woman, paralysed from the neck down, was placed on a ventilator when she began to experience respiratory problems. Her initial request for treatment to be withdrawn was agreed to but then not implemented when the consultant psychiatrists changed their mind about her mental capacity. A month after an independent reassessment at the hospital that was treating her had declared that she was competent to make her own decisions, she applied for a declaration that she had been treated unlawfully for that time.

Held: the ventilator to which she was attached and which was helping to keep her alive could be disconnected. Dame Elizabeth Butler-Sloss P conducted a hearing at Miss B's bedside in an intensive care unit. In response to Counsel for the NHS Trust that was caring for Miss B stating that Miss B's doctors were concerned to establish that she was competent to make it, because of the gravity of the decision, Dame Elizabeth said:

"You seem to be saying that if you want something and the doctors don't think it is a good idea because they want to do something else, the more you disagree the more you will be regarded as unable to make a decision.

"That is a dangerous concept. There is a very paternalistic element. It's a very 'doctor knows best' concept. I really bridle at that as a member of the public as well as a judge."

Commentary

As well as affirming the right of a competent person to refuse medical treatment, even when that refusal would end in death (a principle already established in *Re T (Adult: Refusal of Medical Treatment)* (1992), *Bland* (1993) and *Re MB (An Adult: Medical Treatment)* (1997)), Dame Elizabeth awarded Miss B the nominal sum of £100 in respect of the unlawful administration of non-consensual treatment for the period in which Miss B's wishes had not been complied with.

Deciding for others: Decision-making based on a minimal quality of life

Key Principle: **The common law has recognised situations where a patient's quality of life may be considered to take precedence over the concept of sanctity of life.**

Lim v Camden and Islington Health Authority [1979] Q.B. 196
Dr Lim Poh Choo, a female hospital patient, suffered a cardiac arrest and irreversible brain damage when 25 minutes had elapsed from cardiac arrest to the restoration of normal breathing. In essence, the case (which finally went to the House of Lords) focused on the quantum of damages.

Held: (on the issue of damages) The Court of Appeal upheld the decision of the judge at first instance as did the House of Lords.

Commentary

The more significant aspects of the case for the purposes of this chapter focus on extracts of Lord Denning's speech in the Court of Appeal where he said Dr Lim was brought back to "a life which is not worth living". He noted the agonizing decision that had to be made by the medical professionals involved when he said at [1979] Q.B. 196, at 216, 217:

"... by reason of the advances of medical science, [Dr Lim] was snatched back from death under the operation and has been brought back to a life which is not worth living. The body has been kept alive but the mind is gone. The doctors and nurses, with the aids available today, say that they can keep the body going for the normal expectation of life. ... Many might say: ' 'Twere better she had died.'

...

...the relatives—and the doctors—are faced with an agonising decision: is she to be kept alive? Or is she to be allowed to die? Is the thread of life to be maintained to the utmost reach of science? Or should it be let fall and nature take its inevitable course? [In the circumstances, it may be appropriate to say] 'For mercy's sake, let the end come now.'

...

It is a modern problem—the impact of modern science—in prolonging life in a body destitute of mind."

N.B.: The authority for making decisions on behalf of a patient incapable of making decisions for himself is now provided for in the Mental Capacity Act 2005, and s.4(5) of the Act provides that:

"Where the determination relates to life-sustaining treatment [the decision-maker] must not, in considering whether the treatment is in the best interests of the person concerned, be motivated by a desire to bring about his death."

Key Principle: **The patient's body does not have to be "destitute of mind" before a doctor assists with the patient's "easing of passing", providing the action taken is intended primarily to ease the patient's pain and suffering: the doctrine of "double effect".**

The doctrine of double effect

R. v Adams [1957] Crim L.R. 365

Dr. Adams was charged with the murder of an 81 year old patient who had suffered a stroke. It was alleged that he had prescribed and administered such large quantities of drugs, especially heroin and morphine, that he must have known that the drugs would kill her. During his summing up to the jury, the trial judge, Devlin J., introduced the doctrine of double effect.

Held: Dr. Adams was acquitted.
Devlin J. said:

"... it does not matter whether her death was inevitable and her days were numbered. *If her life was cut short by weeks or months it was just as much murder as if it was cut short by years.* ... but that does not mean that a doctor who was aiding the sick and dying had to calculate in minutes, or even hours, perhaps not in days or weeks, the effect on a patient's life of the medicines which he would administer. If the first purpose of medicine—the restoration of health—could no longer be achieved, there was still much for the doctor to do and he was entitled to do all that was proper and necessary to relieve pain and suffering *even if the measures he took might incidentally shorten life* by hours or perhaps even longer."

Commentary
The accuracy of Devlin J's analysis has been doubted by Lord Edmund-Davies who said: "Killing both pain and patient may be good morals but it is far from certain that it is good law." On the other hand, it has been supported by Professor Glanville Wllliams who says the proposition is easily justified by necessity. There seems to be considerable merit in this argument, given, for example, that a "responsible" body of medical opinion would support a treatment plan of a five-milligram dose of diamorphine every four to six hours to a woman suffering with motor neurone disease and that this would be more likely than not ... the start of a process [that would shorten life] even though the principal purpose of the drugs was to relieve pain: "Dying woman granted wish for dignified end" *The Times*, October 29, 1997. This referred to Annie Lindsell who sought a declaration from the High Court that her doctor, Dr Simon Holmes, would not be prosecuted for murder if he gave her potentially lethal painkillers when her condition deteriorated. After hearing that a "responsible" body of medical opinion supported Dr Holmes's treatment plan, Mrs Lindsell withdrew her application for the court's intervention.

Do Not attempt Resuscitation

Key Principle: **The recognition that a patient had such a low quality of life that circumstances could exist where steps should not be taken to prolong life encompasses "do not resuscitate" orders. This is established at common law and promoted in ethical guidance.**

Common Law

Re R (Adult: Medical Treatment) [1996] 2 F.L.R. 99

R was a 23-year-old man in a "low-awareness state": he had a malformation of the brain and cerebral palsy, was probably blind, deaf and unable to communicate in any normal way. He had been admitted to hospital five times in one year and his weight had dropped to five stones. Nevertheless, a member of staff at the day centre where R was being treated sought a judicial review when he discovered that a DNAR order (do not attempt resuscitation) had been signed by a consultant psychiatrist with the agreement of R's mother. The health authority then sought a declaration that it would be lawful to withhold life-sustaining treatment

Held:

Sir Stephen Brown P said:

> "In this case there is no case of the court being asked to approve a course aimed at terminating life or accelerating death. The court is concerned with circumstances in which steps should not be taken to prolong life. . . . The principle of law to be applied in this case is that of the 'best interests of the patient' as made clear by the Court of Appeal in *Re J (A minor)(Wardship: Medical Treatment)* . . . In the course of his judgment . . . Taylor LJ said:
>
>> 'I consider the correct approach is for the court to judge the quality of life the child would have to endure if given the treatment, and decide whether in all the circumstances such a life would be so afflicted as to be intolerable to that child.'
>
> "Although the present case concerns a handicapped adult and not a child who is a ward of court the overriding principle in my judgment is the same."

Commentary

The clear adoption of a quality of life standard was based on "intolerability" but qualified by taking a decision by reference to "all the circumstances". However, "intolerability" as a *single* test was rejected by the Court of Appeal in *R. (On the Application of Burke)* (2005), below.

Ethical Guidance

Withholding and Withdrawing Life-Prolonging Treatments: Good Practice in Decision-Making (GMC, August 2002)

Cardiopulmonary resuscitation

84. Cardiopulmonary resuscitation (CPR), if attempted promptly in appropriate situations, may be effective in restarting the heart and lungs of some patients. However CPR is known to have a low success rate, especially for patients with serious conditions who are in poor general health. ... if a patient is at the end-stage of an incurable illness and death is imminent, attempts to resuscitate them are likely to be futile and not in the patient's best interests.

85. Advice on when it is appropriate to attempt to resuscitate a patient, and circumstances when it is appropriate to make an advance decision not to attempt resuscitation (DNAR order), is available from professional bodies.

Key principle: **The GMC's guidelines in Withholding and Withdrawing Life-Prolonging Treatments: Good Practice in Decision-Making (GMC, August 2002) have received judicial approval.**

R. (On the Application of Burke) v GMC [2005] EWCA 1003
In February 2004, Leslie Burke, a 44-year-old former postman, challenged the guidelines issued by the GMC in 2002 and published in *"Withholding and Withdrawing Life-Prolonging Treatment: Good Practice in Decision-Making"*. Counsel for Mr Burke claimed that stopping the supply of food and water breached Mr Burke's right to life. Mr Burke won his case at first instance and the Court of Appeal affirmed that he would receive artificial nutrition and hydration (ANH), should he require it, because once a patient was accepted into a hospital the medical staff came under a positive duty at common law to care for him/her. However, the GMC won the appeal (in July 2005) in relation to its guidelines. In effect, the judgment meant that a competent patient who expressed a positive request to receive ANH would receive it: and the presumption that an incompetent patient would also

receive it if it was in his best interests was maintained. The presumption could be displaced, however; i.e. the treatment could be withheld if it was not in the best interests of the incompetent patient's life.

Commentary

At first instance, Munby J. put forward the notion of "intolerability" as the test in determining whether life-prolonging treatment should be administered. He said:

> "There is a very strong presumption in favour of taking all steps which will prolong life, ... *In the context of life-prolonging treatment the touchstone of best interests is intolerability. So if life-prolonging treatment is providing some benefit it should be provided unless the patient's life, if thus prolonged, would from the patient's point of view be intolerable.*"

In the Court of Appeal, Lord Phillips M.R. (delivering the judgment of the Court) rejected "intolerability" as the single test applicable in all circumstances. He said:

> "The test of whether it is in the best interests of the patient to provide or continue ANH must depend on the particular circumstances. ... We do not think it possible to attempt to define what is in the best interests of a patient by a single test, applicable in all circumstances."

Key Principle: **Life-prolonging treatment might include an order to reinsert a feeding tube if it is in the patient's interests to do so.**

W Healthcare NHS Trust v H [2004] EWCA Civ 1324; [2005] 1 W.L.R. 834

The brother and the daughter of a female patient (KH) appealed against a High Court decision permitting W, an NHS trust, to reinsert a feeding tube to keep her alive. The 59-year-old patient had suffered from multiple sclerosis for 30 years and had been incapable of making informed decisions for 20 years. For the last 10 years she had lived in a nursing home and for five years she had required feeding by tube. She was admitted into W's hospital after her tube fell out. Her family unanimously did not want it to be reinserted, but the NHS Trust did. Evidence was adduced that the patient had previously stated that she did not want to be kept alive and that she would now want to be allowed to die. However, in the absence both of the patient's capacity for self-determination and any evidence of an advance directive that clearly amounted to a direction that she preferred to be deprived of food and drink until she died, the judge at first instance decided that it was in her best interests to reinsert the tube.

Held: the appeal was dismissed. The Court decided that when doctors wished to treat an incompetent patient, the court's decision on whether to allow treatment should be based on the patient's best interests (following In *Re F* [1990] 2 A.C. 1) rather on its view of what she (KH) would have chosen if she were capable of doing so.

Commentary

If a patient who had no hope of recovery because (s)he was in a persistent vegetative state, and his /her feeding tube became dislodged, then the decision might be taken not to reinsert the tube: see *Frenchay NHS Trust v S* [1994] 1 W.L.R. 601 (below).

Decisions to Withdraw Treatment

R. v Malcherek and Steel [1981] 1 W.L.R. 690

Here, the Court of Appeal dealt with two cases. In the first, the defendant had stabbed his wife. In the second, the defendant had attacked a girl, causing her multiple skull fractures and severe brain damage. Both victims were put on life support machines that were eventually disconnected *when brain-stem death was diagnosed*.

Held: Both defendants were found guilty of murder based on their acts being *continuing, operating and substantial* causes of the deaths of their victims. Lord Lane C.J. said:

".. it is ... somewhat bizarre to suggest ... that where a doctor tries his conscientious best to save the life of a patient brought to hospital in extremis, skilfully using sophisticated methods, drugs and machinery to do so, but fails in his attempt and therefore discontinues treatment, he can be said to have caused the death of the patient ... Where a medical practitioner, using generally acceptable methods, came to the conclusion that the patient was *for all practical purposes* dead, ... [then discontinuation of] treatment ... did not break the chain of causation between the initial injury and the death."

Commentary
In essence, death "for all practical purposes" means death for all
legal and medical purposes and the courts have a common law
jurisdiction to make this declaration.

Key Principle: **The courts have jurisdiction to declare a
patient "dead" for all legal and medical purposes.**

Re A [1992] 3 Med L.R. 303
When a baby boy, "A", was taken into hospital, the doctors who
examined him could detect no heartbeat ("day 1"). He was
transferred to a different hospital the next day ("day 2"). He was
finally declared brain-stem dead on "day 5". On "day 6" second
opinions reached the same conclusions: "A" was brain-stem
dead.

Held: ("day 11"):
Johnson J. said:

"I have no hesitation at all in holding that A has been dead since ['day
5'—the day he was first declared brain-stem dead].
. . .
. . . I hold that I have jurisdiction to make a declaration that A is now
dead for all legal, as well as medical, purposes, and also to make a
declaration that should [any hospital consultant] consider it appropriate to disconnect A from the ventilator, in doing so they would not
be acting contrary to the law."

Commentary
A declaration of death for all legal, as well as medical, purposes
is certainly death *for all practical purposes*. If death *for all practical
purposes* is another way of expressing death for all legal, as well
as medical, purposes, then we have had a consistent English
common law definition of death for over 25 years. It is a matter of
opinion whether death *for all practical purposes* is sufficiently
explicit to be synonymous with death "for all legal, as well as
medical, purposes".

Key Principle: **There is no legal distinction between withholding or withdrawing life support and that the best interests
test applies equally to both situations.**

NHS Trust v MB [2006] EWHC 507 (Fam)
(For the facts of this case, see Ch.11).
Holman J. said:

[Paragraph 18] "... there is one area of law to which I must make fuller reference, namely the correct approach to the factual distinction between 'withholding' and 'withdrawal' or discontinuance of life support."

[Holman J. then devoted the remainder of para.18 to reporting elements of Lord Goff's speech In *Airedale NHS Trust v Bland* (1993); and in para.19 he reported an extract from Lord Lowry's speech in the same case. In para.20 Holman J. concluded:]

[Paragraph 20] These passages establish and make quite clear ... that there is no legal distinction between withholding or withdrawing life support and that the best interests test applies equally to both situations.

Commentary
Whilst there is no legal distinction between withholding and withdrawing life support treatment (omissions) the criminal law does recognise a difference between acts and omissions. This latter distinction seems illogical when the intended result (the patient's death) is the same "but it is undoubtedly the law"—see the extract of Lord Browne-Wilkinson's speech in *Bland* in the commentary following *Diane Pretty's* case (below).

Key Principle: **Withdrawing treatment from a patient in the persistent vegetative state is withdrawing treatment from a patient who is medically and legally still alive.**

Airedale NHS Trust v Bland [1993] A.C. 789
More than 90 people were killed at the Hillsborough Football Stadium tragedy in April 1989. However, one person, Tony Bland, did not suffer cardio-respiratory death or brain-stem death: he lapsed into the PVS where he remained for the next three and a half years until an application for the declaration that the *Airedale NHS Trust* might lawfully withdraw the medical treatment (feeding and hydration) that was sustaining him. Evidence was given that part of his upper brain had liquefied: there was no doubting that he would never regain

consciousness; his capacity for personal identity was lost. An issue raised by the Counsel for the Official Solicitor was that withdrawing such life-support mechanisms would constitute murder: the *mens rea*—intention to bring about a person's death—was present and, it was contended, that the discontinuance of the regime of artificial feeding would constitute a positive act of commission—the *actus reus*.

Held: It was not in Bland's best interests that his life should be prolonged by the administration of futile treatment. Indeed, according to Lord Browne-Wilkinson: "Unless the doctor has reached the affirmative conclusion that it is in the patient's best interest to continue the invasive care, *such care must cease.*"

Commentary
Lord Goff explained what was meant by PVS before stating his opinion in which he noted that:

> "The central issue in the present case has been aptly stated by Sir Thomas Bingham MR to be whether artificial feeding and antibiotic drugs may lawfully be withheld from an insensate patient with no hope of recovery when it is known that if that is done the patient will shortly thereafter die....

> "I start with the simple fact that, *in law*, Anthony is still alive...

> "[However] The doctor caring for a patient [such as Anthony] cannot ... be under an absolute obligation to prolong his life by any means available to him, regardless of the quality of the patient's life....

> "... the question is *not* whether it is in the best interests of the patient that he should die. *The question is whether it is in the best interests of the patient that his life should be prolonged by the continuance of this form of medical treatment or care.*

> "... for my part I cannot see that medical treatment is appropriate or requisite simply to prolong a patient's life when such treatment has no therapeutic purpose of any kind, as where it is futile because the patient is unconscious and there is no prospect of any improvement in his condition. ... *it is the futility of the treatment which justifies its termination....*

> "... artificial feeding is regarded as a form of medical treatment; and ... in the case of discontinuance of artificial feeding it can be said that the patient will as a result starve to death; [but] the outward

symptoms of dying in such a way, which might otherwise cause
distress to the nurses who care for him or to members of his family
who visit him, can be suppressed by means of sedatives."

Another way of expressing that it might not be unlawful to
remove a patient from a life support machine, even when death
has *not* been diagnosed is if there is "no reasonable possibility of
her ever emerging from her present comatose condition to a
cognitive, sapient, state" per Hughes C.J. in the American case of
Re Quinlan (1976) 70 N.J. 10.

Key Principle: **It may be permissible to withhold treatment
that has been administered via a feeding tube if that tube has
become dislodged and it is not in the patient's best interests to
reinsert it.**

Frenchay Healthcare NHS Trust v S [1994] 1 W.L.R. 601

S had suffered severe brain damage and was in a persistent
vegetative state. He had been fed by a gastrostomy tube which
had been inserted by surgical operation. The tube became dislodged, however, and S's survival required its urgent replacement by surgery. The consultant considered such a step contrary
to S's best interests, given that there was no hope that S would
recover, and the health authority applied to be allowed lawfully
to refrain from intervention. The Official Solicitor acting on S's
behalf opposed the application but did not have time to obtain
independent medical evidence. The judge granted the declaration and the Official Solicitor appealed.

Held: Whilst the lack of independent evidence required the
court carefully to assess the health authority's evidence, it did
not prevent the court making an order. On the evidence, S's
condition was clear and there was no reason to question the
conclusion reached by the consultant. The decision in *Airedale
NHS Trust v Bland* (1993) applied.

Commentary

The straightforward application of *Bland* in the *Frenchay* case
should be contrasted with the decision in *W Healthcare NHS Trust
v H* [2004] EWCA Civ 1324. The wholly different outcomes are
noteworthy given that the decisions in each case were based on
the patient's best interests.

Key Principle: **It is not necessary for a patient's condition to comply with all the criteria in the guidelines issued by a professional body before a decision is made to withdraw life-sustaining treatment.**

Re H (A Patient) [1998] 2 F.L.R. 36

Three years after H had suffered serious head injuries in a road traffic accident, the NHS Trust sought a declaration that it would be in H's best interests for his life-sustaining treatment to cease. However, where there was a unanimous opinion that H was in the persistent vegetative state, a consultant clinical psychologist thought that all the criteria in the guidelines issued by the Royal College of physicians had not been met.

Held: Since H was in a persistent vegetative state it was in her best interests that the treatment should cease.

Sir Stephen Brown P said

> "This is another of the very sad cases of a patient .. who is ... in a state which may well fall within the description of a 'living death'."

. . .

Sir Stephen then went on to approve a passage from Taylor L.J. in *Re J (A minor)(Wardship: Medical Treatment)* [1991] Fam 33 @ 52, viz;

> "First, it is settled law that the court's prime and paramount consideration must be the best interests of the [patient]. . . .
>
> Secondly, the court's high respect for the sanctity of human life imposes a strong presumption in favour of taking all steps capable of preserving it save in exceptional circumstances. The problem is to define those circumstances.
>
> Thirdly, ... it cannot be too strongly emphasised that the court never sanctions steps to terminate life. ... The court is concerned only with the circumstances in which steps should not be taken to prolong life."

Commentary

This was not the only case where there was disagreement amongst experts as to whether the patient was in PVS in accordance with all the guidelines laid down by the Royal College of Physicians: see also *Re D (Medical Treatment)* [1998] F.L.R. 411. In *Re D*, Sir Stephen Brown P said:

> "The court recognises that no declaration to permit or to sanction the taking of so extreme a step could possibly be granted where there was

any real possibility of meaningful life continuing to exist ... In this case ... there is no evidence of any meaningful life whatsoever."

Key Principle: **The withdrawal of artificial nutrition and hydration in PVS cases does not contravene Art.2 of the European Convention on Human Rights as an omission to act does not amount to an intentional deprivation of life.**

NHS Trust A v Mrs M; NHS Trust B v Mrs H [2001] Fam 348
Hospital Trusts sought declarations that they were entitled to discontinue the administration of artificial hydration and nutrition to M, a patient in a persistent vegetative state for three years and H a patient in a persistent vegetative state for nine months. The Trusts sought declarations that they would not infringe the Human Rights Act 1998 if they discontinued the artificial feeding in each case.

Held: Granting the declaration, that where the continuation of treatment was no longer in the best interests of a patient, action to discontinue that treatment would not constitute an intentional deprivation of life pursuant to the European Convention on Human Rights 1950 Art.2(1). Butler-Sloss P said that the phrase "deprivation of life" had to import a deliberate act; and that omission to treat would not constitute a deprivation when continuance would, in fact, not be in the patient's best interests and the decision had been made in accordance with a respectable body of medical opinion.

Commentary
Diane Pretty's case focused on a greater number of Articles of the European Convention on Human Rights. Her case was rejected, however (below).

Assisted Suicide

Key Principle: **Whilst suicide has not been a crime since the coming into force of the Suicide Act 1961, assisting the suicide of another person has remained a criminal act.**

Suicide Act 1961

Section 2 Criminal liability for complicity in another's suicide

(1) A person who aids, abets, counsels or procures the suicide of another, or an attempt by another to commit suicide, shall be liable on conviction on indictment to imprisonment for a term not exceeding fourteen years.

(2) If on the trial of an indictment for murder or manslaughter it is proved that the accused aided, abetted, counselled or procured the suicide of the person in question, the jury may find him guilty of that offence.

(4) No proceedings shall be instituted for an offence under this section except by or with the consent of the Director of Public Prosecutions.

Commentary

A declaration in a civil court that the requirements of s.2(1) have been satisfied by the publication of a book on suicide is most unlikely given that this usurps the function of a criminal court.

Key Principle: **The publication of a book on the subject of suicide is, of itself, not unlawful.**

Att-Gen v Able [1984] Q.B. 795

A booklet was published by the Voluntary Euthanasia Society (now Dignity in Dying) on the subject of suicide. The authors believed that it gave no encouragement to persons reading it to commit suicide. The Attorney General had evidence that the book was associated with 15 suicides, but wished to avoid prosecuting the authors for offences under s.2 of the 1961 Act, however, because their beliefs were wholly genuine and all were respectable persons. Accordingly, he applied for a declaration that distribution of the booklet could constitute a criminal offence under the Suicide Act 1961 (c.60) s.2.

Held: The declaration was refused. The publication of itself was not necessarily unlawful—it might be required for genuine research, or indeed play no part at all in any eventual suicide; and to prove the offence under s.2 it had to be shown that the defendants had aided and abetted, counselled or procured the suicide or attempted suicide of another.

Commentary

The Voluntary Euthanasia Society became "Dignity in Dying" in January 2006. The much-promoted book *Final Exit* (and now 46-minutes long DVD) on "guidance ... for the possible use by a terminally or hopelessly ill competent adult who wishes to avoid further unrelieved pain and distress" is now available from ERGO (Euthanasia Research and Guidance Organisation): *http:// www.finalexit.org* [Accessed February 28, 2008].

Key Principle: **If a competent person travels abroad for the purpose of committing suicide, it is possible, but probably unlikely, that anyone who assists that person will face a criminal charge of aiding, abetting counselling or procuring suicide.**

A Local Authority v Mr Z [2004] EWHC 2817

After a man informed his local authority that he intended taking his wife to Switzerland where she intended to commit suicide, the authority obtained an injunction preventing him from doing so.

Held: The woman was competent, so there was no basis in law for the court to prevent the wife from taking her own life. Whereas the husband could contravene s.2 of the Suicide Act 1961, the court would not of its own motion continue the injunction where no one of standing sought such an order and where the effect of the injunction would deny a seriously disabled but competent person a right that could not be exercised by virtue of the disability.

Commentary

Article 115 of the Swiss penal code considers assisting suicide a crime if and only if the motive is selfish. Assisting suicide for altruistic reasons is condoned. In most cases the permissibility of altruistic assisted suicide cannot be overridden by a physician's duty to save life. It should be noted that Art.115 does not require the involvement of a physician or that the patient be terminally ill. It only requires that the motive be unselfish.

More than 50 Britons have travelled to Switzerland to commit suicide in a clinic run by Dignitas—a non-profit organisation set up in 1998 by Swiss lawyer, Ludwig Minelli. The relaxed provisions of Swiss law have led some people to call Zurich a favourite place for "death tourism".

Key Principle: **The DPP will not grant in advance immunity from prosecution under s.2(1) Suicide Act 1961 for assisting in the suicide of another person within England and Wales nor will the European Court of Human Rights sanction the aiding of another person's suicide.**

Diane Pretty's Case: R. (Pretty) v. DPP [2002] 1 All E.R. 1; & Pretty v UK [2002] 2 F.L.R. 45

By November 2001, 42-year-old Diane Pretty, who was suffering from motor neurone disease, had failed to get a declaration both in the High Court and in the House of Lords that it would not be unlawful for her husband to assist in the ending of her life. Diane Pretty was mentally competent but physically incapable of ending her own life. The DPP refused to grant Mr Pretty immunity from prosecution under s.2(1) Suicide Act 1961 under which he could be jailed for up to 14 years for aiding and abetting the suicide of another person. The decision was upheld on appeal to the European Court of Human Rights where the Court agreed with the House of Lords that there had been no breach of the following Articles of the European Convention on Human Rights: Art.2 (right to life); Art.3 (prohibition of torture or inhuman or degrading treatment); Art.8 (right to respect for private and family life); Art.9 (freedom of thought); Art.14 (prohibition of discrimination).

Commentary

Contrast the cases of Diane Pretty and Ms B. Both women were mentally competent but Diane Pretty required the assistance of another person to *commit an act* that would end her life whereas Ms B was able to get a declaration that as she was competent she was able to *refuse* the administration of treatment: that treating her from the time she was deemed to be competent was a trespass to her person. The law will not sanction a positive act that ends a person's life but a competent person may refuse life-saving treatment. In *Bland*, Lord Browne-Wilkinson addressed the omission/commission debate stating:

> "... the criminal law draws a distinction between the commission of a positive act which causes death and the omission to do an act which would have prevented death. In general an omission to prevent death is not an actus reus and cannot give rise to murder. But where the accused was under a duty to the deceased to do the act which he omitted to do, such omission can constitute the actus reus of homicide, either murder (*R v Gibbins* (1918)) or manslaughter (*R v Stone* (1977)).
>
> ...
>
> How can it be lawful to allow a patient to die slowly, though painlessly, over a period of weeks from lack of food but unlawful to produce his immediate death by a lethal injection, thereby saving his family from yet another ordeal to add to the tragedy that has already struck them? I find it difficult to find a moral answer to that question. But it is undoubtedly the law ..."

Physician-Assisted Suicide and Euthanasia

Key Principle: **The inconsistency in the application of English law has led to proposals for reform—proposals that include permitting a doctor to assist a competent, terminally ill patient commit suicide by providing the means to do so.**

Lord Joffe's Bill:

Assisted Dying for the Terminally Ill Bill [House of Lords, May 2006]

This was a Bill to:

> Enable an adult who has capacity and who is suffering unbearably as a result of a terminal illness to receive medical assistance to die at his own considered and persistent request; and for connected purposes.

Some very brief extracts from clauses of the Bill include:

1. Authorisation of Assisted Dying
Subject to the provisions of this Act, it shall be lawful for—

    (a) a physician to assist a patient who is a qualifying patient to die—

(i) by prescribing such medication, and

(ii) in the case of a patient for whom it is impossible or inappropriate orally to ingest that medication, by prescribing and providing such means of self-administration of that medication, as will enable the patient to end his own life, ...

2. Qualifying conditions

(2) The first condition is that the *attending* physician shall have—

(a) been informed by the patient in a written request signed by the patient that the patient wishes to be assisted to die;

(b) examined the patient and the patient's medical records and satisfied himself that the patient does not lack capacity;

(c) determined that the patient has a terminal illness; ...

(3) The second condition is that the *consulting* physician shall have—

(a) been informed by the patient that the patient wishes to be assisted to die;

(b) confirmed the diagnosis and prognosis made by the attending physician;

(g) advised the patient that prior to being assisted to die the patient will be required to complete a declaration which the patient can revoke.

8. Protection for health care professionals and other persons

(1) a physician who assists a qualifying patient to die, or attempts to do so, in accordance with the requirements of this Act, shall not, by so doing, be guilty of an offence.

Commentary
Dignity in Dying reported that:

"The Bill has 20 inter-related safeguards and the patient would be seen by a wide range of health professionals including two doctors. Only if the patient satisfies a lengthy set of criteria would he be allowed the option of receiving life-ending medication. The life-ending act must be done by the patient. ..."

The whole purpose of the Bill is to make sure that all terminally ill patients have the fullest range of options at the end of life so that they can have the best death possible for themselves."

Moreover, a Monitoring Commission would keep the operation of the Act under review. Adherence to the procedural requirements of the Act (had it been passed) would be essential if criminal charges were to be avoided. However, the Bill was defeated by 148–100 votes in the House of Lords in May 2006.

Legislation outside the jurisdiction

Switzerland
See the commentary following *A Local Authority v Mr Z* [2004] EWHC 2817 above.

Oregon
Oregon's Death with Dignity Act permits physicians to write prescriptions for a lethal dosage of medication to people with a terminal illness. The Act was a citizens' initiative passed twice by Oregon voters. The first time was in a general election in November 1994 when it passed by a margin of 51 per cent to 49 per cent. An injunction delayed implementation of the Act until it was lifted in October 1997, when voters chose to retain the Act by a margin of 60 per cent to 40 per cent.

Euthanasia

Key Principle: **Whilst English law regards euthanasia as murder, not all States regard active voluntary euthanasia as a criminal act: this is so even for another Member State of the European Union.**

English law

in *Bland*, (1993) Lord Mustill said:

"... 'mercy killing' by active means is murder ... that the doctor's motives are kindly will for some, although not for all, transform the moral quality of his act, but this makes no difference in law."

Equally:

"If the acts done intended to kill and did, in fact, kill, it did not matter if a life were cut short by weeks or months, it was just as much murder as if it were cut short by years. per Devlin J., *R. v Adams* (1957)."

Commentary

Clearly, the strict interpretation of the law has been tempered in cases such as *R. v Cox* and in *Brian Blackburn's* case. By contrast with Lord Mustill's statement in Bland, when it comes to sentencing (should a case have proceeded that far), a sentence for "mercy killing" . . . makes all the difference in law. Note that the essential difference between physician assisted suicide and euthanasia is that in the former only the means to commit suicide may be provided by a doctor whereas in the latter the doctor may administer the treatment. It would seem that some people believe that actually administering a lethal dose of medication to a patient would breach the doctor's duty of non-maleficence or *primum non nocere*—first and foremost, do no harm.

The Netherlands

Termination of Life on Request and Assisted Suicide (Review Procedures) Act

Provisions of this Act include the following requirements of due care being placed on the physician who has terminated a life on request or assisted in a suicide:

Chapter II. Requirements of Due Care

Article 2
1. The requirements of due care, . . . mean that the physician:

    a. holds the conviction that the request by the patient was voluntary and well-considered,
    b. holds the conviction that the patient's suffering was lasting and unbearable,
    c. has informed the patient about the situation he was in and about his prospects, . . .

Commentary
It is imperative to note that liability for criminal action is NOT excluded unless the doctor who has terminated a life complies

with the specified procedures within the Dutch Penal Code. This provides as follows:

Article 293

1. Any person who terminates another person's life at that person's express and earnest request shall be liable to a term of imprisonment not exceeding twelve years or a fifth-category fine.

2. The act referred to in the first paragraph shall not be an offence if it committed by a physician who fulfils the due care criteria set out in Article 2 of the Termination of Life on Request and Assisted Suicide (Review Procedures) Act, ...

Belgium

In May 2002, the Belgian parliament approved by 86 votes to, 51 against a Bill to legalise euthanasia.

Patients wishing to end their own lives must be conscious when the demand is made and repeat their request for euthanasia. They have to be under "constant and unbearable physical or psychological pain" resulting from an accident or incurable illness.

Switzerland

Swiss law does not recognise the concept of euthanasia. "Murder upon request by the victim" (article 114 of the Swiss penal code) is considered less severely than murder without the victim's request, but it remains illegal. (*cf.* Art.115 and assisted suicide, above).

Commentary
Whilst legalising euthanasia in England and Wales might not be on the current or foreseeable political agenda, further attempts are being contemplated by Lord Joffe at promoting a Bill to ensure that physician assisted suicide does not attract criminal sanctions. If successful, it remains to be seen if this partial liberalisation of English law will eventually be the springboard for importing provisions legalising euthanasia in very carefully controlled circumstances.

INDEX

LEGAL TAXONOMY
FROM SWEET & MAXWELL

This index has been prepared using Sweet and Maxwell's Legal Taxonomy. Main index entries conform to keywords provided by the Legal Taxonomy except where references to specific documents or non-standard terms (denoted by quotation marks) have been included. These keywords provide a means of identifying similar concepts in other Sweet & Maxwell publications and online services to which keywords from the Legal Taxonomy have been applied. Readers may find some minor differences between terms used in the text and those which appear in the index. Suggestions to *sweetandmaxwell.taxonomy@thomson.com.*

(all references are to page number)